strangers
tend
to tell me
things

strangers tend to tell me things

a memoir of love, loss, and coming home

amy dickinson

 hachette
BOOKS

NEW YORK   BOSTON

Hachette Books
Hachette Book Group
1290 Avenue of the Americas
New York, NY 10104
hachettebookgroup.com
twitter.com/hachettebooks

First edition: March 2017

Hachette Books is a division of Hachette Book Group, Inc.
The Hachette Books name and logo are trademarks of Hachette Book Group, Inc.

The publisher is not responsible for websites (or their content) that are not owned by the publisher.

The Hachette Speakers Bureau provides a wide range of authors for speaking events. To find out more, go to www.hachettespeakersbureau.com or call (866) 376-6591.

Library of Congress Cataloging-in-Publication Data

Names: Dickinson, Amy author.
Title: Strangers tend to tell me things : a memoir of love, loss, and coming home / Amy Dickinson.
Description: First edition. | New York : Hachette Books, 2016.
Identifiers: LCCN 2016027999| ISBN 9780316352642 (hardcover) | ISBN 9781478912521 (audio download) | ISBN 9781478912514 (audio book) | ISBN 9780316352581 (ebook)
Subjects: LCSH: Dickinson, Amy. | Advice columnists—United States—Biography.
Classification: LCC PN4874.D445 A3 2016 | DDC 070.92 [B] —dc23 LC record available at https://lccn.loc.gov/2016027999

Printed in the United States of America

LSC-C

10 9 8 7 6 5 4 3 2 1

*This book is dedicated to the memory of my mother,
Jane Genung Dickinson, and also to my family
of daughters, sisters, aunties, and cousins.*

The best way out is through.
—Robert Frost

Life is a memory.
—Jane Dickinson

Contents

CONTENTS

Author's Note

This book is a work of memory. The experiences I write about are told from my perspective. Much has been left out, but nothing has been added. Some names have been changed.

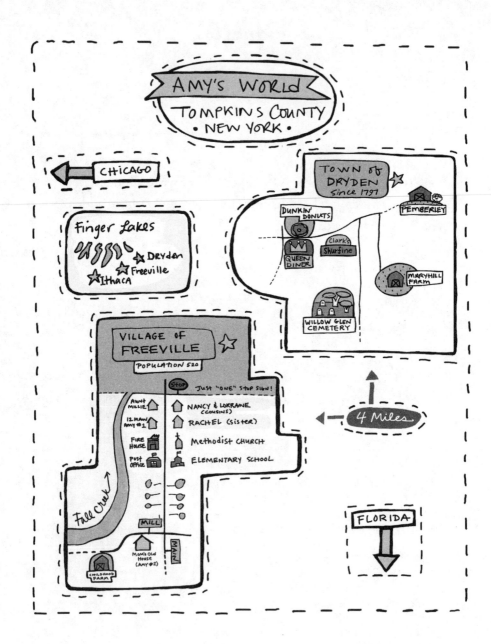

Introduction

Welcome to Freeville

I come from a place that seems to nurture two kinds of people: those who stay and those who leave. I grew up in a family of stayers, but I left. And now, as far as I know, I am the only person in the entire history of Freeville, New York (aside from my own grandfather), to leave—but then return again.

Like me, my grandfather Albert grew up in Freeville, moved to Washington, DC, for his career, and moved back to Freeville later in life. My grandfather died in the house in which he was born—our family homestead on Main Street—where his daughter, my ninety-year-old aunt Millie, currently lives. As I write this, I am sitting in my own little house on Main Street, twenty feet away. Looking out my window, I can see my elderly aunt toddling around in her kitchen.

Freeville is a good place to be from. The village of 520 people has one stop sign marking the end of tree-lined Main Street. Children ride their bikes to the village school, and in the summer you still see kids carrying fishing poles as they walk to the old Mill Dam to fish. On summer evenings, people sit on their porches and slap at the mosquitoes that swarm the lights.

That's what a lot of people probably think about when they remember their childhood in Freeville. But they do their remembering mainly from Florida, where everybody who leaves seems to wind up. The Freeville-to-Florida diaspora is fed by a pipeline powered by low wages and high taxes. Our former citizens are also blown south by the blizzards that rip through the region from Halloween to Mother's Day. Freeville lies near Ithaca, New York, on an axis between the small cities of Binghamton and Syracuse (ranked by the *Farmers' Almanac* as being the fourth- and fifth-worst weather cities in the United States).

Even if you have the constitution to shovel your driveway for five months every year, there is also the cloud cover to contend with. The sky hangs low; much of the time it is gray and gloomy. My mother, Jane, used to call this a "lowery" sky, and while she always claimed to love it, she was alone in her affection for those dusky months, when the sun's low passage in the sky tended to be completely obscured by clouds. When it finally set, you arrived at the realization that it was probably time for supper.

My family has called this place home since 1790, when the first of my mother's family, the Genungs, pushed west after farming for over a century—first in Flushing, Queens, and then in New Jersey. My far-off ancestor was given a land grant in the frontier of the Finger Lakes district in exchange for fighting in the Revolutionary War. The area where he settled and where our family took root and grew is rugged, hilly, and interrupted by spectacular glens, streams, lakes, and waterfalls. Then there are the Finger Lakes—glorious narrow glacial gashes that create miles of shoreline and spectacular vistas. Surely when he arrived in our county with his two oxen, my ancestor felt some ancient Scottish tug in his cells. I know I do.

We who live here are granted four sharp and thrilling seasons (although spring and summer tend to be brief), landscape to make your heart swell, and—when the weather breaks our way and the clouds part—a glorious sky that inspires a full-bodied gratitude just to be alive. On a rare sunny day, you basically want to tear your clothes off and run down the street, crazily rejoicing. We natives do not behave this way, however. Overall, we are a tamped-down, noneffusive people with New England–style reserve and a belief in the power of bootstraps to pull oneself up—as well as the utility of good fences to make good neighbors. We are not huggers, nor lovers of nonsense or drama. We do not suffer fools, gladly or otherwise.

When I was a senior in high school, I told my mother that I wanted to go to Cornell University, just twelve miles away. She responded that of all of her (four) children, I was the one who most needed to leave. Temperamentally, I am a gamboling baby goat pastured with strong and steady draft horses. My mother might have detected a restlessness inherited from my father, who was always on the move but never satisfied. I followed her directive and left home for college in Massachusetts when I was seventeen. After that, I moved from city to city as my life and career dictated, but I always came back home to Freeville. I brought my daughter Emily home for every Christmas and Easter, and for the bulk of many summers. Those years when I lived in New York City and Washington (four and seven hours away, respectively), I would drive back to Freeville for Halloween, just so I could see the trick-or-treaters begging for candy up and down Main Street. I chose to move home permanently when I was forty-eight years old, and it is likely that I will stay here in Freeville for the rest of my life.

During the 1930s, my home county—Tompkins County—was declared officially part of Appalachia. Its poverty seems Appalachian, with rusty trailers and sway-backed farmhouses and sad little settlements ringing the larger and more prosperous county seat of Ithaca.

Freeville is one of the villages that prospective Cornell University students drive through on their way to its sprawling campus in Ithaca. Aside from our handsome brick school next to the old white Methodist church and our busy post office across the street, most of the houses along Main Street are in need of a fresh coat of paint. Two of these houses were half painted a shade of strawberry red by an itinerant crew of housepainter brothers several years back. The brothers took off with their down payment and never returned to finish the job. Will these houses be fully painted before they fall down? Unless the brothers return as suddenly as they disappeared, it seems unlikely.

Next to those structures is a half-built home that has been under construction for fifteen years. The gentleman who owns the lot lost his original dwelling to a terrible fire, and now he, too, seems headed for Florida, leaving his half-built home behind. Fire has also made its mark farther along Main

Street. Our little fire station, now rebuilt, burned to the ground when the village's one fire engine caught fire while it was parked inside.

Surely prospective Cornell students and their families look around and wonder why Freeville exists at all and why the people in those crowded clapboard houses choose to live there.

I am one of those people. From my white house on Main Street (freshly painted, thank you very much), I write the "Ask Amy" advice column, syndicated to 200 newspapers throughout North America and read by an estimated 20 million people each day. I have lived in New York City, London, Washington, DC, and Chicago. Now I live here, working out of a tiny house next door to my aunt Millie, down Main Street from my aunt Jean, my cousins Nancy and Lorraine, and my sister Rachel. My sister Anne lives two hours away in Rochester, and my brother, Charlie, lives…in Florida.

Our mother died five years ago. After her death, I inherited her house, which is just up the road from the fallen-down dairy farm on the edge of the village where we lived during my childhood. So if you're keeping track, I now own two houses in Freeville, which is two more than most people would probably want.

I got remarried in 2008 and moved in with my husband and his family of three daughters to a farmhouse outside of Dryden (population 1,900). This slightly larger town was named for the poet John Dryden and is four miles from Freeville. Dryden is where I went to elementary and high school, after graduating from the Freeville primary school. Clark's Shurfine Food Mart is in Dryden, and that's where people who live in Freeville go for groceries. Dryden also has a good liquor store and a wonderful library, and you can get yourself a decent slice of pizza there. On Friday nights, we might stop over at the Dryden Hotel for beer and hot wings. Dryden is where we go to set out our folding chairs along the curb on Library Street to watch the parades on Dairy Day and the Fourth of July.

Every day, I commute from my house near Dryden, where I live with my husband, Bruno, and drive four miles to my house on Main Street in Freeville to work on my column. Along the path of this short commute is the Dunkin' Donuts, where I stop each day for coffee, and the Willow Glen Cemetery, where I drink my coffee from my car while looking out at the windswept graves of my kinfolk.

Once a month, I travel to Chicago to check in with my bosses at the *Chicago Tribune* (which syndicates my column). I also appear on the National Public Radio (NPR) comedy quiz show *Wait Wait…Don't Tell Me!* While there, I stay in an apartment that is left over from when I was a single mother, and my daughter Emily and I lived there full-time. So if you're counting, I actually have four homes, which if consolidated would be worth a little less than you would pay for a split-level outside Fort Worth, Texas. I also have exactly as many houses as pairs of shoes (boots, pumps, sneakers, and loafers).

All of this is important because homes and landscape and people—and moving around and between them—are part of my story. In most isolated small places where people stay put (rural villages and islands, for example), houses change hands back and forth as the property flows through families via inheritance, financial bailouts, or marriage.

For instance, the white house on Main Street where I am sitting as I write was my great-aunt Jane's home during my childhood. Great-Aunt Jane lived near her sister (my grandmother, next door), just as I live near my sister now (Rachel, five houses down). My mother lived down the street from her mother, and that is what I chose to do in midlife—to live down the street from my mother. I am on the verge of turning over the house on Main Street to my cousins Jan and Roger, who are moving back to Freeville after fifteen years away. Jan is Aunt Millie's only child, and I will vacate this house so that mother and daughter can live next door to one another. Soon I will begin the process of relocating my Freeville workspace around the corner to my mother's old house on Mill Street, and the family population in this little place will gain another two members.

My decision to leave Chicago, where Emily and I had lived for several years, and move back to my hometown changed my life in every way imaginable. It brought me back into the realm of the women who had raised me. It brought me into the orbit of the man I would choose to marry. And it is where, smack in midlife, I resumed the lifelong job of growing up.

This is what it feels like to come from a tiny place: You feel known. My neighbors may not know my inner thoughts, but they know the headlines of what has happened in my life. If I am teary in the checkout line at Clark's Shurfine Food Mart, Mike Clark (who was in my husband's and my sister's class in high school and who I have known for almost fifty years) might assume that I am missing my mother that day. He might clap one of his big hands on my shoulder and ask me how I'm doing. Mike knows many things, and he also understands the void left by loss. We don't need to have a soulful or revealing conversation, because we both know the same important things about each other.

Donna, Donna, and Jean work at the Freeville post office. (We call them Donna #1 and Donna #2. And Jean.) Our postmistresses know who's having a birthday or who's sick or who just died, because of the uptick in the volume of cards being delivered to a resident. They also know that the advice business is booming, because they deliver bins full of letters sent to me from readers (although most of my queries arrive online, via Facebook, Twitter, and e-mail, some people still put a stamp on their question). Whenever I stop in, our postmistresses are patiently talking to one or another of the many elderly people who live in our town, whose daily trip to the post office is a meaningful outing. I am happy to wait until their conversation is done, because what they are doing in that moment is much more important than what I am doing.

There are no doubt people around me who do bad things, who hold terrible secrets, who are unkind and lie, cheat, and gossip—or worse. People around here are fond of their guns and have committed violent crimes and suffered tragic accidents close to home. As I write this, somebody less than a mile away is probably trying to cook up a batch of meth on his camp stove. Bad things as well as good things happen everywhere, but coming home has helped me lend context to life's tragic turns. Small everyday graces make the bad things bearable. Back in Freeville, I've learned to lean toward these graces as I make my way in the place where I was born.

When people challenge the advice I dole out to my readers, they often do so by questioning my credentials. Such as they are, my credentials were earned the way most of us earn—or learn—anything: through experience.

I have lived in poverty and prosperity. I've dodged and settled debts. I have fallen in and out of love, dated blindly, survived infidelity, and blended a new family together. I drove the back roads through marriage and divorce and raised a child as a single mother in distant cities. I've started new jobs, wrestled with unemployment, and struggled to get the bills paid. I have cared for my mother until her death. I've seen things fall apart, and tried to pull them back together. I have lost my faith and found it again. I have loved and lost and been undone by grief. Now, at the tail end of my midlife, I am learning to let go and live on.

The author, top left, with her family in 1963: mother Jane,
Rachel, Charlie, Anne, Buck (center)

Chapter One

We Played with Matches

When we were children, my siblings and I almost burned down the house. Not long after that, our father almost burned down the county. Both times our mother helped put out our fires, and both times, she forgave us.

A surprising number of my most potent memories from childhood involve fire. Most of the questions I continue to wrestle with throughout the rest of my life seem to hinge on the infernal complications set in motion by being raised by one parent who set fires and another who put them out.

Back then, children played with matches. You knew you weren't supposed to, but you did anyway. Matchbooks were everywhere in the 1960s—in the kitchen junk drawer, wedged in the Naugahyde crack of the front seat of our car, rattling around in the bottom of my mother's pocketbook, and in the messy cab of my father's truck. My three siblings and I had ready access to matches, since both of our parents smoked and because we used both a fireplace and a woodstove for heat. There were also a few occasions when our mother illuminated the house with kerosene lamps and candles because our electricity had been cut off.

When I was three years old, my mother discovered me sitting in the gravel driveway of our house, scraping off the ends of matches with my teeth and swallowing the scrapings. I was also eating pieces of gravel, plucked off the driveway. She took me to the doctor. In retrospect I think I might have had pica, which is caused by an iron deficiency (a problem I still have). People who have this tend to eat odd things, like clay or coal dust, because it is their body's way of seeking to redress a nutritional imbalance. The doctor and my mother both told me to stop eating gravel and match heads, and I did. But I can still remember how sulfury good they tasted.

Before long, I graduated from eating matches to lighting them. Though I hadn't yet started kindergarten, I was already a pretty proficient match-lighter when my older brother and sisters hatched a fun way to play with fire. This new game was more exciting than merely flicking lit matches into the road. We sequestered ourselves in one of the upstairs bedrooms in the large and pretty house we lived in at the time (the house and furnishings were given to us by my grandparents). First, we lit little pieces of paper and quickly tossed them into the wastebasket. That was fun for a while, but the thrill of it gradually drained away, the way it does when you're watching a fireworks display. For us, flaming paper was losing its awe factor.

I don't know which of us had the idea to light the toilet paper on fire; it might have been my brother, Charlie, because at nine he was the oldest of the four of us. Or it might have been an idea that sprang up spontaneously among the group, as the best and worst ideas tend to do. I was not allowed to hold, light, or let the strips of flaming toilet paper drift through the room— not because it was too dangerous for a five-year-old but because I had not yet earned the right. As a snivelly gravel-eating tagalong and chronic tattle-tale, my rights were often contested.

Lit toilet paper has a way of floating and briefly rising toward the ceiling that is mesmerizing to watch. It was especially fun to watch the flaming paper bump up against the filmy curtains lining the bedroom windows. My job was to stamp out any remaining flames when the charred pieces hit our grandmother's oriental rug. I was good at this. But as my pyromaniac siblings got more creative, the pieces of toilet paper got longer and more flamey. They rained down with a higher frequency and velocity, and I had a hard time keeping up. Soon enough, everybody was forced to help extinguish them.

Our mother, Jane, heard the stomping overhead and came up the stairs.

It's almost magical how good you can feel in the split second before you get caught. The moment just before everything goes bad feels so much better than all the moments that precede it. Our mother twisted the ball of her foot onto the smoldering rug, like she was putting out a cigarette. Then she ran to the bathroom and returned with a cup of water to dowse it. The five of us—mother and children—stood looking blankly at each other, surrounded by the scent of sulfur (yum) and airborne pieces of toilet paper ash, as Jane shook drips out of the cup and onto the rug.

Jane had never punished us. She would get aggravated, wag her finger, mutter under her breath, and occasionally slam a pot or pan or deliver an empty threat to leave one of us by the side of the road and drive away. Beyond that, she had no system of punishment. If she was disappointed, she told you. If she was furious, she ignored you. She always claimed we were just really good kids and didn't need to be punished. Her limited experience with discipline held no category for what we had just done.

Jane decided to send us to bed without any supper. I'm not sure where she came up with this idea, but as we lay in our beds whispering to each other in the late afternoon of a long summer's day, it felt Victorian and punitive, like something out of a fairy tale. We were told we could not leave our beds, and from our quilted prisons we had lots of time to consider and be sorry for what we had done. Rachel (age eight) immediately started writing notes to our mother, apologizing, challenging the sentence, and demanding clemency. Anne (age seven) was trying to think of ways to coax our dog Tippy up the stairs to join us. Charlie was silent, from his room on the other side of the hallway.

Jane put on a record downstairs: *Slaughter on Tenth Avenue*. She liked its throbbing score when she was feeling riled.

I was worried that she would tell our father, Buck, when he came home. Buck wasn't home all that often. He was either on the road selling paint for Sherwin-Williams, doing construction, or farming. During those years, we were unsure what our father did for a living. But when he was home, he was definitely in charge. Unlike Jane, who could be counted on to eventually side with us, Buck was completely unpredictable. He didn't have to deliver punishments. Mainly, keeping us afraid of him was his primary parenting technique. For instance, that previous Easter, when we bounded down the stairs in the morning looking for our Easter baskets, Buck was waiting for us. He was sitting calmly in front of the woodstove in the dining room, smoking a cigarette, drinking coffee, and smirking. No baskets.

He looked at us. "Oh, yeah. I've got some bad news. Red got out last night. I'm afraid he got the Easter bunny. It was a real mess." Buck took a slow drag and looked at us impassively. Red was our neighbor's psychotic junkyard dog. He often strained powerfully at his chain, menacing anyone who came within his worn-out circle of terror. When passing Red's house, we walked on the other side of the road.

Charlie, Rachel, and Anne looked skeptical. Buck was famous for being a mean tease who nonetheless always referred to himself as "a kidder."

I burst into tears (my specialty). Buck sat there, calmly looking at us, until our mother came into the room, carrying our baskets. She had gotten up early and had been hiding colored eggs and little piles of jelly beans around the house and yard. "Oh now, stop it," she said to me. "He's joking."

Oh...humor, I thought.

Now we lay in fear in our beds after our house-burning episode. Because Buck seemed capable of just about anything, his coming up the stairs was the worst-case scenario. At around six o'clock we heard our mother's footfall on the staircase. I wondered if she would spank or beat us with a switch: These were punishments she had never even hinted at. However, after being sent to bed without supper, anything seemed possible.

Jane opened the bedroom door with her foot. She was carrying a tray on which were cut-up hot dogs, milk, fruit, and pie. She served each of us on our beds. I wondered if this was what it was like to stay in a hotel, having your meal served to you on a tray like that. Jane sat on each bed and asked us if we knew that what we had done was wrong and dangerous. She said how scared she was that the curtains would catch on fire and then the rest of the house would go. She stroked my head when I got sniffly and overwhelmed with remorse. She never told our father.

My parents met in high school. Jane was a 1940s cutie who grew up in Washington, DC, but spent her summers in Freeville, until her father's health forced him to retire from his job as an economist with the Department of Agriculture. Then the family moved full-time to their house on Main Street. My precocious mother graduated early from her huge high school in Washington but then repeated her senior year at tiny Dryden High, where she fell, fatefully, into my father's orbit. Any ambitions she might have had to go to college (as both of her parents had done) were demolished on the tracks of my father's runaway train. They were both twenty when they got married in my grandparents' living room in Freeville.

Buck moved my mother around a lot. They lived in over a dozen different houses and farms around Freeville before I was born. Sometimes they had plumbing, and sometimes an outhouse out back, with a hand pump for water in the kitchen. They rarely owned a phone. Buck had a habit of neglecting to pay the rent. He would come home from his various jobs as a salesman, construction worker, or hired farmhand and say, "We're moving." My mother gave birth to four children in five years. She lived in ten different houses during that time.

Just before I was born, the family moved into the home given to them by my father's (more prosperous) parents. Unlike the broken-down farmhouses and country apartments my mother and her babies had been living in, this house was a large and elegant local landmark. It featured a grand curved staircase and a fancy carved fireplace that a young itinerant carpenter named Brigham Young had made for the house, before he pushed west and founded Mormonism. The house was full of antiques and heirlooms. The immediate family's poverty was well concealed.

Setting fires was a skill Buck encouraged. He had a survivalist streak and went through a phase of taking the four of us into a forested area on some land he owned, in order to test our woodland skills. On one of these trips he gave each of us one match apiece with which to start a campfire. He made us scatter into the woods. My brother, Charlie, had mentioned bears during the ride up the steep hill, as we rattled around in the back of the pickup truck, clinging to its sides. After the bear mention, I lost enthusiasm for that afternoon's goal, which was to survive on your own in the woods for the afternoon, or possibly forever.

My match was quickly spent, due to an overall lack of enthusiasm and the choice of fresh moss as an accelerant. I wandered over to my older sisters' campsites to watch them earnestly try to light their fires, which can be surprisingly hard to do in the damp, dank forests of upstate New York.

Buck had chosen *his* spot outside the woods, in the middle of a pasture of tall, dry, golden grass. Jane spread a blanket on the ground. She had brought drinks and raw hot dogs to cook over our campfires. I have a memory of Buck stomping down a large circle on which to build his, there in the middle of the grassy pasture. It seemed like a good idea at the time, but then again, I was in first grade.

Our father's campfire (lit expertly with one match) spread to the dry grass and quickly raged out of control. We heard whoops and rushed into the clearing. Jane urged us to stand back as she poured Kool-Aid onto the flames and then whipped out the picnic blanket to smother them. Our uncooked hot dogs, cups, and plates went flying. Buck raced to the truck and pulled out the floor mats. He started beating the burning grass as it migrated into an ever-widening circle. My siblings and I started flame-stomping with our boots and sneakers, and we used our jackets to try to beat the flame into a smolder. Flying sparks made new fires in the dry grass.

We got lucky. After about ninety minutes of panicked extinguishing, the fire seemed to be out. An acre or so of grassland was blackened. We stayed on, sullenly circling and watching for fresh flames. Buck got a shovel from the truck and dug around to make sure the fire was extinguished. He seemed furious. The color had drained from Jane's face. "It's okay; it's okay," she repeated as we hovered. As dusk fell, we gathered our dirty, smoky jackets, climbed silently into the back of the truck, and bumped down the hill. Then our mother made a joke about going back to the picnic site for our (now thoroughly cooked) hot dogs, trying to retrieve the day. No one laughed.

It is a unique challenge to be the child of a *character*. My old man, Buck, was one. He was a handsome, chain-smoking loudmouth whose defining characteristics were his vulgarity, his volatility, and his willingness to do whatever he felt like doing, without feeling the consequences. He was a dairy farmer who did iron work on the side, a womanizer (as I learned later), a brawler, a drinker at roadside taverns, and a world-class abandoner.

Jane was his opposite. She was reserved, bookish, and so passive that she would get a sick headache rather than tell somebody no. Where my father sowed chaos, my mother craved and created stability. He was a punisher; she was a forgiver. He set fires. She put them out.

We have only one photograph of our family together, taken on the porch of our aunt Anne's farm in Pennsylvania. Buck is sitting in the center of the picture, his dark hair rakishly swept back, like a 1950s matinee idol. His four children are seated around him. Our mother is leaning to the side, slightly out of focus. She always referred to this photo, wryly, as "the sun, surrounded by the planets."

My father was obsessed with lineage, property, possessions, livestock, vehicles, and everything he saw as rightfully his. As young children, my siblings and I followed suit. I remember tamping down a line of grass in our yard and declaring it to be the "official property line." Along with my brother and sisters, I taunted the neighbor kids—a band of toughies whose uncle, it was rumored, was doing time in Attica. (Like our father, these kids rolled their own cigarettes, using dried leaves instead of tobacco from the mulberry bush that was on our side of the official property line.) I was emboldened by my belief in the magical properties of the invisible force field protecting our yard. "Stay off our land!" I yelled over the imaginary line, until one of the neighbor boys twitched in my direction, and I ran into the house and told my mother.

When I was seven, we left the lovely historic house with its antique four-poster beds, empire furniture, oriental carpets, and mahogany spinning wheel. Buck had started farming eight miles away in Freeville, on a farm and a hundred acres that my mother had recently inherited from her father. Without notice, Buck sold the furniture, the piano, the rugs, and moved us to the ancient drafty farmhouse at the edge of Freeville. Our new house had started life as a cabin, which had been added to over many different eras. The rooms were small, the floors sloped, the doors didn't shut, and the ceilings were low, but the barn was spectacular and cavernous. We became full-time farm kids.

The next few years of my childhood were a pastoral complication of living on our rough dairy farm within walking distance to the village. My siblings and I tramped through the fields and woods. We learned to swim at the base of a glorious waterfall and swung from a rope tied to the cupola in our enormous hip-roofed barn. Charlie took an axe and broke through the winter ice on Fall Creek, which flowed through our property, ran a line of muskrat traps, and sold their pelts for spending money. On the village pond, Rachel and Anne let me skid behind them wearing my rubber boots as they skated and played hockey with other kids.

Jane was physically isolated, probably bored, and was starved of television, radio, and other entertainment during my early childhood. She owned every Broadway musical LP she could get her hands on and played them all day long during those times she had a working record player. She had perfect pitch and played piano by ear, picking her way through show tunes and pop hits on our wheezy wooden Edwardian pump organ, which she had taken from the Freeville church when they were getting rid of it.

I would lie in bed at night in our farmhouse and listen to my mother power up the pump organ by stomping on its wooden pedals until its bellows filled with air. Then she'd start to play the chords to Burt Bacharach's "This Guy's in Love with You." Given the organ's overall creepy pipe tones and asthmatic volume changes as my mother pedaled faster or slower, it sounded like a lounge act in a horror movie.

As soon as I was old enough, I followed my two sisters and joined the Freeville United Methodist Church choir. Walking by ourselves up to the church on Main Street on Wednesday nights for rehearsal felt like an important privilege. Our grandmother had been choir director and organist. After her death, Mrs. Ayers, who lived on Main Street and taught music at our school, took over the choir. I remember the moment when I realized I could finally read music. It was like tumblers clicking into place.

On the farm, I trundled along beside my father on his tractor or in his truck, rolling cigarettes for him as he drove. When I turned eight, he started letting me ride my bike to the store on Main Street with a note for the shop-keeper and a dollar to buy him rolling papers and tobacco.

During the evening milking, Buck would crouch beside our muddy Hol-steins, who were lowing and locked into their rusty stanchions. Cigarette dangling from his lips, he would attach the milkers to their teats and hop, crouching, from cow to cow. He swore prodigiously at the cows, calling them "the Girls" or "Goddamn Filthy Bitches" as they shifted their bovine weight and switched their powerful tails into his face. My job was to hold their manure-encrusted tails as my brother and two older sisters carried full pails into the milk house. In between chores, my sisters and I sang to the rhythm of the milking machines and practiced being cheerleaders or baton twirlers on the long concrete floor of the barn, until Buck barked at us to cut it out, goddamn it.

My father seemed blind to both his behavior and the tough luck conse-quences that always followed. Every skirmish he waged was lost, but it was somehow always the other guy's fault. The people running the milk plant didn't know what they were doing. The superintendent on his latest con-struction job was an idiot. Our neighbor didn't know where the property line was and needed a solid punching in the nose.

Buck insisted on seeing himself as a winner, despite overwhelming evi-dence to the contrary. When the latest of our broken-down cars finally quit for good and Jane drove us to school events in a dump truck, he pointed out that this goddamn truck was more expensive than a limousine.

Buck expressed contempt for professionals and intellectuals, whom he referred to as "eggheads." He hated the government in every form. His way of expressing affection toward his children was to declare that we were better-looking and smarter than everyone we knew.

Even as I gained a growing awareness that our father was a bigoted gas-bag, I was still fascinated by him. He moved through the world with the ease and optimism of someone who knew he would simply move on if things didn't work out.

Our way of life ended when I was twelve years old, when Buck suddenly moved on from us. He took a construction job up north and only came home on weekends. Charlie, then sixteen, kept milking the cows, along with Walt, our hired man. During the slurry season of a dismal March, Buck simply stopped coming home. We later learned that he had taken up with a local waitress and was living with her in a sad town on the Black River.

Without telling my mother, Buck sold our herd of fifty cows to a nearby dairy. One day I got off the school bus to see the dairy's cattle trucks pulled up to the barn. They were taking the Girls away. Like all farm kids, I had a complicated relationship with our livestock. I both loved and loathed our Holsteins fiercely, and I knew I would miss them.

My childhood changed in that moment. I was the daughter of someone who'd convinced me that everyone not connected to him was a loser. By leaving, he put us in that category. Jane, always the grounded center of our home life, spent the warming evenings that spring sitting on our front stoop, listening to the peepers on the creek and smoking, as she played a Seals and Crofts record over and over on our stereo. She was quiet and sad. Her sisters—my aunts Lena, Millie, and Jean—pulled in close. I would hear them talking at the kitchen table. I suspected they were giving her money. Buck had taken our mother's inherited farm and mortgaged it without telling her. Jane was forced to sell everything in our barn—all of the equipment, the milkers and milk pails, and even the leftover hay—in an auction held in our driveway.

I watched from the house as our neighbors and some Amish farmers from Pennsylvania bid on our belongings. Jane told me to go ahead and run into the barn and bring out anything I wanted to keep. I found an old Victrola record player in the barn's granary and put it in my room. I still have it.

Up until the time my father left her, Jane had been a full-time farm wife and had never held a paying job (after her teenage years). Now she went to work as a typist in an office at nearby Cornell University. My father charged my mother with "cruel and inhuman treatment" as a way to get a quick divorce, but he said he didn't mean it—it was just the only way to get the goddamn thing done.

Buck mainly kept his distance after that, although from time to time in high school I'd hear that he was surfacing locally. When I was sixteen and performing in a community production of *The Music Man*, I learned from some of the adult cast members that Buck was drinking with them at the local bowling alley. "He's a riot!" they said. I just nodded. He was a riot, all right.

My father married Joan, the woman he left my mother for, adopted her children, and then left them three years later. He picked apples in Nova Scotia. He started a business making cattle harnesses. He sold silos. He moved around, eventually establishing himself in a dying factory town on the Allegheny River in Pennsylvania. After Jane and Joan, he married Jeanne, and then Jean, and then Pat. He met women at church, taverns, diners, or the community center, and also through mail-order dating services found in the back of farming magazines.

My mother graduated from her role as the passive witness to Buck's failed ventures. The out-of-focus face in our family photo gained definition. The utility bills got paid. She bought a working car. Being separated from my father's chaos became her liberation. The year I graduated from high school and went to college, Jane quit her typing job and then got her undergraduate and graduate degrees at Cornell, later becoming a professor there before retiring from teaching at Ithaca College.

Jane was eventually able to leave our farm, when she unexpectedly inherited a house from our neighbor, John Sager. It happened in 1982, when I was twenty-two. The small Greek Revival style house was 500 yards up the road from our broken-down dairy farm, with its rambling, drafty house and enormous barn, which was in the process of falling down. John was a bachelor farmer. He had never married or had children. He grew his own food and cut his own wood and made a small living as a local "dowser" (also known as a "water witch"), finding wells with forked divining rods. John was well over six feet tall and had huge hands, like a smithy.

When we were growing up, my sisters and I would walk or ride our bikes past John's house on our way to Main Street several times a day. If he was outside working, he would welcome us into his small, crude kitchen to let us splash water into our cupped hands and drink from his big metal hand pump. John's house had no indoor plumbing, and he heated it with a wood-burning stove. We were particularly fascinated by his one-hole out-house, which stood next to his small barn.

John showed us how he held his forked divining rods in his giant hands and how the point of the stick jammed toward the earth and vibrated when he found water. John said he had so much magnetism in his big body that he couldn't wear a watch; its hands went haywire when strapped to his wrist.

Later, when John got very old, my mother would leave casseroles or pies on his porch or invite him down the road for supper. She was looking out for him, in the way that people do.

One night when I was sixteen, John walked down to our house through a blizzard and ate with my mother and me. Our farm had failed and all of my siblings were gone. It was just the two of us now, rattling around in our house. The blizzard was howling, and my mother offered to drive John the short way home after supper. As he was getting his coat and scarf, he said he had some-thing important he wanted to talk to her about. I left the table but decided to eavesdrop from the next room. I heard John say that he had decided to leave his place to my mother when he died. She was stunned. She protested, nam-ing other people she knew he was close to. John said that he wanted her to have his house because he knew she loved it and knew she would keep it.

Jane always told us that her friendship with John began when she was a young child, spending her summers on Main Street (like my daughter Emily, my mother grew up in DC and lived in Freeville during the summers). Jane said that, starting when she was about five, she had a habit of walking down Main Street in the mornings and visiting several households on her way to John's house, which was always her final destination. She would sit with John and his spinster sister, Georgie, on the porch while they read the com-ics aloud to her. Georgie and John saved their newspapers all through the winter to read to my mother during the summers while they sat and drank their coffee together.

Fifty years later, John told my mother that he and Georgie had decided together to leave their place to her and that their decision was final. Georgie had been gone for decades; this fateful choice was made when Jane was in her twenties.

After John's death, this inheritance was the lucky good fortune that enabled my mother to finally shed our hundred acres and its complicated memories of my father's desertion, debt, and failure. She installed plumbing and heating in John's house and undertook a passionate wallpapering and painting campaign. After surviving married life with Buck, where he kept her off kilter and moving sometimes twice a year (just ahead of the bounced rent check), Jane craved stability. She also seemed to love change—as long as it was confined to the small seven-room house.

Jane carved out a small back bedroom in the unheated upstairs of the house, and Emily and I would stay there, bundled under a thick layer of quilts during our Christmas visits. Even after I spent my divorce money on my own house on Main Street, Jane's sweet house remained our daily destination.

Occasionally during my visits home from whatever city I was living in, my mother and I would see an unfamiliar vehicle cruising slowly down the street as we sat on her porch drinking coffee. Over the years my father drove through Freeville in a painted-over laundry van, an army jeep, a lime-green International pickup truck, and a Cadillac. If he saw my mother's car in the driveway, Buck would pop in for a cup of coffee. I have a small collection of homemade business cards he presented over the years for his harness business, his silo selling, and his home-bottled honey. Jane's house in Freeville seemed to be on the outer ring of his sales territory.

During his visits, Buck's attention span lasted for the length of one cup of coffee. He would spill out his line of malarkey about whatever nonsense he was up to, and then he'd leap up suddenly and leave.

Jane often said that if Buck hadn't left her, she would have landed in a trailer somewhere in the hills and would still be waiting for him to come home. I can only wonder about a parallel life with my father in it. I only know about the life without. Both of my parents provided stellar examples to me about what I wanted for my own life. I wanted to be the tolerant and forgiving mother Jane had been to me, and I wanted to avoid any Buck-like men at all costs.

Chapter Two

Romance: A Brief History

I've fallen deeply in love only twice in my life: once when I was young and then again in middle age. Both experiences were joyful, intense, lusty, and crazy-making journeys into the wonderment of deep attachment. My first love involved a relatively brief foray into marriage and parenthood and ended in heartbreak. The second time I fell in love felt like a true forever-after.

When I first fell in love, I didn't ponder my moon tide of crazy emotions and think to myself, *Wow, I feel giddy as a schoolgirl.* It was the week before my twentieth birthday when love first crashed down on me, and I thought, *This is what it means to be a grown-up.*

I entered this state perhaps more naïve than other girls my age, because I didn't have boyfriends in high school. The only boys I did go out with went to other schools. This was a deliberate attempt on my part to keep my two selves separate. At Dryden High School, I was a striving and ambitious blur: cheerleading, competing in sports, participating in student government, and starring in the spring musical. Outside of high school, I was probably a bit of a mess. My basic philosophy about boys seemed to follow a "don't poop where you eat" guideline, and I carefully limited my mild risk-taking to places where my local reputation as a Goody Two-shoes would be intact, even if I screwed up.

In high school, our social lives were dominated by the various sports seasons and the few dances held in the cafeteria each year. Our sports teams played against the same small schools over and over, so you'd see the same cute boys on opposing teams several times over the course of a season. A rumor would circulate about a party, usually held in someone's cornfield or barn, and a group of us would share a ride into the other school's territory in someone's rusty car. We'd park in a circle and shine our car lights into the center. There might be a keg in the back of someone's truck or bottles to pass around.

Alcohol mainly made me loud, repetitive, and vomit-prone, but occasionally it also made me brave enough to make out with somebody at one of these cornfield parties. I almost always regretted it later, but fortunately, because I didn't go to the same school as the boy in question, I wouldn't have to deal with the hallway drama. I only had to suffer through occasional awkward glances across the gym during an away game.

During high school, I also sang in regional choirs, giving me additional opportunities to meet guys during weekend-long music festivals. These festivals were usually held on a college campus in Rochester or Buffalo and were attended by 250 choir and band kids from around the state. I was not a choir slut, exactly, but there were definitely girls and boys who fit into this category (sopranos and tenors, mainly). I fancied myself more the Make-out Queen of the alto section.

The typical choir encounter went like this: We'd be intensively rehearsing a tricky Benjamin Britten piece. During a twelve-measure rest, I'd lock eyes with a sixteen-year-old baritone or percussionist. We'd stand near one another during the water break, sit together while eating our box lunches, swap sloppy kisses between performances, and promise to (but not) keep in touch.

Fortunately, the boys I was attracted to were nice people, but aside from these clumsy encounters, I found the prospect of being in a romantic relationship of any duration pretty embarrassing. There seemed to be a code to courtship that I could never quite crack. First of all, in order to have a boyfriend, you had to *want* to have a boyfriend. I was deeply ambivalent about this. I had seen my two older sisters tangle with the drama of teenage dating. I saw how relationships could turn a person's life inside out. It was hard to see an upside.

Jane's parenting, post-divorce, was a form of benign neglect. She cared, but she also seemed spent. My mother was a survivor of Tropical Storm Buck, picking through the rubble of her home life and trying to take stock of what remained. Jane was trusting and permissive, but she was also powerless regarding the rebellion that sometimes accompanied my sisters' and my teen adventures. She had nothing she could threaten to take away from us. We had no money, no college fund to hold over a child's head, or car privileges to threaten to revoke. Her brown Plymouth Duster was reserved exclusively to get her back and forth to work.

All Jane had was her disapproval, but even that seemed in play. She wasn't like some of my friends' parents, who lived their lives one way and hypocritically advised their children to make different choices. Jane's attitude seemed to be "What the hell do I know?" She only spoke to me about boys and sex once, and in typical fashion, she alluded to the topic indirectly. I was sixteen, and a boy was on his way to pick me up in his car. "Ahem," Jane said. "I knew that boy's father in high school. I want you to call me if you want me to pick you up. It doesn't matter where or when. Understand?" Ummm, not really. And yet I still got the message.

After high school, I attended Clark University in Worcester, Massachusetts. I was seventeen and had never been away from home. I had also never spent time in a city. I suspected fairly quickly that Clark and I were a mismatch, but I threw myself into college life with gusto, all the while wrestling with bouts of debilitating homesickness. I ping-ponged back and forth between playing field hockey for the school, starring in theater productions, and crying in my dorm's stairwell. I worked in the college cafeteria, scraping plates as they came through on a conveyor belt. After the dinner service had ended and the plates stopped coming through, I washed enormous, industrial-sized cooking pots. Washing giant pots in the big stainless steel sinks in the kitchen reminded me of washing milking machines with my sisters, in the milk house attached to our barn.

My cafeteria supervisor, James, was ten years older than I was. I first met him when I exited the cafeteria accidentally by way of a fire door. Piercing alarms interrupted the meal service. I stood frozen in the open doorway as several hundred students applauded, until James came with his keys and turned off the alarm.

By Christmas, James and I were dating. By Easter, I was fairly certain that he and I were (also) a mismatch. I didn't love him, but he was so nice, funny, mature, and kind to me that I selfishly stuck it out. Plus, he was cute, well liked, didn't have homework, and had the keys to the cafeteria for occasional late-night snacking.

James drove me around Worcester in his old Toyota. After work, we would go to an all-night diner and sit in a booth drinking coffee, while my butter-covered corn muffin sizzled on the grill. James and I dated through my sophomore year, when he encouraged me to consider transferring to another school, which he thought would be more challenging for me. I applied to Georgetown, was admitted, and fairly quickly broke up with him. James went to a friend of mine for an explanation and solace. Two years later, I went to their wedding. They have been married now for thirty years.

My mother took me to Washington for my college orientation at Georgetown. I was nineteen. During a welcome session on the school's sweeping lawn, Jane lay back on the grass, rested her head on her purse, and dozed in the sun. I took this as a sign that this new school would offer a soft place for me to fall into. My mother had spent her childhood in Washington when her father worked at the Department of Agriculture. I think we both felt at home there.

At Georgetown, I was riding on scholarships and the work-study program. I worked hard to prove myself worthy at the challenging school and behaved the only way I knew how—by flinging myself at everything. I sang in the gospel choir, the show choir, and the madrigal choir. I fell in love with the broad, leafy avenues of Washington and got a weekend job taking tickets for the midnight show at the Biograph Theater on M Street. For the first time in my life, I stopped relying on my sisters as a feminine backstop, and I met and made solid female friends.

The guys on campus were a far cry from those ruddy boys in their rusted Chevy Vegas I knew back home or the older man from Worcester. These boys came from Greenwich, Shaker Heights, and Grosse Pointe. They wore pastel-colored cashmere sweaters tied around their necks and sported boat shoes and stiff L.L.Bean canvas coats in the fall. They switched to duck boots and Brooks Brothers cashmere coats in the winter.

Andrew was the one I fell hard for. I spotted him on the first day of my junior year. We shared one class together and worked in the same college office. He was tweedy, quiet, witty, and cool. He was so handsome he was hired to model the fall fashions for the Georgetown Shop, a preppy clothing store where some of the boys on campus had accounts. I could feel my eyeballs burning whenever I glanced his way, which was often. I immediately cast Andrew as Hubbell in my mental production of *The Way We Were* and engaged in a full-out assault to get his attention. I careened between the only two behaviors I knew: attention-hogging verbal razzle-dazzle in Shakespeare class (sample: "Professor, methinks I doth have a question...") and inadvertent spaz—once actually falling over and pulling down an entire filing cabinet onto myself, in front of him.

In short, I behaved the way you might if you were trying to repel someone. But it's a true fact that when it comes to attraction, we do what works for us, and this worked for me. By my twentieth birthday in November, Andrew and I were a couple.

He was a polished New Yorker who summered in Southampton, which he and his family referred to as "the country." (As someone who has spent time in both places—the country and the Hamptons—I can testify that the Hamptons are to "the country" as Paris Hilton is to Minnie Pearl.) During many weekends of the first winter we were together, Andy took the train home to New York, where he would escort debutantes to cotillion balls at the St. Regis and the Pierre. He owned his own tuxedo.

My relationship with Andy was both passionate and sweet. We loved reading the same books and going to the movies together. We seemed attracted to the obvious contrasts between us. I was intrigued by what I perceived as his wealth and prep school polish; he seemed to find my small-town upbringing and gothic tales of farm life charming. Our perceptions of each other were based only on our own descriptions, with the glossy overlay that happens when you decide you love every single thing about someone and are oblivious to the dull slap that reality delivers later on.

During school vacations, I took the Greyhound bus home to Freeville, with its layover in Scranton, and he went home by train to the Upper East Side. We wrote each other letters full of descriptive longing and called each other late at night—he sitting on the floor of the hallway of his father's seven-room pre-war apartment and me from my mother's old desk in the living room of our drafty farmhouse. I would sit and silently finger the keys on her powder blue Selectric, typing out phantom messages as we talked.

Andy and I stayed together through college graduation, geographic separation, and two breakups of several months' duration. Each time he broke up with me, I felt utterly heartbroken, walking the Washington streets in the rain and writing extensively in my diary.

Three years after graduation and just when I had recovered from our most recent breakup, Andy traveled to DC and stood underneath my apartment window. He asked me to please come down to the street, and then he asked me to move to New York. I eagerly quit my lonely job working solo as the overnight editor at NBC's Washington bureau and moved to New York, feeling not one moment of hesitation. We lived in a tiny basement apartment on the Upper West Side that had a little fireplace and a shady garden full of leggy impatiens. We worked for competing news stations in New York—he in front of the camera as a reporter and me on the production staff of a network news show. One night after work, while waiting at a bus stop on Sixth Avenue, I turned around and saw that every single one of the dozens of television screens in the Crazy Eddie store was tuned to his station, featuring a close-up of his face on that night's newscast.

I was desperate to get married. I wanted to seal this deal. In retrospect, I think I was trying hard to get ahead of Andy's next departure. Plus, I loved him.

Andy and I engaged in months of passive negotiations, full of heavy hinting (on my part) and resistance (on his). One Saturday afternoon I went to a salon and got my first-ever expensive New York haircut. They asked me if I used "product" (no) and if I wanted a sparkling water (also no). What I wanted was the Meg Ryan in *You've Got Mail* haircut. I even brought a picture with me.

After what I can only describe as a vicious weed-whacking, the stylists in the salon seemed to know things had gone south. They gathered to gush over my new look, which I felt was actionable and worthy of a segment on *Judge Judy*. But because I was spending too much money on something undeserving, I became a silent and sullen co-conspirator in this hair crime. An hour and $110 later, plus tips (I am an inverse proportionate tipper), I left the salon looking like Meg Ryan's slutty low-foreheaded cousin Tammy.

I did the hair fail walk of shame back to our apartment, darting through back alleys and hiding behind Dumpsters until I reached our brownstone. I stood outside the apartment door, sniffling, unable to enter. From the hallway I heard Andy walk to the door.

"Did you forget your key?" he called through the door.

"Don't open it!" I whimpered. Through the closed door I told him about the hair disaster.

"Well, how long do you want to stand in the hallway?" he asked.

"Forever," I said. When I finally entered the apartment, I picked a fight with him and essentially said that we had to get married or I was leaving.

"Uh, okay, we can get married if that's what you want," he said.

"Andy," I said, "I will love you forever."

"That's nice," he said. "I really appreciate it."

We told my mother during a rare visit of hers to New York City. We took her to lunch at the Plaza and shared our news with her. Jane seemed happy about it but was a little quiet. Through the restaurant's massive windows we could see Central Park South. Horse-drawn carriages stood at the ready as the snow drifted down. "It's like Edith Wharton," my mother said, and I knew exactly what she meant.

Andy and I took a day off from work and went shopping for engagement rings up and down Fifth Avenue. That afternoon, a gypsy cab jumped a curb and plowed into a bunch of pedestrians near where we were. Andy had to run off and cover the story for that night's newscast. We abandoned our ring search. At some point several weeks later, I bought a small emerald ring from a vintage dealer in Rockefeller Center, where I worked, but I only wore it briefly. Something about it felt not-right, and I was embarrassed that I'd bought it for myself.

I remember my mother trying to talk to me about how in many relationships, it was her perception that one person seemed to like the other person a little bit more. I knew she was talking about me, but I didn't care. We had a beautiful wedding on Block Island and traveled to London for our honeymoon.

The marriage was over before our fifth anniversary. By then, we were living in London full-time. He was climbing the broadcasting ladder as a network correspondent. I wasn't working but instead was living the life of a prosperous expatriate housewife. Going to art galleries, browsing up and down the Kings Road, and meeting people for lunch consumed a fair part of my day. Soon enough I was pregnant with Emily. We bought an apartment on a leafy square in Earl's Court, filled it with antiques and chintz pillows, and prepared to start life together as a family.

But something was off from the start. I was lonely, with near-crippling homesickness and a feeling of almost overwhelming nostalgia for a life I hadn't even experienced yet. I felt a sort of wistfulness that came from looking both forward and back but not at what was right in front of me. Andy traveled constantly. His job was to cover disasters and conflict throughout Europe and the Middle East. When he was home, he still acted like he was away. I began to withdraw as well.

Aside from some lovely moments nuzzling our baby, our family never hit its stride. On the surface, we tended to get along very well, because we basically buried our problems by buying things and decorating. We swept all of our tougher feelings under antique kilim area rugs. All the same, as our apartment became ever more lovely and pulled together, I felt Andy drifting and our relationship starting to pull apart. We talked very easily about the headlines of the day, but he seemed detached and uninterested in things I was starting to find fascinating—namely everything having to do with babies and children. I didn't hide my own frustration and disappointment. I was panicking. I felt like a spoiled brat for wanting what I wanted, which was a romance both secure and enduring, as well as everything else I thought went along with it—namely children and domestic happiness. Not only had I never had this, but I had also never even witnessed it. My own parents' marriage was, I supposed, terrible before my father left my mother with four children to raise and a barn full of Holsteins. All of the young couples I knew were just like we were—busy buying things and talking about babies and granite countertops. I could only imagine what a good love would be like.

No one knows how to make love stay. Still, Andy chose a cowardly way out by finding someone else, and then telling me about his infidelity, and then leaving me standing on the street in London as the cab pulled away with him in it. We parted peacefully, but just as I had been during our breakups while we were dating, I was utterly heartbroken. I took Emily, then two, and moved back to Freeville.

It was March, the dismal season of freeze-and-thaw and driving cold rain. I didn't know where we would ultimately live, so I left our possessions in storage in London. Rachel had gotten a head start on life as a single mother and was living with her daughter, Railey, in a little bungalow in Freeville. Rachel displaced five-year-old Railey from her twin bed and turned the room over to Emily and me. At night, I would lie next to my daughter and stare at the silhouette of my niece's prodigious collection of toy horses. I pictured Emily's toys and her baby bed, stashed away in a shipping container with no forwarding address. I tallied up my losses as I listened to the rain pound down on the roof.

Andy said he would take my calls, in case of an emergency. I was instructed to communicate only through the network's London switchboard. I tried this once, although it wasn't really an emergency, and Andy's disinterest was so humiliating that I decided never to do that again. I didn't have a car, so in the afternoons Emily and I walked down Main Street to Jane's house. My mother and I drank coffee and looked at the daffodils in her garden, while Emily played with the old wooden blocks that had been left over from my grandfather's childhood. My toddler breached the generations by making her blond-haired Barbie ride shotgun atop a hundred-year-old tin stagecoach. My sisters and aunts gathered around me, and my mother petted me like a cat. Jane had always liked my husband. I knew she would miss him, too.

Three months later, I cashed in my divorce settlement and spent it on the down payment of the house on Main Street for us to use during visits home. Then Emily and I moved to Washington, DC. Andy moved to Moscow.

Chapter Three

Dating Blindly

I've had several fresh starts in my life, but the one I took with my two-year-old daughter didn't just feel like a transition—it felt like a Hail Mary. Emily and I moved into a small apartment in a sprawling Art Deco apartment building next to the National Zoo in Washington. At the time, the building was slightly down-at-the-heel and full of elderly people. Most of them were long-retired functionaries who seemed left over from the Eisenhower administration (Lyndon and Ladybird Johnson had lived in the building in the 1930s, when he was a junior congressman). After we moved in, I realized that Emily was literally the only child in the 200-unit apartment building. Every day as we walked through the lobby on our way to the store or the zoo, we would run a gauntlet of elderly cane-wavers and walker-thumpers. My little girl got a lot of outside attention.

Apartment buildings are really a lot like small towns. Over the course of the day, you have many glancing connections with a revolving cast of characters. We said hello to Charles the doorman, Damon the maintenance guy, the postman, and the proprietor of the little convenience store in the building. In many ways, this reminded me of life on Main Street in Freeville. In the late afternoons before supper, Emily and I would walk through the National Zoo, which we treated like our front yard. Emily pushed her doll-sized stroller in her toddler way—circulating in a serpentine pattern that covered very little ground. I had always found this extremely irritating, but now I tried to stride less and stroll more. As a newly single parent in a new city, my instincts were to freak out and worry excessively about my future. But I wanted to slow down. I tried to let my little girl's perambulations teach me how to do that.

When I talked to my mother on the phone, I could tell she was avoiding pressing me on my life plans, but one evening she couldn't stand it anymore and raised the big question of my future. Emily and I had been in Washington for a couple of months. The last of the boxes had arrived from London and were unpacked. I'd shoved a fan into the apartment's window to try to suck in some cool evening air.

"So. What are you going to do now?" Jane asked. Her question seemed to cover lots of categories at once: Work, Life, Love.

"I think I'm going to stop trying so fucking hard," I told her. I'm not sure this was particularly comforting to my mother. "Trying so hard" had always been my defining characteristic. Jane reminded me that she didn't like hearing me use the F-word and left the rest alone.

My life in Washington picked up from the running start I'd gotten during my time in college there. Several of my friends from school had settled in DC; I reconnected with them and was gathered into the fold. In our early thirties, everyone was having babies, so there was always something fun to do. Pool parties and birthday parties, nursery school field trips and trips to the circus dominated my social schedule. I tagged along on others' family outings with a brigade of married moms, always with my daughter in tow. I didn't know one other single parent. This seemed like a statistical impossibility, and on a trip home to Freeville, I pointed this out to my mother. I told her I feared I was living in a marriage cluster; it was like the water carried a contagion, creating an odd geographic pocket of fidelity. "Give it time," she said. "The divorces are around the corner."

The divorces did, in fact, happen. For a thirty-five-year-old person, there are really only two segments of datable people—the newly divorced and the never-married. (Once in a great while, an age-appropriate widowed man would float past. These guys were snapped up faster than a drapey linen dress at an Eileen Fisher sale.) The newly divorced are often basket cases who can't stop talking about their exes (I was in this category for a long time). I strongly sensed that the never-marrieds were not likely to start with me, a single mother who sometimes wore my heartbreak on my sleeve.

We drove everywhere in my old 1967 Morris Minor, which I had shipped from England, along with the other spoils of my divorce. The car was a shiny jalopy with no radio, heat, or air-conditioning. In the winter, Emily and I froze as we slid on the car's flimsy tires on DC's icy streets. In the summer, it was a heat-conducting sweatbox. But the Morris was cute, and I quickly learned that my vintage car was man-bait.

"That guy is looking at your car!" my friend Gay exclaimed as we stood outside her nursery school during afternoon pickup. "Go! Go talk to him!" Gay herself was an irresistible people magnet. Men, especially, seemed drawn to her. Within a few minutes of entering a crowded room with Gay, I would be elbowed closer and closer to the coat closet as a scrum of people vied for her attention. I noticed that Gay's technique with grown-ups was really a version of what made her such a gifted teacher of young children. She focused completely on the other person, made flattering and insightful observations, asked great questions, listened attentively, and remembered telling details from previous conversations. My flirting technique, left over from the last time I had used it in college, was to babble incoherently about myself and then act prickly whenever someone tried to connect with me.

Because of my divorce settlement, I wasn't under tremendous financial pressure to work full-time. However, I applied to two jobs in newsrooms as assistants to busy and famous (male) journalists, who each told me that I was overqualified—with a twist. It's not that I was overqualified professionally, necessarily (I had been out of the workforce for several years), but more that I was somehow overqualified personally. One gentleman explained himself by saying he would find it challenging to ask me to get a sandwich for him because I was older than his typical assistant and had a child at home. I told him that being a mother made me the perfect candidate because I was used to fetching things and could also wipe his nose for him if need be. He hired someone else.

In the second case, when the journalist called to tell me I had *not* gotten the job, he also volunteered that he had instead decided to hire a recent (male) law school graduate instead of me because he simply felt more comfortable around him. "I mean, what if your daughter gets sick?" he asked.

"Um... I don't know, what if *your* daughter gets sick?" I asked him. My experience interviewing for jobs wasn't that different from my experience trying to date. Both involved patting down my sweaty underarms in the ladies' room before and then fearing I'd said and done everything wrong afterward.

Eventually I was handed a job by a friend who personally passed it along and gave it directly to me. I became a temporary worker filling in for people on maternity leave at NPR. Thus began my career as a job doula for new moms, where I bounced from being a receptionist to being a booker. By the time Emily started kindergarten, I had landed a permanent part-time position as the commentaries editor for *All Things Considered*. My job was to find fresh voices to run on the program, and I admit to occasionally using my position as a way to try to meet writers I thought were cute. This never worked—not once—and yet it seemed like something that really *should* work. I had two friends who had met their romantic partners at book signings. How cool would it be to show up at a signing for your favorite (talented, available) writer, only to have him write his phone number along with the inscription in your book? This was the sort of adorable meet-cute I envisioned for myself, but it never happened.

It is a tempting and romantic thought to believe that someone is out there, waiting patiently for you, but in my case he was not. I bought new outfits for blind dates and fix-ups—always excited by the possibilities and always returning dejected to our apartment to pay the babysitter. I had two (very) brief relationships with two different men who each said to me, "You make me want to be a better man." I thought, *Well, that makes two of us who want you to be a better man!*

I did not find love around the corner. Instead, gradually I fell in love with what was there all along—my daughter, our friends, their children, my nieces and nephews, and the fun and overall peaceful engagement in work and family. Emily and I had a life in Washington and a life back in Freeville, where we spent holidays and summer vacations. But sometimes I dropped my guard. I got tired of making the effort to be happily alone.

After the last day of school, I would pack Emily and our cat into the car and drive from Washington seven hours due north to Freeville. I worked on my editing and freelance jobs in the early mornings, and in the afternoons our chief occupations were riding our bikes to Jane's house down the street and drinking lemonade with her on the porch. As the summers ticked by, my family members expressed surprise that I was still single. Jan and Roger set me up with a man they knew. I went on a movie date with a professor my age who seemed far more interested in his research than in me. Jane even got into the act, throwing a small dinner party featuring the one single man my age she knew. Each time, excitement was followed by disappointment.

Every summer I enrolled Emily in a day camp, where at the end of each two-week session the campers put on a show. One summer when she was ten, I went to see their performance on a Friday night. It was a goofball mash-up featuring kids forgetting their lines and running into each other during the production numbers.

There in the camp's overheated old theater, I saw Bruno. Bruno was a remnant of my childhood. Like many people I ran into locally when I wasn't expecting it, I had to source this particular connection from my mental Rolodex, gathered through time and the different places I had lived. And then I placed him: Schickel, Bruno. Birthplace: Dryden, New York. Family's occupation: dairy farmers. Bruno and I went to Dryden High School together, but I hadn't seen him in twenty years. On this night he was in the auditorium with his wife; their daughter Clare was enrolled in the camp.

Bruno was no longer the rangy farm boy I remembered from childhood but was now a burly man with a receding hairline and a beard. We shook hands. His was massive and calloused. "Wow... you're smaller than I remembered," he said. I put the meeting into my mental file of Random Encounters and forgot about it.

When Emily was a teenager, we ran into Bruno again. This time he was with another daughter at a local ice-skating rink. He was no longer married. I knew this because I had been single for several years and could spot a wedding ring from the International Space Station. Bruno's ring finger was absent the telltale band. As I laced up my skates, he asked about my family, and I asked about his.

Afterward I said to Emily, "Hubba, hubba."

"Mom, stop," she replied.

As Emily was entering ninth grade, we moved to Chicago when I was chosen by the *Chicago Tribune* to write the "Ask Amy" advice column. From the start, I fielded many questions from people searching for love. My advice reflected what I knew, which was to get out there and meet lots of people in order to increase your odds of finding the right one. It's simple math, people! I suggested joining clubs and online matching. "You'll never find someone in your living room," I wrote.

As I typed that line, I was sitting in my own living room, definitely not finding someone. I followed my own advice and took a swing dancing class, where I was paired with a stranger with an excessive sweat issue who talked about refinancing my mortgage. I had a few coffee dates and drinks with people I had met on dating sites. Twice I went out with men who I assume by now are happily out of the closet, and twice I was rejected by other men who told me straight up, "You're too good for me." This observation was not necessarily delivered like a compliment. I felt like I was being told that I was too fancy, haughty, or demanding. As if something about me wasn't right. But now I countered with, "No, I'm not!"

It's a uniquely low moment when you find yourself trying to convince someone that you're the lesser person.

I went through very long stretches of not trying at all. In Chicago, I fell in with a crowd of five single women roughly my age, gathered from the *Tribune*'s newsroom. We made plans every weekend to go to the movies, out for drinks, or ice-skating in the park. My friends in Washington had all been parents, but in Chicago I knew very few other parents. Instead of me sharing in the social life of a child, Emily, now a teenager, was folded into the life of a middle-aged single woman. There was a lot of cooking, eating, talking about work, and laughing—and sometimes we all went bowling.

There were moments riding the bus to work in downtown Chicago when I'd look out at the grand gray expanse of Lake Michigan and feel a deep well of sadness about my divorce. My ex was married to the woman he had left me for. They were living in a wealthy suburb of New York and had two children together. Well over a decade later, I still found the tears for the romance I had started but that had always felt unfinished, because it had not been my choice to end it. It's not that I was lonely—or even that I wanted him back—but I wondered what it would be like to have an adult partner. Although Emily saw her father from time to time, I had raised her essentially by myself. She had become my perennial sidekick. As we would make our weekend plans to go on walks or to the movies or to hang out with friends, I would often think about how much fun it was, and how very uncomplicated it was, to essentially be dating my daughter.

But furtively, I watched elderly couples holding hands in line at the movies. I watched these old people with the same intensity that, decades earlier, I had once watched young intact families frolicking at the beach—with a combination of awe and envy. For singletons of a certain age, looking at old people holding hands is relationship porn (we don't admit we watch it). During those moments, I thought I would happily trade romance and sex, if necessary, for companionship. I just wanted to hold hands with someone again.

Chapter Four

Night of the Chipmunk Hands

I should have known better than to entrust my romantic life to the mercy of comedians. Generally, people who devote their lives to making other people laugh are too maladjusted to grasp something as high-stakes as a middle-aged woman's search for love. And yet, I willingly climbed down to the bottommost rung of the dating ladder when I involved my colleagues on NPR's *Wait Wait...Don't Tell Me!* in what I now assume is the last blind date I will ever have.

I have always treated my monthly appearances as a panelist on NPR's quiz show as the realization of my lifelong fantasy to be Sally Rogers, the comedy writer played by Rose Marie on the *Dick Van Dyke Show*. I secretly cast myself as the wisecracking feminine presence in the male-dominated backstage writers' room. (Like Sally, I turn up for my appearances wearing '50s-style shirtwaist dresses and sometimes even tease my hair into her trademark style.) By offering to introduce me to a potential date, Peter Sagal, *Wait Wait*'s host, was Carl Reiner on this particular night, producing my imaginary sitcom's episode: "Amy's Last Blind Date."

Blind dates are like relationship Rashomon; each participant has their own version of events. Since my memory of the night itself is a little fuzzy, let me start with the ending, which is two people going their separate ways. That outcome is indisputable, while other details are mutable.

This blind date was with a guy I'll call Steve. I will call him Steve in the hopes that it is not his real name. Other details of this night are seared in my memory, but his name has escaped, along with, I pray, his ability to find and sue me.

Peter told me he wanted to fix me up with Steve, who was someone he had met but didn't know very well. This is the ideal situation for a blind date fix-up, because it lowers the octane on the event. No one party has too much skin in the game. This is a good thing because in my experience, blind dates, like my long-ago swing dancing lessons, never work out. For me, they are the triumph of hopeful enthusiasm over experience. Peter told me he would invite Steve to attend a taping of our show, and then Steve would join the cast and crew when we went out to our regular bar afterward.

I was excited. I was excited in the way a poodle gets excited for walkies, with the dumb, raw energy of someone who suffers from blind date amnesia.

The cast gathered backstage before the show. I was on that night with Adam Felber and Mo Rocca, two of the nicest, kindest, and funniest people I know. I briefed both men on the situation: Peter was fixing me up with a guy who was going to be sitting in the audience that night. We turned to Peter for confirmation and details. Steve was a media person of some kind. He did political PR for the hot-button Chicago market. *How cool is that?!* I thought. Steve sounded yummers. *This time next year, Steve and I will be partying with James Carville and Mary Matalin. Maybe they'll lend us their country house.*

Backstage before the show, Peter commenced the blind date prep: "You don't have a problem with baldness, do you?" he asked.

I looked at Peter, whose baldness is a weekly audience warm-up joke. "Um, no. Not at all. I don't have a problem with that."

Adam (also bald) jumped in: "Oh yeah, the ladies love the bald men. Everybody knows this." He ran his hand in a seductive waxing motion over his pate.

Peter continued. "And you don't mind dating someone who is short, right?" He had hit upon his second warm-up joke. I looked at Peter, who is not short, exactly, but he's also not tall (though appreciably taller than I am). Peter is a serious athlete and marathoner who has run the Chicago and Boston marathons. And while I would definitely send Peter running to the next village to deliver an important message, I wouldn't necessarily ask him to get a book off of a high shelf. "Um...no. I don't have a problem with height," I said warily.

Mo weighed in. He was gathering data and felt he needed more information. He wanted to know just how short and how bald *was* Blind Date Steve. Peter's answer was "Height appropriate" and, well, bald wasn't a gradual state. You either were or you weren't. Peter observed that because I was short (5'2"), I couldn't possibly mind being matched with a person who was also short. It was the physics of the thing.

I called Emily from the ladies' room and relayed Peter's description. "Sweet Jesus, no," she said.

I need to state for the record that I myself have been judged and found wanting physically. My former husband chose a woman prettier, leggier, leaner, and several years younger than me. I couldn't help but take this as a personal affront to my own less-pretty, less-leggy, less-lean, and older reality. In the years since this rejection, living as an aging singleton, the Pilates revolution seemed to have altered men's expectations about what a grown woman should look like. Although I played sports through high school and college, I had not devoted myself to regular workouts. I'd never taken hot yoga or belonged to a gym and had always considered my daily early morning walks with my friend Margaret to be sufficiently vigorous. My middle-aged body had settled and become ever-so-slightly lumpy. I was not, and had never been, a babe. I paid for this when one man, an architect, dismissed me purely for structural reasons. The architect might have chosen to merely fade away after our first encounter, but instead he chose to be very specific about the parts of my body he didn't like as he was rejecting me. I was genuinely hurt but took some comfort in the fact that while I could probably hire a trainer and tone up nicely, he would always be a jerk.

Backstage before our show, I was aware that I did not want to harshly judge someone else as I had been judged, and yet I was starting to get nervous. "Um, is Steve life-sized? Like, if I saw him from behind, walking down the street, would I assume that he was an adult, or might I think he was a ten-year-old boy?"

Peter thought about it. He said something to the effect of, "What season is it? If it's summer and he's wearing shorts, sneakers, and a baseball cap, I'm not sure. Winter, you're good because he probably carries a briefcase."

Mo tried to explain that Peter's reasoning was like when people try to match gay people together with the only common quality being that both parties are gay. "Short doesn't automatically like short!" he offered.

"Everybody needs to stop, because I have a really good feeling about this!" I insisted. Blind Date Steve would be sitting in the front row of the audience, so we could all get a good look at him during the taping of the show.

I was very nervous heading out onstage that night. I tried to surreptitiously scan the front row to spot my date. Basically I moved my eyeballs but tried to keep my head very still, because I didn't want Steve to notice me looking for him. But I couldn't see anyone matching his description.

We started the show, which is an onstage trivia quiz show based on that week's news. It is a completely impromptu experience, so paying attention is called for. I was seated between Adam and Mo. Adam wrote something on a piece of paper and slid it toward me. It said: *I see him. He's five people over from the left aisle.* I shifted my eyeballs and counted seats.

The fifth seat from the aisle was occupied by an eight-year-old boy, wedged between his parents. The child's feet dangled off the edge of his seat. He was licking a giant lollypop. (Okay, he wasn't licking a lollypop, but you get the picture.)

Like I said, never give a comedian access to your emotional world, for he will place a PEZ dispenser on your leg during a piano recital, and you will have to feign a coughing fit to excuse yourself in order to stop laughing.

After the show, Blind Date Steve approached the group and introductions were made. He was in fact a small bald man wearing a peacoat, which he might or might not have purchased in the boys' department at Marshall Field's. I shook his *tiny* hand; we all got our coats and headed to the bar.

We sat together in a big group, as Steve and I circled one another, the way you do—stealing occasional oblique glances, in the hopes of easing into a conversation.

Blind Date Steve was funny. He had an interesting job, and he told us all about it. I could tell he was more oriented toward impressing the impressive people we were with than me—but I'm used to that. In fact, I also find my funny fellow panelists more interesting than myself. I realized that Steve was really on a blind date with the others at the table. As I listened, I hoped I was wearing my "resting amused face," versus the face I was trying to suppress, which was the "If-I-leave-now-I-can-catch-*Storage-Wars*" face. As Steve held forth, I considered him—his hands, especially. His hands seemed proportionally smaller than they should have been. I pictured him washing his food in a nearby stream, using his tiny digits to scrub an apricot.

The evening wound down and Steve walked me a couple of blocks to the taxi stand. Walking together, I realized that we were, in fact, proportional. The union with my tall ex-husband had yielded a daughter who had passed me in height when she was in fifth grade. Emily was now a 5'10" statuesque beauty who could rest her chin on the top of my head. Sometimes my daughter and I didn't even seem like we were the same species. I reconsidered my previous harsh assessment of my date. If we got together, Steve and I could have tiny chipmunk babies. They would sleep in little nests in our tree house, like Keebler people.

Steve didn't seem all that into me (maybe he prefers tall women), but I decided to go for it anyway. I was ashamed of myself for taking the measure of this man in such a superficial way. I wanted to spend one evening with him when he wasn't distracted by my friends' star power. And we could take it from there.

Walking down the street, Steve asked me how to get an editorial into the *Chicago Tribune* for one of his clients, and I offered my help. I said he could call me, and I asked him if he would like my number. He said, "No, that's okay," and I never heard from him again.

Blind Date Steve delivered the perfect comeuppance to my own hubris: flat-out rejection.

When Emily graduated from high school, I decided to keep our apartment in Chicago but move to Freeville to spend more time with my mother, who was becoming quite frail. I had spent seventeen years as a single mother. I was tired. I was going home. "*You* try going on blind dates for seventeen years," I would tell people, as if I was exhausted from all the single-lady sex I was having. What I didn't mention was that in seventeen years, sex had happened so few times that I thought my virginity may have actually grown back. Nor had I fallen in love. I missed my sisters, nephews, nieces, cousins, and aunts. I missed my hometown. And I missed my mother.

I dropped Emily off at college in Virginia on a 102-degree day. The most enduring and uncomplicated love affair of my life had been with my daughter, but now I was saying good-bye. I knew that aside from brief visits home and summers, we would probably never live together again—unless, of course, twenty-five years from now she decided to make a choice like the one I was making now, to return home to be with her mother.

I drove through the rolling hills of Maryland and into Pennsylvania, past the ancient battlefields of Gettysburg, the last lovely autumn blooms of crown vetch and goldenrod lining the ditches and pastureland. I felt myself also starting to change and hoped for my own sort of late blooming. I was leaving my urban life and friendships, moving ever northward, toward the village where I was born and the people I knew best.

Whatever I was looking for, surely I would find it there.

Chapter Five

Journeys End in Lovers Meeting

For me, love has always been a cold-weather sport. Almost every important relationship I've ever had has commenced in the fall. Emily was born in October; we brought her home from the hospital through a shower of yellow leaves drifting down from the sycamores that lined our London square. All of my siblings were born in the fall, and my dearest and most enduring friendships all began with the start of school and college.

Fall is a friend to this middle-aged woman, with its soft, indirect sunlight, opportunities for crispy leaf-play, and cellulite-hiding leather coats. Plus, the whole sleeveless problem is eliminated in colder weather.

I would like to tell the story of how I fell in love with the man who is now my husband, but there is no way to do so without sounding like the plot of a Lifetime movie. The elevator pitch goes like this: Withering writer meets hunky contractor. Sparks fly!

But the thing about clichés is that sometimes they are true. And stepping into a cliché doesn't make something any less true—or less of a cliché. It just makes it what happened.

Moving back to my hometown after leaving Emily at college didn't seem like a momentous decision at the time but more an extension of where my life already seemed to be headed. We were spending our summers in our house on Main Street. My employers at the *Chicago Tribune* were exceptionally understanding of my desire to spend more time with my mother as she became more frail. Filing a column 365 days a year can be a grind, and I assume they were hoping to avoid the Mike Royko syndrome, where the world-famous daily columnist basically moved into his office, chain-smoked, drank, and yelled at the world. Ann Landers, who set the standard for advice-giving for forty-five years, worked from her palatial Michigan Avenue apartment, sometimes in her bathtub. Her bushels of daily mail were opened by assistants at the *Tribune* and delivered to her home by limousine.

I had neither their reputations to uphold nor the compensation to support such eccentricities. My employer quietly let me do what I wanted, as long as I got the work done. I returned to Chicago once a month to check in at the *Trib* and also appear on *Wait Wait…Don't Tell Me!* My bosses knew where to find me.

In Freeville, I had set up the tiny back bedroom of the house as my office. It had a large window, through which I could see Fall Creek gurgle past. The walls were lined with cowboy kitsch, which I had gathered during a phase inspired by my grandfather's amateur oil paintings of cowboys and Indians. My grandfather Albert was born in the house next door, where my aunt Millie now lives. His knowledge of cowboys and Indians was gleaned mainly through books and magazines. His small paintings betrayed his fascination with horses, dogs, men moving through nature, and the Western landscape, which I don't think he had ever seen in person but which he captured beautifully. I had owned my house for fifteen summers before moving there full-time. It was furnished inside with uncomfortable twig porch furniture and odds and ends I'd found in my mother's barn or left by the side of the road.

I had not spent a fall in Freeville since leaving for college thirty years before. Now I watched out my window as the teachers from the primary school led their students single-file through the village for their annual walk to Toads ice cream shack before Kathy shuttered it for the winter. I emptied out the leggy geraniums from my porch boxes and put my bike into the shed. As autumn slid past, I could feel myself changing seasons, too. It was like an exhale. I was settling in.

I spent my forty-eighth birthday raking leaves into giant piles. That night I took my mother to the annual Election Day turkey dinner at the church. She was using a walker now, but so was everyone else at the dinner. I remembered a time when I was surrounded by children, messing with fold-up umbrella strollers, car seats, blankies, and binkies. My sisters' kids and my own roamed in a pack during holidays and summers. Now I was surrounded by old people, and the dynamic was startlingly similar: driving people around, fussing with equipment, obsessing over food choices, and making sure scarves and mittens were accounted for.

There in the basement, across steaming bowls of Methodist mashed potatoes, I saw Bruno. Now he was bald and clean shaven, with a fringe of close-cropped white-flecked gray hair along the sides.

Women of a certain age divide our definition of handsome men into two categories: Ed Harris or Sam Shepard. If a handsome man has hair, he is Sam Shepard. Bruno was Ed Harris, with notes of Liam Neeson. He was helping his mother with her coat. He caught my eye. A wave and a nod. A look of recognition: Hi. It's Tuesday. We Are Here with Our Mothers.

It was not yet time for us to meet.

I was single for most of my adult life, and during that time I pondered long and hard the universal questions every long-term singleton asks:

Is it really like everybody says, that if I stop looking, my partner will suddenly appear?

Is that guaranteed, or is that something people just say after the fact because they don't want to reveal themselves to have been lonely, needy, pathetic, and searching?

Can I stop wanting and expecting love and yet at the same time (down deep) really want and expect love?

If I purposely and intentionally stop wanting and expecting love in order to make love appear, aren't I just gaming the system? Will the karmic wheel in the great game show of romance land on the Kenmore side-by-side washer/dryer, or will it reward me with the Brand-New Car?

Do I need to double down and be more intentional about everything? Be more declarative and confident about it all?

Do I need updating or improving? Can everyone tell I bought this jacket in 1989?

Have I become so quirky that what used to be endearing and adorable is now a spinsterish turnoff?

Was I ever really endearing or adorable?

If I really am such a catch, then why are the only people who tell me this my gay friends and my mom?

Which Golden Girl am I?

You wake up one day and realize with sudden clarity that every single professional athlete, and many of the coaches, are younger than you are. The majority of the cabinet of the United States government is younger than you are. The president of the United States was graduating from law school the same year you had a baby. You are almost old enough to be Jimmy Fallon's mom.

Aging makes it harder to meet appropriate people, but there is also an easing, a comfort, and a surrender to the reality of who you are and what you are about. In addition, because I both like to be alone and am frequently surrounded by family, I have never felt the urgent need for company.

My daughter might have had other plans. The very last thing Emily had said to me after I left her at college was both an admonition and a permission. She knocked on the driver's side window just as I was about to pull away from campus: "It's called Match.com, Mom. You just type in your zip code, and a list of guys pops up." In the quiet evenings that fall, I typed in Freeville's zip code, and the available men who popped up all looked frighteningly familiar. They were guys I had gone to high school with, ex-husbands of girls I had gone to high school with, lonely adjunct professors from Cornell or Cortland State, and truckers posed next to their motorcycles. I tabled my search and decided that if I was to meet him—whoever he was—then he would have to come to me.

Chapter Six

Meeting Mr. Darcy

Looking into Emily's bedroom in the mornings on my way down to make coffee, the tiny room was just as she had left it. In the time I had owned the house on Main Street, she and I had moved three times and changed cities twice. Her other bedrooms in Washington and Chicago kept pace with the change and growth in her life. This was the only place that had been a constant for her since the age of four.

Tacked onto the cheap sound-conducting plasterboard walls were pictures from camp, Harry Potter memorabilia, and several "newspapers" her father had hand-made to celebrate various accomplishments in her life, featuring photos and hand-lettered headlines with charming mock news stories starring her. During summers, Emily and I both had the habit of starting our mornings by reading in bed. All through high school vacations, I would peek into her room in the morning and find her awake and reading or doing sudoku puzzles in pen. Unlike my taste in books, Emily's was both broad and deep. She had graduated from Harry Potter to Trollope, lying in her creaky spool bed in her little bedroom. I considered this to be the place where she had grown up, and now I wanted to ready it for the next phase of her—but mainly my—life.

I don't think I would suggest in my advice column for a middle-aged singleton to shelve her romantic yearnings to focus instead on a house renovation, and yet that is what I decided to do. My house attachments have always been almost as strong as my romances; my house-proud mother often said that while people sometimes let her down, her house never had. Like much of Jane's wisdom, this seemed both practical and true. My fantasies about meeting a partner started to morph into a dream about making my house bigger and more beautiful.

Much time in my cowboy office was now spent imagining how great it would be to push out the back of my house, just a few feet. I wanted an upstairs sleeping porch overhanging a screened-in area off the kitchen. During our regular Wednesday morning breakfasts with my mother, aunts, and sisters at the Queen Diner, I drew my plan on a napkin. "You should call Bruno," Rachel said. A few weeks later, Bruno's brother Jacques came to my house one night with a group of friends from high school. When I detailed my plans to him, he also said, "You should call Bruno."

Given his reputation as a designer and builder, I thought Bruno was probably too good for my little renovation project. But I called him anyway. Soon after catching his eye at the Election Day turkey dinner, I left a message at his office. He didn't call back.

Just before Thanksgiving, Rachel and I went to Ithaca to see my nephew Jack sing with a regional children's chorus. In our musical family, Jack was particularly talented. He had inherited Jane's perfect pitch, and with his blond curls, he both looked and sang like an angel. Rachel and I sat next to each other in the pew at the Unitarian church wiping tears away. I nudged her. "This is why I came home," I said.

"I know," she whispered.

During the intermission, we ran into Bruno. Two of his daughters were also in the choir. I told him I had left a message about my house renovation, but he'd never called me back. He laughed. "Sorry."

I sidled in for a hug and noticed that I fit nicely under his armpit. He took out a mechanical pencil, wrote my cell number on the back of his business card, and put it in his pocket. When Rachel and I took our seats again,

I could feel him looking down at me from the balcony. I found it hard to concentrate.

I was at the Bright Day Laundromat doing my whites when Bruno called me. He said he was going to be in the village, and he'd like to stop by and take a look at my house. I threw my sopping sheets into a basket and raced to meet him there.

Bruno entered my house like John Wayne darkening Maureen O'Hara's doorway in *The Quiet Man*. His large silhouette was backlit against the open door, and a cyclone of leaves kicked up on the porch behind him. His giant red Chevy pickup truck filled the driveway.

He came into the house and we shook hands. Tingle. I took him upstairs to show him my plan to push out the back of my house. I noticed the unmade bed and the horrible clutter of my cowboy room. I was wearing the same clothes I was wearing the day before (laundry day), and I'd forgotten to brush my hair. We descended the creaky stairs and he sat on my uncomfortable twig couch. I offered him a cup of warmed-over coffee, which he accepted.

Bruno and I first met when I was twelve and he was sixteen. I became aware of him when I entered the orbit of his unusual and enormous family. His parents were proto-hippie Dorothy Day Catholics who farmed a ramshackle 225-acre place they called Maryhill Farm, three miles from our own falling-down farm.

Both dairy farms—theirs and ours—were failing enterprises but for almost opposite reasons. My father white-knuckled his way through the early 1970s farming crisis by doubling down on his debt and drinking at roadside gin mills after the evening milking with men named "Speed" and "Rusty." My old man supplemented his passion for farming by working on construction sites during the day. Bruno's father, Norbert, was an educated and erudite World War Two test pilot, philosopher, and dreamer. Born to wealth in an illustrious family of architects and designers, Mr. Schickel built and developed apartment properties in Ithaca. He kept the dairy farm as a way to give his thirteen children *character*.

The Schickels' farming operation didn't necessarily work out so well—though they somehow kept it going for forty years—but the character part took root. All of the children had been homeschooled by their mother until sixth grade, when they hopped the Greyhound bus for their daily commute to St. Mary's in Cortland, fifteen miles away. By the time they entered our local high school, their legend had preceded them. The eight Schickel boys were all big, good-looking, athletic, weirdly named, and— due to their prior isolation and innocence of the communal dark knowledge of high school society—they didn't seem to care what other people thought of them.

Bruno and two of his older brothers, Sarto and Norbert, entered our high school as upperclassmen, when St. Mary's shut down its upper grades. They were a sensation in their cutoff jean shorts, T-shirts, shit-kicker boots, and flowing silky Jesus hair. My older sister Rachel (also beautiful, with flowing flaxen hair) immediately started dating Bruno's older brother. For the entire summer before I entered eighth grade, Rachel took me and Anne over the hill to Maryhill Farm almost every day. I was Rachel's tagalong and romantic beard so she could hang out with her boyfriend. I knew this, but I didn't care because I liked being there.

Bruno was a blur. Though he was only sixteen, he seemed like a grown man to me. He ran the family's farm operation—he started overseeing his elder brothers and the hired help on the farm when he was a bossy nine-year-old. As a rawboned teenager, Bruno always seemed to be leaping onto or off of a tractor, pitching apples at a wayward kid, pointing out things to do, and yelling. I remember hiding from him because I was afraid he'd find a job for me.

I spent the summer of my twelfth year diving into the farm's pond and trying to teach Bruno's younger siblings (three of them were around my age) synchronized swimming moves and show tunes. Unfortunately, the only song this cloistered and very Catholic family seemed to know was "She'll Be Coming 'Round the Mountain," a song whose jauntiness cannot make up for the fact that it is really just a song about waiting. Even at the age of twelve, I already knew that she would never actually make it 'round the mountain driving her six white horses, but the Schickel kids had not been acculturated to anything recognizable. They seemed to exist in a bubble of perpetual curiosity about things I was born knowing, such as the lyrics to the Carole King songbook and the punch lines to *Laugh-In*.

The family had no radio but did have a tiny black-and-white television, purchased just before John Glenn orbited the earth. It lived in a closet and was brought out only for momentous occasions, such as papal visits and Richard Nixon's resignation. Their only discernible technology was an old record player that played two records: an old Spike Jones 78 and a Bob Dylan album. One teenage sister eventually smashed the Spike Jones record in a fit of cultural rage (and I stand with her on this). After that, they were left with only Dylan, the indestructible troubadour. At Maryhill Farm, the answer always seemed to be blowing in the wind.

Mrs. Schickel ran an open household. Every night after chores, around twenty people crowded on benches around their long table. Dinners resembled a cross between a food riot during the French Revolution and a current-events seminar. They prayed before eating and hollered at each other throughout. Their house was a haven for neighbors (the closest also had thirteen kids), cousins, long-term visitors from other states, hippies passing through, and runaways with nowhere else to go. Although I was none of these things, I was also harboring my own secret: My father had just left our family, our cows had been sold, and the contents of our barn auctioned off; our way of life was gone, my mother was sad and searching, and I was completely at sea.

In the evenings at dusk, my mother would pick us up at Maryhill Farm. I would find her waiting in the Schickels' driveway with the engine running in her brown Duster. Then we would return to our newly quiet house and hollowed-out world.

Bruno played football in the fall and basketball in the winter. He once refused to play a whole season of basketball when the coach told him to cut his hair. He wasn't the only teen I knew who seemed to feel the secret to his power resided Samson-like in his tresses, but his stance was notable—there weren't many boys who stood up to Coach Smith. The Schickels were on the vanguard of the hair wars. Their parents seemed not to care in the slightest how long their sons' hair grew, while my father would roll down the window in his pickup truck and wolf-whistle at any boy he saw sporting hair below his ears (including my own brother). "Hey there, princess!" he'd call.

Throughout high school, Bruno and I circulated in our own orbits, only occasionally intersecting. I was a cheerleader on the sidelines during the legendary undefeated 1973 football season, when Bruno shoved his football helmet over his Comanche braids (he wore the coach down) and knocked a lot of opposing players over. Bruno and I had a nodding acquaintance in the high school hallway as I came into my own, stuffing down my own sadness and running myself ragged as I raced through high school—always on my way to a meeting, practice, rehearsal, or game. With no cows in the barn and no evening chores to go home to, I devoted myself to every after-school activity I could find: field hockey and cheerleading through the fall and winter, and band, chorus, and the school musical in the spring.

The year Bruno graduated, Rachel did as well and headed to college. Anne left for Europe as an exchange student, and Charlie went into the Navy. Practically overnight, Jane and I were left alone. She would come home after her job as a typist at Cornell University's College of Engineering and lie down on her bed, still wearing her coat and holding her purse. After about a half hour she would get up, take off her coat, and make dinner for the two of us.

My mother and I rattled around in our old house. I couldn't bring myself to pull open the heavy doors leading to our now-empty barn, a place I had always loved. Our enormous and beautiful barn stood just at the edge of my periphery. It was a worn wooden palace to a faraway life. The only livestock we had left was a small tribe of barn cats, who with their black-and-white markings were a mocking reminder of the Holsteins we had surrendered. By day, our big red barn merely looked massive and forlorn, but at night it loomed like a leviathan outside my bedroom window. Its dark and brooding outline interrupted the passage of the stars against the night sky. I couldn't wait to get myself to college.

Bruno stayed home. After high school, he stopped running the family farm and turned the job over to a succession of younger brothers and then on to his sister Ruth. Bruno took a job as a carpenter and laborer for a local construction company and continued to live with his parents, siblings, and assorted others in their rambling farmhouse. Mrs. Schickel got up at six o'clock each morning to make Bruno's coffee and braid his hair before he headed to the job site.

These worn memories came flooding back to me as Bruno sat in my living room, reviewing my renovation and sipping his coffee. Bruno's braid was long gone. He was starting to resemble his father. He now owned his own construction company. I had seen his signs in front of handsome houses and construction sites around the county. As I pondered my house's prospects, I wondered if I could afford him.

Bruno drew a diagram of my renovation plan on the back of my utility bill, which he had lifted from the coffee table. He pointed out that my house was old and small. He said the renovation would cost more than the house was worth. He didn't think it would be a good idea to renovate a house with so little promise. He said if I wanted a bigger house, I should probably just move. He earnestly made eye contact. I tried to think of a word for the blue of his eyes. I decided their unique hue was somewhere between that of a Tiffany box and a June sky. I remembered how he looked in his shiny tiny nylon basketball shorts in high school, back in the '70s before basketball shorts started looking like knee-length culottes. This was what I was thinking about while Bruno was describing why he was turning down my renovation.

Then he asked me if I had heard about his divorce, and I pulled back into focus. I had not.

The warmed-over coffee grew cold (again) while I listened to Bruno describe what his life had been like over the past several years. He was raising three of his four daughters at his house four miles away in Dryden (his oldest, Clare, like Emily, had just started college). Suddenly, he jumped up. The flimsy furniture he'd been sitting on clattered on the plywood floor. He said he had to pick up his youngest daughter from school. Before I could say, "Don't leave me. Ever," he was gone. So was I. I wasn't quite sure what had just happened, but I thought something had definitely happened. At least something had happened to me.

A couple of days went by. On Wednesday morning I was sitting in my car in the parking lot of the Queen Diner, waiting to have breakfast with my mother, aunts, and sister. I looked at the diner's drab brick façade. I knew what we would do that morning. We would talk about curtains, and joint replacement, and movies, and who was bringing what to Thanksgiving dinner at my cousin Nancy's house on Main Street. The previous Wednesday we had diagrammed sentences. We might do that again.

I dialed Bruno's cell. He answered on the first ring. "Well, you turned down my renovation, so I feel like the least you can do is buy me a cup of coffee," I said. He asked me to meet him in downtown Ithaca in twenty minutes. I ran into the Queen and faced my Greek diner chorus. "I think I have a date!" I said. It was nine-thirty on a Wednesday morning. They laughed, and I left.

Bruno and I met in Ithaca. We drank a gallon of coffee apiece. He talked and talked. He asked me if I had any hobbies, and I couldn't think of any. He asked me if I liked to travel and I said, um...not really. Mainly I wanted to ride bicycles down Main Street with him. I wanted to go ice-skating. I forgot to be my show-offy self and retreated to the quotidian. My mind had become a soft blank. Two hours went by. His cell phone had been ringing continuously, and he finally stood up to go back to work.

It was a beautiful and rare sunny late-November day. I asked Bruno if he wanted to go for a walk with me around the small downtown park. "No," he said. "I mean, I *can* walk—I just don't want to."

Oh, Mr. Darcy, how you do toy with my affections.

The abruptness of Bruno's response took me aback. It seemed that my magical ability to repel someone I was interested in had kicked in, yet again.

I drove home, hopped up on coffee, and went back to work. I couldn't wait for the day to end. That night I went upstairs, pushed my books and papers aside, and climbed into bed, still wearing my clothes. I lay awake, looking out my bedside window onto the dark silence of my hometown. When the dawn broke, I got up, changed my clothes, and tried to reframe my renovation plans. I drove to Dunkin' Donuts and then past the farm where Bruno grew up and where his mother and brother Jacques still lived.

I drove over to the pretty little lake just beyond their farm. When I was in high school, this was where people gathered for beer-drinking parties, tailgating out of pickup trucks. It was a park now, a gathering place for kayakers and ice fishing.

I sat sipping my milky coffee, watching the slate-colored November sky. The last of the geese were fleeing south. I could hear their faint honking overhead. Throughout my adult life, my romantic efforts had been tinged by rejection, but this felt different. My plucky youth had disappeared. My hopes themselves were migrating south. There would be no more of this for me. It was all too exhausting. My diaphragm would sit in its pink plastic case forevermore. After my death, Emily would find it, tossed under the sink with the curlers I also never used. She would say to someone, *"What the hell is this thing?"* And she would be told, *"That is an artifact of your mother's empty hopes."*

There was no room large enough in my little house to contain my longing. I didn't even seem to have the language for what I really wanted, which was everything I would never have. This felt like the end, and I knew I needed to find a way to adjust. I might never find a life partner, or even a swing-dancing partner. But adjusting to disappointment...now, that was something I'd had a lot of practice with.

Thanksgiving morning, a week after meeting with Bruno, I was still smarting from his rejection(s). I got up early and went with Rachel's husband, Tim, to take his falcon out to hunt ducks for dinner. Tim's kestrel lived in a hutch in their attic. They fed it microwaved frozen mice, and Tim took it out hunting during duck season. Tim worked at Cornell's famed Lab of Ornithology. He hunted with other falconers all over the world— with British barons and Arab sheikhs. And sometimes with his heart-sore sister-in-law.

It had snowed the night before, and the landscape was in Wyeth tones of white, brown, and gray.

Tim and I drove to an open field near a pond. He brought out the hooded bird, perched atop his big leather glove, and unleashed his bird dog, Skeeter. Tim removed the hood and set the bird free. It shot up, soared and circled far overhead. Skeeter flushed some ducks from the pond, and we watched the kestrel stop, change direction, and dive toward them like a sleek, duck-seeking bomb. The kestrel slammed into a duck midair with the sound of a crack of a baseball bat, and we watched the duck flutter to the ground. Skeeter charged off to retrieve it. Tim held some rabbit meat for the kestrel and called it back to his glove.

Watching this ancient dance, I couldn't help but notice the parallels to my own hunting style. I was the heat-seeking kestrel, forever soaring and then dive-bombing. That was my problem. But now I was done. I felt a calm that accompanies the end of nonsense. I awaited the sweet relief from sexual longing I was sure menopause would bring. In a decade or so more, this would be done.

My family and I ate the duck along with our store-bought turkey for Thanksgiving dinner that day. Marinated and grilled, and it was delicious.

The day after Thanksgiving, Bruno's brother called me. Jacques and I had become closer along with other friends from high school during my visits home over the years. I would sometimes take my coffee over to his pottery studio on the edge of their farm's cornfield to talk while he put pieces into the kiln. Jacques said that his many brothers and sisters had gathered at the farm for Thanksgiving, and he wanted to invite me over for dinner. Jacques was unaware of my recent encounter with his brother, but Bruno's recent renovation rejection was still smarting. That night I planned to go to a movie alone, but I promised to stop by beforehand.

I was swinging a bottle of wine by my side as I picked my way through the many cars parked in their farm's wide driveway that night. I checked my watch; I hate to miss previews and figured I could pop in for a half hour and then make it to the film. I noticed Bruno's red truck parked and idling. The cab light was on, and he was sitting inside. I ducked under a pine tree to avoid him and got a few yards from the kitchen door, when he lowered the driver's window and called out to me. He waved me over.

"That's okay. I...I'll just head in," I stammered.

He got out. "No, come here for a minute. Please?"

I did. He opened the door for me and I climbed into the passenger side. It was warm inside the truck's cab. It smelled like pine, Carhartts, and dusty

Muck boots. My self-consciousness was acute. Bruno said he was driving over to his house to pick up his nephew. Would I come with? I glanced toward the crowded house but felt a magnetic pull toward the truck. *You can take me anywhere,* I thought.

Bruno took the two-lane road away from town. The moon was full, white, and hanging directly through the windshield like a giant romantic beacon. I had to stifle a laugh at the brutal irony of it. I was trapped in a moving vehicle with my crush, and the moon itself was mocking me.

We drove along quietly. Bruno seemed utterly at ease. I was quaking. I felt the truth emerging like a full moon rising.

"You know I have a crush on you, Bruno, right?" I said, staring straight ahead at the road.

He was quiet for a moment. "Well, Amy, I'm very flattered...," he said.

I didn't hear the rest. I knew that when someone was *flattered* by your attention, you were done.

Gamely I tried to recover. We drove through the snow, up a quiet lane with trees on both sides meeting overhead. We pulled into the long driveway of his beautiful farmhouse, surrounded by fields and hedgerows, illuminated by the giant white moon. *Pemberley.* I walked inside with him, and we retrieved his teenage nephew Ben and drove back to his mother's farm. I told Bruno I was going to leave to catch my movie. "My mother will be very sad if she doesn't get to see you. Just come in to say hi to her," he told me, and because he'd played the mother card, I entered his family's party.

The house was crowded with adults and their children. I greeted his many siblings, most of whom I hadn't seen in decades. I saw Bruno talking to his mother, and then he led her to me. Like my own mother, Marnie was white-haired, stooped, and frail.

She said, "My son says you are a proper young lady and that you won't stay without a personal invitation from me, Amy. I hope you'll stay to eat with us."

I made sure to sit with a group as far away from Bruno as I could manage, but I noticed him watching me from the periphery. All night long, he was just at the edge of my field of vision. At one point during the crowded and noisy meal, I could see only his elbow, and I knew I was in love with it.

Chapter Seven

The Antidote for Longing

Female companionship is the only treatment I know to remedy a case of terminal longing. Women who have experienced this tender state will assist by sharing their own stories of romance and heartbreak before telling you what to do. Right after my rejection by Bruno, my sister Rachel and my cousin Jan took me out for drinks. We sat at the deserted bar of a beautiful lakeside hotel with a view of Cayuga Lake, which on this day was the color of iron and whipped into whitecaps by late-November winds. I told Rachel and Jan about what had happened with Bruno. We broke it down into components and storyboarded it on the bar. Who said what, when? What were you wearing? What was he wearing?

Both women countered by telling the stories of their adult courtships with their (second) husbands. While my mother and my aunts had all stayed single after their divorces, it seemed all of the women in my generation of the family were making successful second marriages—Jan with Roger, my sister Anne with Brian, and Rachel with Tim.

Basically, their advice boiled down to this: Grab him and kiss him, move in with him, marry him.

Boldness was certainly not my problem, and yet it *was* my problem. Since high school, I had always behaved as if a prospective relationship were an audition for a Busby Berkeley musical. This time felt entirely different. True, I had thrown down the gauntlet by telling Bruno that I had a crush on him (I had done that before with other people). But I said that only so he would know something important about me. I had no specific expectations, although his claim to be flattered by my attention seemed the worst possible response.

It would be disrespectful to throw myself at someone I thought I'd fallen in love with, versus someone I was merely showing off for. With Bruno, I moved beyond my own impulses. I didn't want him to feel bad or uncomfortable. I would *not* grab Bruno and kiss him. I would leave Bruno alone, because I was in love with him. "Fly, Bruno, fly away!" I declared at the bar, cupping my hands and releasing them skyward. My tiny imaginary Bruno fluttered ceilingward. He was wearing his satin high school basketball uniform.

We were laughing so loudly I almost didn't hear my phone ringing. I looked down and saw his number. I showed my phone to my companions: "Excuse me, it's my husband calling." More peals of laughter.

I went into the other room to take his call. He said he wanted to talk. He said he was confused by what was happening. He sputtered, saying that he didn't feel ready for a romance.

I interrupted: "Hey, don't worry about it. I've moved back home and I'm going to stay put. I'm not going anywhere. You can drive over to my house when I'm seventy years old, and I'll still come out onto the porch, leaning on my cane. We can be friends. I'm good with that." Even though I meant what I'd said, I still felt my sinuses start to sting—back there where the tears come from.

Bruno was quiet. I was thinking about his elbow and how much I loved it.

"Really. I mean it," I said.

"Um...that's not going to be good enough for me," he said. "That's not what I want."

I was heading to Chicago the next day to visit my office at the *Tribune* and tape an episode of *Wait Wait*. I told Bruno that we could talk when I got back. I snapped my phone shut and returned to my drinking companions.

"I think we'll have the wedding reception right out there on the lawn," I said, sweeping my arm toward the hotel's lakeside property.

The laughter from my sister and cousin indicated that they thought I was joking—and I was. But I wasn't.

Few dating books are bold enough to state it out loud: Courtship works. I'd never really tried it before. The few relationships I'd ever had commenced with the fireworks of physical attraction, followed by anxiety, missed connections, recrimination, and an eventual parting of ways.

During that week's taping, I was onstage with Roy Blount Jr.—another comic genius who miraculously combines the qualities of being both hilarious and kindhearted. I told Roy about the hometown contractor I had gone to high school with who was, I thought, interested in courting me. Bruno had called and left a message, but now I was trying to play it cool. Should I call him back? Roy had heard about the night of the chipmunk hands. He had been to the rodeo a few times himself. Roy told me not to play games and to get on with it.

Encouraged by Roy's enthusiasm (and because it was what I wanted), I embarked on a courtship with Bruno that felt both timeless and surprisingly well adjusted. During my week away from home, we started talking on the phone. We talked for hours each night and several times during the day. We talked about our work, our children, our mothers, our schedules, politics, current events, religion, music, and vacations. We wracked our brains for memories from our shared childhoods that might link us together. We reviewed our failed marriages and tried to be honest about the parts we'd played in what had gone wrong.

Bruno said, "I have an idea, Amy. Let's do everything differently this time." This commonsense concept was something I had never considered. I'd always built upon my own relationship failures by simply trying harder and hoping to get lucky. I promised Bruno (and myself) that I would embrace doing everything differently.

Emily called me from college. I told her, "I think I have a boyfriend!" When I told her who it was, she said, "Hubba, hubba. Good job, Mom."

I returned to Freeville on a Friday. Bruno asked if he could come and see me. He said he would bring lunch.

Bruno walked onto my porch bearing takeout meals and a huge bunch of lilies with fat pink buds, just on the cusp of bloom. We embraced. He said, "I can feel your heart beating," and then he placed his hand over my sweater, and I could feel both my heart and his hand, pulsing together. We sat down and held hands. "You know what I like about you?" Bruno asked me.

Hmmm, probably my minky hair. Wait. Maybe my sense of humor. Or no—my goodness. My overall goodness. Or maybe he likes my boots. But what if he says I "look good for my age"?

"You're reliable," he said.

Reliable? This is what he comes up with when he's trying to win me over? Bruno explained how much my reliability meant to him: that when I said something, I meant it, and when I said I'd do something, I did it. I had never pondered the impact of being reliable on other people, perhaps because I was raised and surrounded by people who could be counted on. Hearing this strange compliment made me think differently about Bruno. He was not like other people.

Bruno and I knew we were in love early on. We said as much to each other after two or three weeks of seeing one another. We were sitting on my rickety couch in front of the fire, holding hands. He said, "Amy, I have something to tell you." I had already learned that whenever Bruno said, "I have something to tell you" or "I have an idea," what came next would be very good for me. I was in love with his thoughts, many of which seemed to be about me. I had simply never had that much—or that quality—of attention poured onto me. That was when we told each other that we were in love.

Every evening, after I had eaten dinner with my mother and he with his daughters, Bruno drove over to my house in his red pickup truck. I stood by the front window, scanning Main Street for the familiar headlights. I threw on my coat, ran outside, and scrambled over Main Street's eternal snowbank to jump into the overheated cab with him. I scooched over on the leather panel seat to sit right next to him, just like a girl in a Garth Brooks video. I flung my arms around him and sang along with the radio into his ear.

He asked me to sing his favorite—a pop hit by Ingrid Michaelson, which he dubbed "the Rogaine Song."

The song's lyrics, about a woman who promises a man that she will do lots of everyday things for him (including buying him Rogaine when he starts losing his hair) held so much meaning for two old people like us who had found each other. I whispered it to him like a promise.

Bruno and I toured the countryside of our childhood together, driving over moonlit roads in the snow, pulling over to gaze at the starry winter sky and the rolling snowfields, hedgerows, and formerly cultivated farmland turned to forest. Bruno seemed to want to show me everything—all of the houses he had built, the vet hospital going up near the mall, and the community of adorable candy-colored rental cottages he had designed and built outside Ithaca. We celebrated the next full moon by wishing each other a happy mooniversary.

Emily came home for Christmas vacation, and Bruno gingerly tried to get to know her. I could tell she was wary, but she also behaved as I would have hoped. She was open to my romance and didn't seem to take my absences personally. Still, middle-aged women in love are by definition schoolgirl-ishly annoying.

Emily and I were headed to the mall one day to finish our Christmas shopping. She had just gotten her driver's license and was practicing. Bruno was building a nearby building; I saw his company sign posted on the street in front. "Let's do a stakeout!" I squealed. I made her drive over to the construction site, but I lost my nerve when I saw Bruno climbing out of an excavation hole and ducked under the dashboard.

Emily was horrified. "Ohmygod, Mom. This is so high school!"

I said, "I know, but I never acted like this in high school. In high school, I was mature."

Bruno saw the car and walked over. He was wearing heavily insulated canvas Carhartt overalls against the bitter wind. He put his hand on the car roof and ducked down to say hello to Emily. I quietly righted myself and said, "I . . . I just dropped something on the floor." Emily rolled her eyes.

On Christmas Eve, Bruno left a package on the porch. Very late that night, after church and long after Emily had gone upstairs to bed, I sat alone in front of the fire and opened it. It was a small painting of a luminous bunch of white bleeding heart blossoms, spilling from a vase. A friend of his had painted it. The heart-shaped blossoms were tumbling, delicate, and wild. I carried the picture upstairs and put it next to my bed.

Christmas morning, I went to my mother's house very early to help her get up and to get Christmas breakfast started for my sisters, their husbands, and all of our children. Mom's illnesses all collided that morning; she stayed in her bed in the living room in front of her fireplace and we tried to have Christmas around her. There, surrounded by wrapping paper, we decided that she needed to go to the hospital, and so the day became about something else: carrying her out through the snow, getting her into a hospital room, and taking shifts to be with her. I was driving to the hospital for my shift during her overnight stay when Bruno called me. I pulled over and unleashed all of my anxiety, frustration, worry, and sadness. While I was talking to him, he pulled up beside me, got out of his truck, and held me close while I sobbed.

We started telling people about our relationship. I broke the news to my mother, aunts, and sisters. At Wednesday morning breakfast at the Queen Diner, we all clinked our coffee cups together in a toast. Bruno came to my mother's house to visit with her. Like Emily, Jane was polite and acted delighted. But really, what are you supposed to say when two people tell you they're in love? It's a setup without a punch line. In addition to his mother, Bruno had eleven siblings. He called each one of them, and then he started working outward from there, calling aunts and uncles, family friends, and business associates in the building trade. He even reached an elderly cousin in Germany who didn't speak English.

Bruno had three daughters living with him: Angela, seventeen, Dominican by birth and living with Bruno and his family from the age of ten (Bruno adopted her when she was fifteen); Michaela, also seventeen, born to Bruno and his former wife; and Avila, age eleven, adopted from China when she was a baby. Clare, Bruno's oldest daughter, who like Emily was nineteen and had just started college, lived with her mother nearby during school breaks. Bruno and I never declared ourselves with our children the way we had with other people. We both assumed that our children knew that we were together and would be staying together. Because all of our children behaved well around us, we were certain that they would welcome our relationship. We were loving and involved parents, but we were also blind to the impact that our coming together would have on everyone in the family.

Chapter Eight

Let Me Get My Puppets

There is no more fearsome creature on the planet than the daughter of a single father. I know this because of questions I receive for my advice column from pissed-off and vengeful daughters. I have also seen at least forty Disney movies pivoting on this ancient plotline, including both the original and the remake of *The Parent Trap*. I figured that even if Bruno's lovely girls *were* inclined in my direction, fairy tales, YA novels, and basically every other outlet in American popular culture would have taught them how to terrify a woman in love with their father.

Bruno and I slowly brought our relationship out into the open. We met for lunch at the Queen Diner, equidistant between our houses. We further closed the distance by squeezing into the same side of the booth together. We talked on the phone during the day and, when possible, got together after dinner. I mainly stayed away from Bruno's house, because he had his hands full with his three daughters—Angela and Michaela were juniors in high school, and Avila in fourth grade—but also because I was afraid of them.

These daughters were unfailingly polite to me, but I knew they were giving their father the business at home in the way that adolescents do: through door-slamming and occasional tantrums, expressing their own anxiety by punishing their father. It would be easy to interpret this as a child's desire to interrupt a parent's happiness, but I recalled my own experience as a teen with a single parent. The lesson was later reinforced by my experience as the divorced mother of a teen, who occasionally acted out. I knew that:

Our children do not care if we are happy.

Our children care if they are happy.

Introducing any new relationship, certainly one that seems from the out-set so serious, upends the tender balance in a one-parent household. Hell, my little Emily (then age four) had briefly acted like a maniac when I brought home a cat. The very few dating relationships I had engaged in while a sin-gle mother were conducted offstage; I didn't introduce my daughter to any men I might have been feebly trying to know. But Emily had occasionally given her stepmother a hard time, and as the wronged first wife, I watched this from the sidelines with uncharitable satisfaction. Now, fifteen years later, the tables were turned and karma was handing me a bitch-slap. Fur-thermore, I suspected that if Emily hadn't gone back to college after winter break, she would have found a way to join forces with Bruno's daughters to attempt romantic-interruptus.

Throughout the late winter, I got to know Bruno's girls as gradually as possible (given the speed at which my relationship with their father was pro-gressing), mainly through attending school events with Bruno and watch-ing his daughters do things. Angela was a cheerleader for the basketball team, Michaela ran track, and Avila sang in her school choir. Sitting next to Bruno in the high school gym, we would let our knees touch. *Zing.* We kept our PDA to a minimum, but there was no mistaking the look in our eyes as we gazed at each other.

Bruno wanted to keep our relationship, um…chaste, because he is Catholic as well as old-fashioned and had been giving his older daughters the somewhat quaint "no sex until marriage" talk. This was also part of our campaign to try to do everything differently. Frankly, this was one area of our lives where I did *not* want to do *anything* differently, but I respected his views and his desire to court, date, and get to know each other intimately before getting to know each other intimately. When one partner wants to go full speed ahead but the other wants to wait, the person who wants to wait usually prevails. I decided to trust him on this score, that delaying physical intimacy would be a good thing for us. At times this was a tough agreement to keep, and yet we did.

After Bruno and I had been seeing one another for three months, I decided to test the mettle of everyone involved by taking the family on a road trip to New York City. It was mid-March. Angela, Michaela, and Avila came with us, and Angela brought a girlfriend. I had bronchitis and was both feverish and wracked by coughing spasms that sounded like a Canada goose being sawed in half. But a friend had a large furnished apartment in New York City, which I rented for the weekend. I had purchased tickets to *The Lion King* for this Broadway-starved family. Bruno and I were in love and thought we could conquer anything. Even New York.

The weather in the city was bitter and March dank. Crusty gray snowbanks lined the sidewalks, which were scattered with leftover road salt and newspaper tumbleweeds. The girls did what groups of girls do: They wore each other's boots and took turns being alternately wonderful and difficult. When they were done cycling through their impressive spiral of feelings, they cycled through them again. Whoever wasn't sulking at the time got to be my sidekick, walking beside me while I gasbagged on about the wonders of the city and delivered wracking coughs into my sleeve. Although I knew he had been to New York before, Bruno didn't seem to have any particular point of view or reference to the place. Not one thing was special the way I wanted it to be, but New York always does that to me. New York dangles its spangly charms like a tennis bracelet in a Tiffany window but then snatches its magic back like a homeless guy peeing underneath a Tiffany window.

The Lion King was family-friendly, epic, and expensive. The show features magnificent giant puppetry. As the massive puppet giraffes came striding down the aisle and onto the stage, it occurred to me: What else was I doing but trying to put on a puppet show for this family? The last time I remembered working so hard to ingratiate myself was in the early '80s, when I worked on the overnight news desk for NBC. Part of my job was to call and wake up a prominent broadcaster whom I'll call "Brandi" at 4:15 a.m.

for her *Today* show live shot. Every morning I staged a mini-opera while I begged Brandi to get out of bed. "Brannnnn-d-iiiiiiii! It's me, your wake-up pal, Amy! America needs you to tell them what's going to happen today!"

My epiphany during *The Lion King* alarmed me. I was embarrassed by my eagerness to please these teens, whose ages, combined, barely equaled my own. Two of the four girls seemed moody and silent throughout the show, and afterward no one mentioned liking it. Instead, everyone only wondered what we would be doing the next day. Bruno held my hand.

That night I lay awake on my friend's couch in the living room (the girls got one bedroom, Bruno the other). I could hear Bruno snoring just beyond the door. It was a particular form of old-fashioned hellfire to be so close to my beloved and yet not be able to simply crawl in with him and call it the end of an exhausting day. Our no-sex rule was working my last nerve.

The next morning, the group looked at me with an expression that read: "…And?" So I flew into action and acted like, "Wait—let me get my puppets!" I took them to Dylan's Candy Bar, which on a Saturday was packed, sticky, and depressing. I took them to Serendipity, but the wait for a table was two and a half hours, so instead we ate lunch at an upstairs burger emporium on 10th Avenue, the New York City equivalent of sharing a slice with Pizza Rat. Then I force-marched the whole group to Roosevelt Island on the tram. The Roosevelt Island tram is my full-on New York fantasy thrill ride. I love to dangle over the river, pondering the magnificent skyline and listening to the soaring Gershwin soundtrack in my head.

As the tramcar dipped and swayed and the girls blankly gazed out the window, I entertained a brief fantasy that the cable would snap and dump me into the river. Only me, mind you. I would swim to shore by myself, and Bruno and his daughters would go on without me, which was, after all, what they seemed to be very good at. I suspected I wouldn't be missed.

Once we got to Roosevelt Island, I instructed everyone to disembark and then walk around the tram station to wait for the ride back to Manhattan. This only underscored the fruitlessness of the entire journey.

After that, I basically gave up. The sun was starting to go down. We would be leaving the next day. I led the group into a gourmet market near the Queensboro Bridge, and we picked up bread, cheese, and fruit. We returned to my friend's apartment, and I collapsed on the couch. Now it was my turn to sulk. After a while, I heard cabinets opening and voices in the kitchen, and when I hoisted myself up, I found all of the girls in the dining area, with bread cut and cheese and fruit laid out on plates. They pulled up a chair and made room for me at the table. We all relaxed into something that resembled normalcy. I stopped tour-guiding and started listening. Michaela announced that they all wanted to go to a movie that night. Without us. They had found a theater, figured out how to get there and back, and wanted to shake us off for the evening. I suspected that they were also deliberately giving me a break, and I was grateful.

After they left, Bruno and I wandered through the Upper East Side. It started to snow, giant snowflakes that floated like feathers against the streetlights. We found a little Italian bistro in a brownstone with the entrance located below street level. Steam had crawled up the restaurant's windows; the little place looked like a Tuscan postcard. We ate together, leisurely and languorously. It was our first New York City meal, just the two of us. I dropped all of my nonsense and pretense; it seemed I'd left my puppets in my other coat. I stopped waiting for New York to wow me and leaned back into enjoying this wonderful relationship, which seemed to be growing like a buried daffodil bulb, getting ready to push up through the snow.

Until this dinner, Bruno had passively tagged along while I charged around the city. After dinner, he walked me up East 84th Street. We stopped on the sidewalk and he asked me to look across the street. There, dominating the block, stood the massive and elegant Church of St. Ignatius Loyola, which Bruno's great-grandfather, Wilhelm Schickel—architect of many New York landmarks—designed and built in 1898. After admiring his ancestor's handiwork, we decided to take the girls there for services the next day, Palm Sunday, before we left the city.

Bruno looked down at me. I was hopping from foot to foot in the cold. "Amy...I have to ask you..." (Bruno has the habit of announcing a question before he asks it.) "Where do you think our relationship is headed?"

I stopped hopping. I hadn't thought about where our relationship was headed. It just seemed to be…headed. Going full speed somewhere. I waited. I looked down at the sidewalk, momentarily at a loss for words.

"I…I want to get married," I blurted out. Until that moment, I don't think I'd possessed one serious thought about marrying Bruno. In seventeen years of singlehood, I had never once actually entertained the idea of remarriage. But the certainty seemed to have been there all along, waiting for me to shut up long enough for it to express itself.

He said, "That's what I want, too. So will you?"

In my mind, I danced. I danced, and sang, and spread my arms wide, twirling like Maria von Trapp on a heather-blanketed mountaintop.

"I will."

As we stood on the sidewalk, embracing, I asked Bruno to do me a favor. I didn't want to share our news with anyone. I wanted to walk around inside our private snow globe for as long as I could. I said, "No planning, no wedding talk, no telling anyone until Dairy Day." I'm not sure why I chose Dairy Day, which is in June, except that I love the parade in our little town and thought it somehow fitting to attach our happy news to a parade that celebrates cows. Heck, maybe we'd decorate our own Bruno-loves-Amy float and parade it down Main Street.

The next morning, we coerced all of the girls to get dressed for the Palm Sunday service at St. Ignatius Loyola. We walked up its broad limestone staircase and entered through the massive and grand bronze doors. The interior of the stately church was a startling baroque mosaic of pinks, yellows, blue, and gold. Bruno and I sat in the pew, bookending the girls, and worshiped together, knowing what no one else knew—that we would become a family. My eyes were drawn up, following the slender marble columns toward the vaulted ceiling. There I saw a springing forth of light and color, like celebratory fireworks blooming overhead.

Chapter Nine

Life Renovation Offer

FROM: Amy Dickinson
TO: Bruno Schickel

March 2008

Dear Mr. Schickel,

Thank you so much for your recent offer to assist me in renovating my life. I understand that you are a very busy person and that your services are much sought after in the tricounty area and beyond.

You mentioned that you don't do estimates, so my understanding is that this is a firm bid. I'd like to review the terms as I understand them.

LIFE RENOVATION: You have agreed to help me renovate my life. This renovation will include but not be limited to:

FOUNDATION: Building a sturdy foundation using the best materials you have at your disposal. As you may have noted from your limited inspections of my structure (thank you, by the way), this particular foundation has its strengths and weaknesses. Various alterations over the years may have compromised it somewhat, but I hope you have found that it is basically sound.

RESTORATION: Finding the hidden gems in my existing structure and restoring, rebuilding, painting, and polishing them, if necessary.

Insulating and protecting the premises against cold and other outside elements.

Inspecting and stoking the furnace, if necessary.

EXTERIOR: On the exterior of my structure, you will add:

Beautiful trim and beautiful children.

MAINTENANCE: You have agreed to perform all the work personally and not subcontract this work out to others. You will personally maintain the structure for a lifetime.

PAYMENT: You will not charge me for this life renovation but may expect payments from time to time, to be negotiated separately.

I am so happy that we will be working on our beautiful building project together. You are probably aware that I have interviewed other builders over the years for this particularly challenging job and have found all of them sorely wanting. When choosing contractors, I decided only to work with the best. I feel lucky that you happened to be available for this particular job.

In return for my life renovation, I offer to love and cherish you for the length of the contract. I will also be nice to your kids, pets, friends, and immediate and extended family, take long walks with you, lie under the stars with you, bake pies for you, laugh with you, sing to you, love you to the core, steal glances at your handsome face, and in general let you complete me. I will also do my best to complete you.

I will continue to let you make me happier than I ever thought possible, and I will return your affection and attention in equal measure.

I hope you find these terms satisfactory. If so, I'd like to get started right away. Not only do I look forward to living in the finished structure for the rest of my life, but I also think this might be one building project where I will enjoy the work itself.

Chapter Ten

The Grenade in the Kitchen

I am a singer of show tunes, not a keeper of secrets. Don't worry, I'll keep your secret, but I don't keep my own. Generally my life goal is to lead the sort of drama-free existence that doesn't require anyone to hush up. Like any of us, I lead a life that is both public and private, but unlike many people, my work depends on people trusting me with their anonymous stories (which I then—it needs to be said—share with the world through my advice column). Unlike discretion, which involves thought, judgment, and choices, secret-keeping is a dangerous business, especially for someone like me, whose poker "tell" is otherwise called "my face."

My propensity to live my own life as a fairly uninteresting open book was seriously tested when I fell in love. Suddenly my personal life seemed very compelling and high octane. Very Kim and Kanye, but with a red pickup truck.

Bruno and I stood on a snowy sidewalk in New York City and exchanged a promise to marry. We made a second promise to keep our news completely private for three months. I wanted to have more time to get to know each other before involving other people. I also found it somewhat embarrassing after almost two decades of being single to so suddenly pivot toward marriage. It had been only ten weeks since Bruno had turned down my renovation project, and now I was in for a wholesale life reconstruction—one that involved five children.

I didn't want an engagement ring. My previous experience with a ring, the one I had purchased for myself and seldom worn, had soured me on the whole concept. It seemed an antiquated idea and somehow unseemly for a middle-aged woman. Sparkly engagement rings are a young woman's game. I couldn't imagine my own left hand, gnarled from gardening and knuckles swollen with arthritis, sporting anything blingy. I'd always put rings in the same category as hats: fine for some women but silly-looking on me.

"No engagement ring, okay?" I said to Bruno. I assumed that in addition to stating my own preference, I was also letting him off the hook, ring-wise.

Bruno looked surprised and a little wounded. "Amy, I'm getting you a ring. I want it to be a giant ring, and I want you to wear it."

Instantly, I changed my mind. I recognized this as part of his campaign to do everything differently. He wanted to be declarative. He wanted to lock this thing down. And I understood, because I felt that way, too. I realized that I'd never before been in a relationship that didn't involve at least a little coercion, where two people manipulated each other into a compromise. I had also never been in a relationship where everything felt so easy.

I did, however, stay firm on the idea of keeping our plans completely secret until Dairy Day. I told Bruno I didn't want to discuss a wedding or do any planning or even think about a wedding until the second weekend in June.

I started driving over to Bruno's house most evenings and having dinner with him and Michaela, Angela, and Avila. They made a place for me at the table, and we exchanged small talk about their school assignments or weekend plans. Sometimes I would share a tricky question I'd received from one of my readers and ask their advice about how to answer it. I got to know some of their friends. Occasionally I still found myself pulling out my puppets, trying to amuse or entertain or win over the girls, but they didn't seem to require (or want) that. They knew that their father and I were a couple and seemed to accept me being tangentially in their lives. (Although Bruno told me that during this period one of his girls asked him, "Dad, why does Amy keep showing up at dinnertime?")

The winter snows stopped swirling, and the snowdrops and crocus emerged in dots of color. Once spring was really blooming, in addition to showing up in the evenings, I also started driving the five miles to their house (which we now laughingly referred to as Pemberley) very early in the morning, bearing donut holes from Dunkin' Donuts and coffee for Bruno. I sat on the front porch in the sunshine watching the sheep in the pasture across from the house, drinking coffee and working on my laptop while the family woke up. The girls would come downstairs in the morning, wearing "You again?" looks on their faces. With Emily at college, my own house was feeling quiet and lonely, and also I simply wanted to be with Bruno at the beginning and the end of each day.

Bruno found an antique ring made in the 1920s—not a giant ring, but a simple band with diamonds clustered in a circle that looked like a blossom. The ring, we were told, came from an estate sale in Beverly Hills. I invented a backstory for it that involved a silent movie star who, like me, was also involved in a secret engagement but who had to sell her ring when her career hit a rough patch during the transition to talkies. It seemed very Myrna Loy. I loved my beautiful blossom ring and kept it by my bedside. I wore it to bed and whenever I thought I wouldn't run into anyone I knew. I slipped it off during my Wednesday breakfasts at the Queen Diner with my sister, mother, and aunts, but as I chatted with them, I could feel it in there, burning a hole through my pocket.

As it turns out, I *can* keep a secret, especially one I am convinced will have a joyful resolution. In fact, I relished holding our relationship close. Our choice locked us into intimacy, while also forcing us to be discreet and careful. Being careful is an underappreciated quality in relationships. So is being reliable. And in this one, there were no surprise letdowns, waiting for phone calls, or waiting at the bar for my date to arrive. We each did what we said we would do.

Bruno and I used the time of our secret engagement well. We reveled in our relationship, without dwelling too much on the details of our future. We continued to tell each other our stories (in middle age, there's a lot of ground to cover); we talked about our children, our work habits, our religious beliefs, and political points of view. There were many areas where we did not see eye to eye, and we learned how we behaved when we disagreed—sometimes sloppily and tearfully but rarely loudly. More important than our disagreements was our ability to fight and forgive. One night we had an argument about global warming that, years later, I could still diagram (where he was standing, where I was standing, what I was wearing) because it got so heated (so to speak). It wound up with my tearful declaration, "I DON'T THINK I CAN MARRY A GLOBAL WARMING DENIER!!!"

I left Bruno's house that night wondering if I could actually marry a man who held what I considered to be an obnoxious view on the topic of global warming. I know, the heating of the earth is a pretty big thing. Okay—it's the biggest thing there is. But my list of nonnegotiables was actually pretty short and mainly involved being mean to people or animals. Bruno's political views forced me to reconsider some of my own assumptions. We could agree to disagree, which concerning certain topics was what we did.

In general, I avoid personal discord (I'm a little tougher professionally). I'm more a "flight" than "fight" type and thus didn't have much experience with how to recover when a disagreement turned into something more. As someone who had been dumped, first by my father and then by my first husband, all I knew at the time about how to manage unhappiness involved either me or the other party leaving. I was like Bill Murray's character in *Groundhog Day*: "Stay? I can't even make a collie stay!" But Bruno did stay. I saw that his bullheadedness was matched by his loyalty. Plus, he is a world-class apologizer. A real look-you-in-the-eye, "I'm very sorry, will you please forgive me" kind of guy.

We continued not discussing the wedding, aside from agreeing to have one at some point over the summer. The courting also continued. Bruno occasionally stopped at my mother's house in the afternoons while I was with her; he seemed like such a big man perched on her little chairs. He drank coffee with us and tried to talk politics with my mother (she demurred). He looked around the old house and found things to fix. Jane had never had anyone around who could fix things and had become accustomed to hiring someone or doing without. It was a major turning point when she asked

Bruno to do something. She also asked me, "Do you think Bruno could take a look at..." (whatever part of her old house needed duct-taping together). That made me feel good.

In mid-May, Emily returned to Freeville from her freshman year in college. Memorial Day weekend was coming up. Bruno expressed his opinion that my Dairy Day declaration plan was sort of dumb (I agreed), and we decided to finally exit the snow globe and start telling our families about our decision to get married.

We chose a day to announce our intentions in late May. We decided to tell our children first and then go to our mothers with the news. We would tell our children separately. I would tell Emily, and he would tell Clare, Angela, Michaela, and Avila on his own. Because our children were wonderful and loved us, and because they knew we were happy together, we felt completely confident that they would accept, even welcome, this news.

Announcement day was cold and dank. Sporadically through the day the heavens opened and rain pelted down. I warmed Emily up for the big news by taking her to a matinee. Going to the movies together had always been one of our favorite pastimes, and in some ways I saw this as the symbolic last "date" of our mother-daughter dating relationship. We saw *Iron Man* at the mall. We had each already seen it once—she while at school, and me with my mother—but we hadn't seen it together, so our previous viewings didn't count.

After *Iron Man*, I drove home and pulled into our driveway. Although the windshield wipers were on high, they were unable to keep up with the rain, which was coming down so hard that the front door of the house looked like a waterlogged mirage through the windshield. My peony bush— just starting to bloom in the front garden—was being flattened into a crop circle. Emily and I were chitchatting about the movie, when I said, "I have something to tell you..."

She turned toward me. "What, Mommy?"

"Bruno and I have decided to get married. He's telling his girls now, and I'm telling you because we want you to be the first to know." Emily was silent. I saw the irises of her beautiful dark brown eyes start to turn black.

My daughter is overall a calm, low-tension, "easy" person, but since early childhood she has had the ability to shoot lightning bolts from her eyes. Lightning bolt eye-shooting happens to be one of her superpowers. I saw the telltale storm gathering. I tried to fill in the ominous silence: "It's going to be fine, honey. You'll see."

Emily burst into heaving sobs, threw open the door, ran out of the car through the rain, entered the house, and slammed the door behind her.

Meanwhile, five miles away at Pemberley, Bruno had assembled Michaela, Angela, and Avila in the kitchen. "Girls, I have something to tell you…"

Michaela stood up and yelled at her father and left the room, slamming the door. Then Angela stood up, yelled at him, and marched off in a different direction. Having been abandoned by her two older sisters, little Avila burst into tears, yelled at him, and stomped off, slamming yet another door. Bruno stood in the now-empty kitchen and called me on my cell phone. I was still sitting in my car, afraid to enter the house, fearful of the daughter-monster stomping around within.

One aspect of adolescence that parents sometimes overlook is the central question that children hold close: *What about me?* We parents don't like to dwell on this—or even acknowledge it—because it inconveniently discounts our belief in our godlike power to take any choice *we* make and spin it into something that will benefit *them*. But our children are more worried about themselves than they are about us. We tell ourselves (and sometimes even say it out loud) that if we are happy, they will be happy. This is what we say to our kids when we are leaving them with a sitter because we want to go out or when we are moving them away from their friends and family for a work opportunity. But our personal happiness does not guarantee our kids' happiness, and deep down, we know it.

I well remember the time my very wise friend Gay schooled me on the subject of older adolescents. At the time, I was sitting in her kitchen, bemoaning some now-forgotten issue with my fifth grader. I believed that separations were tough for Emily, but Gay—who has observed countless parent–child interactions in her forty-five years of teaching children—begged to differ. She rightly pointed out that separations were actually hard for *me*. Gay gave me a piece of wisdom I've never forgotten. It was so simple and so true that I have quoted it in my column, as well as let it influence my own parenting choices. "For our children, their job is to eventually leave us," she reminded me, "and our job as parents is to let them."

Parenting is a drawn-out and occasionally terrifying process of letting go. I had let Emily go her own way, running her own college application process and making choices about her major, her job during college, her grades, and where she wanted to spend her time when she wasn't in school. But now she was having to let *me* go, and she wasn't ready.

Like any parent, I do not like to disappoint my offspring. But because of the nineteen years we had spent raising each other, Emily and I had a somewhat unusual closeness that felt like a deep and fulfilling friendship. I could think of only a handful of times I had ever had to say no to her or knowingly disappoint her, and those times were preceded and followed by a lot of discussion and persuasion—and some puppetry. I wasn't the kind of parent to bring the hammer down. Some of that is due to my nature, but I also have to cop to being occasionally afraid—afraid of being the agent responsible for a loved one's disappointment. Overall, my parenting style involved moving toward easy things and avoiding hard things. In Emily's life, I could think of only one time when I had presented her with a rock-solid nonnegotiable, and that was when we moved to Chicago before she entered ninth grade. Emily's eyes went coal-black on that occasion, too, but she worked hard to adjust, and eventually she did.

This time, however, I was so utterly convinced that things would work out that I didn't get overly caught up in Emily's reaction. I had told her that things would be okay, and I felt they would be. This was one time when I needed to cash in my chips on a lifetime of being boringly reliable.

My phone call with Bruno went like this: "*That* went well…" He told me about his grenade toss and his daughters' reactions. I was hiding in my car; he was standing alone in his kitchen. All of our daughters were sobbing, and while this was a surprising and unexpected development, he and I remained relatively unconcerned.

I left Emily to cool down and bravely drove over to Bruno's house to face the reality of what we had done. None of the girls would emerge from their lairs. He and I shared a cup of coffee and ruefully compared notes about how badly our happy news had landed. But aside from being hit by some emotional shrapnel, we were not mortally wounded.

After about an hour, I returned to my house. Emily was gone. I assumed she was commiserating with her cousins down the street. Wearily I climbed the stairs to my little bedroom. There on my bed was Emily's DVD of *Roman Holiday*. This was her unspoken offering. Emily had heard me belly-aching about how I didn't think Bruno's girls had seen enough classic movies. She had placed it there for me to share with these daughters—her future stepsisters.

Chapter Eleven

Paying the Piper

Getting married is in some ways very good preparation for being married. There are planning and paperwork, arguing and making up, and endless conversations about money, clothes, food, friends, and music—with a final emphasis on cake. Every marital challenge should somehow end in cake.

My first wedding was beautiful. I'm not just saying that; it really was. Decades after the marriage failed, I still remember the wedding as magical, despite some unexpected bumps.

My former husband and I chose to get married in September on an island that was socked in with fog for several days before our wedding weekend.

When I think back on that weekend—now so long ago—I remember waking up on my wedding day and fighting with my future husband about the fog. Who has the energy to fight about the weather? Only people who are getting married that day. By the morning of our wedding, things were already off course because my unfortunate future in-laws' charter plane couldn't land in the fog. Several times on the day before, Andy and I had raced to Block Island's tiny airstrip because his family's plane had left MacArthur Airport and was on its way. Each time we stood listening to the plane circle, unseen above the fog bank, before the pilot gave up and headed back to Long Island.

Andy's stylish mother and stepfather and brother and sister-in-law finally arrived on the island from their home in the Hamptons just hours before the ceremony, dressed to the nines and riding in the prow of a small whale-watching boat, looking like yachters who had somehow wandered onto the set of *Jaws*.

I also remember an unfortunate encounter with the manager of the inn where the wedding was being held and where we and all of our guests were staying. Half of our guests had been inconvenienced or delayed by the weather. I walked through the inn's dining room on the day of our ceremony and saw pearl-gray tablecloths on the tables that were a little wrinkled and (I thought) sort of shabby-looking—in addition to being the "wrong" color. I brought this to the attention of the manager, who was also a police officer on the island. This man was also my former boss from several years before when I had lived on the island, working in a bicycle rental shop and singing at night in the hotel during summers and after college. Like most people who live on islands, he held at least three jobs. I'm assuming he was pretty tired and that I was being pretty tiresome.

He pulled out a chair and motioned for me to sit. I felt so disappointed. The fog had lifted and the sun was streaming through a cloud in cinematic beams of light, but the flowers were wrong, the tablecloths were wrong; so much was wrong. I smoothed out some wrinkles on the tablecloth as I sat. I was so distracted I could hardly pay attention to him. I wish I could remember the exact words he said to me that day, but it boiled down to this: "Knock it off. You're getting married today. If you continue to obsess about this stuff, you'll miss everything meaningful." I remember him also suggesting that I might want to lie down for a little while and take a nap. This is what you say to a kindergartner having a tantrum, of course. This fact was not lost on me.

Thank you, kind sir. I didn't have a father in my life. I didn't have anyone in my corner brave enough to tell me to stop. The only thing I can say in my own favor is that, despite being something of a control freak basket case, I was somehow able to listen. I felt I'd been slapped into consciousness. And right there, I dropped it. I released everything. I can still feel the enormous relief of that moment.

I have wonderful memories of that first wedding. But I'm also aware of how selfish we must have seemed to plan something so inconvenient for so many people. That's the sort of choice you make when you're twenty-five. When you're that age, you sincerely believe that a wedding really is all about you. Marriage *is* all about you, but weddings are all about everyone else.

For my second wedding, I was almost fifty and anticipating blending together a family of five daughters. Because Bruno is one of thirteen children, I would be acquiring literally dozens of in-laws. Both of our mothers were elderly and frail. I harbored no fanciful illusions. The "it's my day" concept seemed as quaint as the bouquet toss.

I receive lots of questions from "Ask Amy" readers about weddings. Although I sincerely believe that the rules of etiquette exist in order for all of us to share our space respectfully, too many people seem to use formal etiquette rules to control, scold, and shame other people. And really, who gives a fig about how an invitation envelope is addressed? What's inside is what's important.

For my wedding to Bruno, I decided to avoid my home church. I have never attended a wedding at the Freeville United Methodist Church (our church, like much else in the village, skews elderly), but I've attended far too many funerals there. Thoughts of my dear aunt Lena's funeral service, just months before, still filled me with a weepy sadness. I did not want to stand at the church's small altar where so many caskets had been placed. Instead, I called the office of the chapel on the grounds of the George Junior Republic, which is a residence reform school for juvenile offenders two miles from my house. My great-grandfather Calvin Derrick had helped found the school and pioneered its (at the time revolutionary) teaching technique for juveniles, which is focused on self-governance, outdoor exercise, emotional rehabilitation, and education.

The small, shingled chapel with dark green trim on the school's campus was built in 1915 and sits on a rise overlooking Freeville. The little Gothic-style building looks like something out of a storybook, like the frontispiece of an illustrated version of "Little Red Riding Hood." Because Bruno is a Catholic and I'm a Methodist, this nondenominational chapel seemed like liturgical neutral ground for our two families. I had never been to a service there, and unlike the Freeville church, it held no memories of any kind for me. The chapel had an open date in August, and we took it. We would marry in the chapel and have our reception at Bruno's childhood home, Maryhill Farm, five minutes away.

Because Bruno and I remained resolute about our plans, all of our daughters eventually calmed down and accepted our marriage as inevitable. We did not insist that anyone else get excited for us or share our bliss—only that they accept it. Bruno and I didn't discuss our wedding plans with anyone. We decided that if people asked, we would disclose them; otherwise, we would carry on with our work and our lives and quietly handle our wedding ourselves.

Soon enough, our daughters couldn't contain their curiosity and started asking about dresses. I had asked all of our daughters to be my "bridesmaids" and told them I'd buy whatever nonmatching dresses they chose. This kept everyone busy, as we spent entire evenings perusing websites and exchanging links and filling virtual shopping carts, only to empty and refill them the next day. There were trips to the giant monster mall in Syracuse, a consumer wasteland so vast and depressing (to me) that I wanted to lie down on the floor and sob myself into a coma. And then the shoes. Did I care about shoes? No, I did not. I still owned only four pairs. But we shopped for shoes and tried on shoes and practice-walked in shoes, and purchased and returned shoes.

We also talked about hair. My own hair options usually boil down to whether I've remembered to brush it that day. But Angela has gorgeous curly Dominican hair, and Avila has beautiful straight Chinese hair, while Clare and Michaela have soft Irish tresses. Emily has my hair—heavy, ponytail hair. How would they wear their hair? I didn't care. But *they* did.

And so we moved on to nails. I don't hold the universal truth that mani-pedis are a vital prerequisite to a wedding, but my bridesmaids did. So I made an appointment two months in advance for my five bridesmaids to visit a salon on the morning of the big day.

Most evenings, Bruno and I rode around in his red truck after supper and talked over details. With only two months to plan, we powered through a long list. We met with a caterer. I declared my preference for Methodist chicken barbeque and corn on the cob. Bruno then tossed me off of the catering committee and decided to choose the food himself. We met with my cousin Roger, a Methodist minister who had agreed to travel from his home church near Rochester to perform the ceremony. Bruno seemed to care less about the ceremony, text, and music, and so I tossed him off of that committee and handled that myself. I asked Rachel to assemble the Gene Pool Choir—made up of family members—and I asked my soon-to-be-step-daughters if they wanted to sing with the group. They said they would sing, and then that they wouldn't, and then again that they would. Rachel came to our house with her children and mine and force-marched the nine-person choir through several hymns. Some of my girls seemed to be lip-syncing during rehearsals, but that didn't matter. Made up of loud harmonizers, my clan can override any silence.

Bruno's brother Jacques said he would handle the flowers. He decided to use bright-colored zinnias everywhere. He designed special bowls and vases in his pottery studio and planted extra zinnias, timed to bloom in August. I asked Jacques to also do something with corn. By August, the fields around us are lush with it. I freaking love corn, and if we wouldn't be eating it for our wedding dinner, surely I could welcome some stalks into our chapel.

Then the rains came. Our part of the world is famous for its extreme and unpredictable weather, but this is most heartbreaking in summertime, which can be either glorious or unbelievably awful. One Fourth of July when Emily was little, we abandoned our optimistic plans for an outdoor picnic and instead spent the day shivering in down jackets as we watched a freezing rain come down in sheets from the shelter of my sister's porch, while we pathetically waved our sparklers at each other. This year, we had already had a very wet spring. I watched our neighbors plant their corn from their rain-slicked tractors in May, and then the corn grew into seedlings in puddled fields in June. The Dairy Day parade was a soggy mess of sad-looking papier-mâché Holsteins, melted crepe paper–festooned floats, and sopping legionnaires saluting from underneath umbrellas. Sometimes the rain would cease long enough for the fields to dry, and everyone ran out and hastily mowed their shaggy lawns or harvested their early hay. This particular summer, the sun only came out on Tuesdays. Every single weekend was sodden.

If you want to know the long-term weather prospects for your August wedding, you need to ask a farmer. Every afternoon through June and July, I drove to Fall Creek Farm and loitered at the farm stand, pretending I was carefully considering their vegetable selection while I pumped the proprietors, sisters Kim and Karin Lamott, for weather updates. I had gone to high school with both of them, and I trusted them to give it to me straight. Kim and Karin are locally famous for their sweet corn. They grow it from some sort of miracle seed stock fertilized by the manure of angels and unicorns. The corn these sister-farmers grow is not like the tough, big yellow kernels that offend me from lesser sources. The Lamott "butter and sugar" corn sports small kernels the size of baby teeth, lined up perfectly in alternating colors of white and pale yellow. This corn is sweet as nectar and pops as you scrape it off the cob with your teeth. The sweet juice runs down your chin as you reach for another piece.

When I asked Karin to prognosticate about that summer's weather, she would only say, "It's weird. We get pockets of cloudbursts every day that hit in one part of the field but not another. And the sun only shines reliably on Tuesdays." Could I somehow arrange to get married on a Tuesday? No, I could not. It rained for seventeen days straight that June. July saw eighteen days of rain. That summer the sandals stayed in the closet; everybody wore Muck boots and shorts. I begged and then cursed the weather gods. Then I gave up thinking about it when I realized I didn't have a wedding dress.

I briefly considered wearing my previous wedding dress—a 1920s flapper number I'd found in a consignment shop—but that idea was shot down by my now-vocal bridesmaids. On a blazing Tuesday in late July, I went to New York City for a meeting. I brought Emily with me, because we hadn't spent much alone time together in several weeks. After a very hot lunch meeting at an outdoor café, Emily and I walked up Madison Avenue to a small dress shop, a place I had been to many times over the years. I remembered that they made one particular frock that I thought could double as a wedding dress. By the time we had trudged twenty blocks on the sizzling pavement, Emily was looking flushed. I was almost violently focused on my dress caper at this point and didn't pay much attention to what was going on with her.

By the time we got to the small shop, Emily asked to sit down and was given some water. I was nearly naked behind a curtain with the one available dress halfway over my head when I heard the chair turn over, followed by a loud thump. I peeked out to see my daughter on the floor, out cold. I ran over to her, dress flapping, and called 911 while the clerk tried to zip me up and close the sale.

By the time the paramedics arrived, Emily had come to but seemed very woozy. The clerk took my credit card and shoved the dress into a bag, and I rode in the ambulance to Lenox Hill Hospital, which turned out to be around the corner. "Dang, we could have walked here," I whispered to her. Emily looked back at me like she hated me, just a little bit. She was diagnosed with heat stroke and was admitted for several hours while tethered to an IV.

I called my mother and then Emily's father, Andy, who held her insurance. I hadn't seen Andy since Emily's high school graduation in Chicago, two years before. Although he lived and worked in New York City, he traveled almost constantly, often overseas. Over the years I had come to expect that he was simply not often available in the way that other parents are. As it happened, on this day Andy was in his office, just across town, and he offered to leave work and come to the hospital to see her.

Andy and I sat, flanking our daughter's bedside, and talked over her as she dozed. Emily is blessed with robust health, and neither of us had ever experienced so much as a sick visit in a doctor's office with her. Seeing our daughter in a hospital bed was a shock, but as the IV dripped slowly, her normal color recovered.

Andy and I caught up on each other's families. He showed me pictures of his two other children, now adolescents, and I described the complicated new family I was about to enter. We talked about our work, falling into the easy topics we had somehow managed to carve out in our almost twenty years of practice as divorced parents. As our daughter slept, we crept out of the room and into the hospital's café, where, over sandwiches, we did something we had managed to avoid since we'd separated: We spent time together. Both of Andy's parents had recently died after long illnesses, and he and his brother had performed the dance of children of divorce, continuing to race back and forth between parents, keeping everything separate and discreet as they tried to give equal time to each of them at the end of their lives. I was very fond of both of his parents, again separately, because I had only ever seen them together one time, at our wedding on Block Island, where one arrived by ferry and the other by whale-watching boat, and they circled one another politely without speaking.

During our long courtship and short marriage, I often felt that Andy's parents didn't quite accept me. Perhaps, like my own mother, they saw us as the mismatch we were. But after my divorce from their son, each of his parents had kept in touch with me, and over the years a warmth that felt more genuine than cordial had grown between us. Andy told me he had been at his father's bedside at the end. He said that he'd told his father about my recent engagement and that his father smiled and whispered, "Tell Amy I'm happy."

He died the next day. I dried my eyes on a hospital napkin as I pieced together what now seemed like a small miracle: A trip to New York. A hot day. A wedding dress. A fainting. A hospital visit. Two estranged parents finally coming together. A loose loop that stretched over great distances and two decades tightened and closed. Emily had managed to do what children of divorce often fantasize about but rarely achieve: She had reunited her parents.

That summer, the tiny miracles continued. Bruno graded and seeded the lawn at Maryhill Farm, and somehow, despite the nearly relentless rain, grass sprouted and grew thick. We found a tent large enough to shield the caterers and guests from the weather. Desperate to find someone who could make a cake for us on short notice, we stumbled onto a nearby master baker who created masterpieces out of her kitchen. My favorite lounge band from DC said they'd load their gear into a van and drive north to play at our reception.

This is what happens when you keep your eye on the ball and don't obsess over the small stuff. Things either fall into place or they don't. When they do, you celebrate. When they don't, you do without and move on.

Bruno held out some hope that we could get a Catholic priest to participate in our nuptials to bless our union. This led to a surreal meeting with a young priest, where he dispassionately unraveled and explained our situation. Bruno's first marriage had been in a civil ceremony; I'd been married in a religious ceremony. We were both divorced.

As the priest explained it, in the eyes of the Catholic Church, Bruno was never actually married (because he hadn't been married in the church). He was free to do whatever he wanted. *I* was the problem. Because I had been married in a religious ceremony and because the Catholic Church does not recognize divorce, according to this priest I was still married to my ex-husband of almost twenty years. I was welcome to pursue an annulment in the Catholic Church for my Protestant marriage. This would take between two and five years.

In the church's parking lot, Bruno and I held an impromptu meeting of the sort that sometimes devolves into yelling and gravel-kicking. He carefully expressed no particular point of view. I did all of the talking. I told him I felt I was being punished. I pointed out the obvious absurdity of it all—that his lengthy marriage somehow didn't actually exist, while my relatively brief one was eternal. I might have used some bad words, there in the shadow of the church. I told him that no matter what, I would not erase my other marriage. Why? Because it really happened. And you can't just petition someone to undo the truth. Would we call off or postpone our wedding? I wasn't sure. I had a brief vision of all those bridesmaids' dresses and shoes languishing in the closet forever. But Bruno said, "I understand." He seemed sadly resolute. He put his arm around me and quietly walked me to the car.

Two weeks before our wedding, I took my mother to the funeral of her best friend from high school. Joan was her own miracle of humanity. Temperamentally, these two friends of almost eighty years were opposites. Joan had her first of five children while still in high school. She had been married and divorced several times and had married and divorced two of her husbands twice. Through it all, these lifelong friends were always Joan and Jane, Yin and Yang. Joan was the loud extrovert, while Jane was shy, reserved, and thoughtful. Joan was lively and funny and daring. Jane was careful and risk-averse. After settling in Atlanta, Joan became an actress late in life and had a small part in a couple of the *Scream* movies. My mother, ever the movie fan, framed Joan's headshot and had it on her desk. She and my mother talked on the phone every week, visited one another, and wrote long letters back and forth. Joan eventually found a much younger partner and left this life as she had lived it—fiercely and on her own terms. Joan and Jane kept talking, almost to the very end.

Joan's burial was in a tiny scruffy cemetery near the house where she had grown up, in a crossroads hamlet two miles from Freeville. After the service I took my mother in her rickety wheelchair toward the little cemetery, which was overgrown and scattered with ancient lopsided headstones. The ground was uphill and extremely uneven. Mom was worried about getting up the hill to her friend's graveside. I bent down and looked at her. Her gray eyes were watery with tears. I made a decision: "Hang on, girl—we're off-roading." She gripped the armrest of the wheelchair. I got a running start and muscled her up the hill, teetering and tripping over exposed tree roots and through stands of goldenrod, to her friend's grave. A dozen people were gathered there. A bagpiper appeared out of nowhere and walked up the hill. Dressed in full Scottish dress, he wheezed out a high-decibel version of "Amazing Grace." It was surprising and beautiful. Afterward, I caught up with the piper as he was headed to his car. I asked him if he would play our way into the chapel for our wedding. I wanted to do this as a surprise gift to Bruno. The piper told me he lived down the street from Bruno's mother and that he would be honored. I reminded him to bring an umbrella. He said he couldn't hold an umbrella and play the bagpipe at the same time, but maybe he could find an awning to stand under.

And so Bruno and I ticked item after item off our list—tasks either completed or abandoned. We would be marrying each other on this day; that was all we knew for sure.

The weather seemed to break the day before our wedding. The clouds suddenly scattered in the afternoon to tease us into thoughts of the dreamy summer we'd been denied. Our out-of-town guests arrived in Freeville and about eighty people gathered for the rehearsal dinner at Rachel and Tim's big pink house on Main Street (our invitations had said only, "Friday night dinner at the Pink House on Main Street"—we knew people would find it). Bruno had erected a large tent on their front lawn; we borrowed tables and chairs from the United Methodist Church down the street. Clark's Shurfine Food Mart supplied the chicken, and Fall Creek Farm the corn. The barbeque committee at the church set up their grills and cooked a hundred chicken halves. They transported the food down Main Street in wheeled coolers. My friend Margaret arrived from Washington and somehow single-handedly handled the food and table service. Margaret was a blur that night.

I made my entrance by walking down Main Street from my house, dressed in a mint-green cocktail dress I'd found at a church rummage sale and hastily hemmed that morning. I joined my future husband and his and my many siblings, our children and our nieces, nephews, aunts and uncles, and our close and distant friends. There on Main Street, we ate Methodist chicken and fresh sweet corn and potato salad. The moon rose. It was the first time I had seen it all summer. It was giant, white, and full.

Chapter Twelve

We Did

My people are marrying people but not wedding people. Our divorces seem to be more dramatic, drawn out, and impactful than any weddings we could possibly host. Of my siblings and cousins, I am the rare family member to have a public wedding. My parents were married in my grandparents' living room; Rachel and Tim were married on my mother's porch. Anne has had two private weddings and has only told people after the fact. My father, Buck, has been married and divorced many times, but he seems to marry (and divorce) women more or less on the fly.

Given this marital legacy, one might conclude that I take marriage lightly. But I do not—not at all. For most of my adult life, I have been alone and without any romantic partner. I have researched and observed marriage, personally and professionally. I make my living trying to help people unravel what went wrong with their relationships. I am intimately familiar with issues that can undermine a marriage, as well as the approximately one in two odds of an American marriage failing. I know all this, but I also understand the pull toward marriage, because I have felt it.

Standing on that snowy New York City sidewalk with Bruno, I experienced an instant realization that we must marry. After many decades of thoughtfully trying to anticipate and then second-guess every romantic choice I've ever made, my decision to marry Bruno was, quite literally, a no-brainer. It happened somewhere on a cellular level, and from the day of our proposal to the day of our wedding I experienced not one moment of the slightest doubt.

What will always be something of a mystery to me is why I (and so many others) are drawn to being married in a public way. I can only explain it as a very human pull toward powerful witnessing. A community that witnesses an important ritual makes it more real and resonant. This same community may then draw close again to be supportive during tough times. I think a joyful moment is amplified when it is shared.

My mother, who did not seem to like weddings, accompanied me once to a beautiful, large, and elegant wedding, which featured a dozen identically gowned bridesmaids, groomsmen in tuxedos, a couple hundred guests, a delicious meal, and dancing and champagne. "Queen for a day," she sniffed. In addition to considering large displays wasteful, Jane couldn't imagine a person being willing to experience any private emotion in public.

Years ago, I covered a story for National Public Radio about a mass wedding held by the Unification Church. For several years in the '80s and '90s, these mass weddings—featuring up to 1,000 couples matched by the church—were a sort of annual curiosity. The "Moonie weddings" would be held in arenas or soccer stadiums, and the photos that emerged from these events were of row upon row of identically dressed brides and grooms, none of whom had even met before the church assigned them to one another on their wedding day.

This particular ceremony was held in RFK stadium in Washington. Up close and not viewed through a photo filter, the whole thing looked surreal, cruddy, and profoundly depressing. To me, it played like some sort of unintentional meta-exposure of the underlying absurdity of wedding ceremonies. Hundreds of couples sat on folding chairs set up on the stadium's field. The grooms wore dark suits and the brides wore identical white dresses (which I assume the church had supplied). But what I noticed on that day, and which I had never seen reported before, was the undeniable surplus of brides. The whole back section of the stadium's field was filled only with brides—a couple hundred extra brides seated side by side, like identical wedding-cake toppers. Each bride held an 8 x 10 framed photo of the groom with whom she had allegedly been matched. My understanding was that these brides were simply told their grooms were unable to attend the ceremony. Talk about a leap of faith! It's one thing to marry someone you just happen to be seated next to at a mass wedding; it's another to pledge your troth to a photo, which—who knows?—could actually be the photo that came with the frame.

After the very short and not at all sweet wedding "ceremony," which dispatched the hundreds of brides and grooms toward the exits, I did what I always do whenever I'm at a stadium: I had a hot dog and a beer and then joined the line for the ladies' room. There was no line at all for the men's room, of course, but the line for the ladies' room was lousy with leftover brides, standing there in their pinned-on rayon gowns, holding their photo-husbands, and shifting from foot to foot as they waited to pee. These brides, many of them quite young, had received their public wedding and witnessing, and yet in their case I worried about who would stand with them later, after they had finally met their husbands.

On my own wedding day, I realized that, because of my stage in life, I had been experiencing a wedding drought lasting for well over a decade. My most recent wedding attendance had been at the long-ago Moonie wedding. I often wonder what had ever become of the leftover brides and their two-dimensional husbands, but I hope they had escaped the confines of an organization that would draw them in on such a flimsy promise.

The first thing I did on my own wedding day was to quickly part the vintage tablecloth I use for a curtain in my bedroom, look outside, and rejoice that the weather was holding. This particular Saturday was dawning into sunshine; there would be no bridal snits over weather on this fine wedding day.

There was a lot of distance to travel between that early morning moment and eventually saying "I do," but instead of obsessing over details, I realized I mainly wanted to get this thing done and start a new life living with Bruno. I definitely wanted the ritual of the church service, and I absolutely wanted to celebrate, but I had already enjoyed my rehearsal dinner of Methodist chicken and corn on the cob, and now I wanted to move it along. I had found the person I wanted to spend the rest of my life with, and I was itchy for the rest of my life to begin.

My first stop was to bring Dunkin' to the household at Maryhill Farm. Bruno's siblings and their families had been gathering there over the previous several days. Bruno had already been to the farm that morning, spraying pesticide around the seams of the tent to try to keep out the chiggers and no-see-ums and mayflies that would swarm with that day's moist warmth. I hadn't seen Bruno since we'd kissed good night standing on the sidewalk in Freeville the night before, and I didn't expect to see him again until we met at the chapel for our three o'clock ceremony.

I walked into the Schickel family's old farmhouse and saw that it had been scrubbed and polished by Bruno's visiting sisters. The tents and tables were set, the gardens were gorgeous, the lawn trimmed tight, and someone had repainted a door and trim. I hadn't asked anyone to do it; I wasn't even aware of this monumental labor happening. It dawned on me for the first time since exiting our secret engagement snow globe: A lot of people were working very hard to get us hitched.

Next I stopped at my mother's house on Mill Street. She had missed the rehearsal dinner at my sister's house. Jane had been waffling back and forth about attending the ceremony; it seemed that she was unsure if she could physically manage it. But I had found an outfit for her to wear, Aunt Jean had altered it to fit her, her caregiver was helping her to get dressed, and Elsie, her eighty-year-old friend from high school, was going to transport and assist her in the chapel and at the reception. Although I was desperate to have my mother witness my marriage to Bruno, I was at peace over whatever last-minute choice she might make. I did not want to feel disappointed over anything today.

I met all of my bridesmaids for their salon date in Ithaca. Declining any services for myself, I nervously leafed through a magazine while the girls were all made beautiful. The reason I didn't submit to any professional fluffing is this: I always look the same. With the exception of the few times I've been a guest on Fox News—when I have been made by their makeup department to look like a man in drag—I always look like myself. I'm not vainly declaring that I don't need any improvement, but in my experience, when the beauty professionals get ahold of me, I emerge from the process looking worse, sometimes dramatically so, than when I went in. This is never the case with other people, and I have never heard another woman complain of this phenomenon. Because of this, my beauty philosophy consists of: Leave well enough alone.

When my five bridesmaids emerged at 11:00 a.m., polished and pretty, I realized there was a yawning gap of a few hours where we were basically unprogrammed. There aren't many amusements for underage bridesmaids with upswept, bobby-pinned hair. We decided to go to the Queen Diner for lunch and call it our bachelorette party.

It was over patty melts at the Queen that the enormity of the afternoon started to bear down on me with real force. Many years ago I had read a quote that when First Lady Nancy Reagan wanted to hurry Ronnie along, she said, "Zip zip, let's go!" Now, for some reason, that phrase was running through my head like a ticker tape. I was jumpy and excited. I declared to our waitress Lorraine, "I'm getting married today!" and she said, "I know!" Lorraine had watched my courtship with Bruno progress over countless bowls of chili as I sat crushed up next to him in our regular booth. She knew everything.

By one o'clock, my five bridesmaids and I had landed back at my house on Main Street, where we would all get dressed. I helped them steam out their dress wrinkles, and they pulled out makeup bags loaded with eyelash curlers and eyeliners (liquid and solid), jumbo folding palettes of eye shadow, lip glosses and lipsticks and deodorants and perfumes. They stood on the porch and displayed their newly painted fingernails and toenails, comparing colors and wiggling their digits to catch the afternoon sunshine. They either did or did not like their hairstyles and took turns in front of the full-length mirror as they critiqued and propped up one another and fussed with their tresses and dresses.

If I could get away with it, I would doll myself up at every opportunity. I'd wear hats and opera-length gloves and flowing scarves and boots with buttons. But I have a small stature and a largish head. I can take a cool-looking, "fun" or artistic garment into a dressing room and emerge wearing Garanimals. The only accessory I seem to get away with is a strand of pearls. One additional thing—even a hair clip or a handkerchief—is too much.

My wedding dress was a simple champagne-colored sleeveless dress with a fitted bodice and full, twirly skirt. I know that brides commonly refer to their layered, tucked, seed-pearled, lace-festooned gowns as "simple"—but this one actually was. The dress had no buttons, no pattern or adornment, no internal wiring to keep it up, and no dragging train. I slipped it over my head and zipped it up the back. *Zip, zip, let's go.*

I was so eager to get married that I insisted Emily leave the house a half hour early to go to the chapel—a drive that takes three minutes. She started to protest, then took one look at my face and got the keys.

We parked behind the chapel. I didn't see Bruno's truck there. I walked around toward the front entrance, which was flanked by two fat sheaves of cornstalks. I later heard that Bruno's sister Ruth had snuck into a neighboring cornfield in the middle of the night to gather the eight-foot stalks and lash them together. Inside, the simple chapel bloomed with brightly colored zinnias in white pots of different sizes and shapes. Jacques had solicited zinnia contributions from neighboring gardens throughout town. The bagpiper I'd asked to play pulled up in his car. I'd forgotten all about him.

What I felt in that moment was the simple joy of something coming together. This was not the manic satisfaction of ticking boxes off a long list and of having my best-laid plans realized. This was the absolute absence of anxiety. I realized that I was surrounded by people who were pulling for me and happy for me—and who also were reliable.

The bagpiper stood off to the side, playing to the soft hills and cornfields as our guests found their way into the small chapel. I hustled the girls into position for the procession. Bruno pointed out to me that we were starting five minutes early. I told him that I simply could not wait one more minute to be married. I signaled to the pianist to start, and as he started to play, I pinwheeled my arms toward the bridesmaids in the universal symbol for

"Hustle!" Avila started up the aisle, and then Bruno grabbed my hand and motioned me off to the side. His ninety-year-old uncle Bud wasn't in the church yet. And so we stopped the pianist, midnote. Avila returned to her place, our congregation shared a knowing chuckle, and Bruno got his uncle seated.

We started again. Cue the piano, cue the beautiful bridesmaids. Lined up at the front of the chapel, our daughters looked like individual brightly colored flowers. Bruno and I held hands and walked up the aisle together. On the way I saw Jane, seated just behind the Gene Pool Choir at the front of the church. We stopped just short of our destination to greet and kiss our mothers. I whispered my thanks.

The ceremony was not a blur. It was beautiful. I told myself to stay in the moment because this would be my last wedding. Reverend Roger started by asking, "Who presents this woman and this man to be married, one to the other?"

Our daughters/bridesmaids responded as one: "We do."

Together with our guests, we read:

O Divine Master,
grant that I may not so much seek
to be consoled as to console;
to be understood, as to understand;
to be loved, as to love;
for it is in giving that we receive,
it is in pardoning that we are pardoned,
and it is in dying that we are born to eternal life.

And then the Beatitudes:

Blessed are the poor in spirit . . .

Bruno and I sat on chairs to the side of the altar during the sermon and the music portions of the service. I looked out at the crowded little chapel.

Somehow we had managed to squeeze almost 200 people into the old wooden pews. In addition to our family members, there were friends and colleagues through every stage of my life. And, just as importantly, neighbors from Freeville who knew my grandparents and my parents, people who had gathered with me to mourn my aunt Lena's death and who were helping my mother when she needed help now; people who quietly pitched in and built things and sowed gardens and left casseroles or seedlings or jars of preserves on the porch. I sought out my sisters, cousins, and aunties, sprinkled throughout the congregation. I was so moved by their presence and their willingness to increase my happiness by adding their own joy on this day. My bridesmaids were all smiling, and that made me even happier.

Rachel wrangled the choir together and they sang for us: "The King of Love My Shepherd Is."

And then a surprise—the wonderful, schmaltzy old song "I Love You Truly," which is most familiar to some from its brief appearance in the movie *It's a Wonderful Life*, when Bert and Ernie sing it beneath George and Mary Bailey's window on their wedding night.

I love you truly, truly dear,
Life with its sorrow, life with its tear
Fades into dreams when I feel you are near
For I love you truly, truly dear.

I was so happy, I thought I would inflate and float, balloon-like, over the crowd, out of the chapel, and fly and drift over the village and the hills, fields, streams, and lakes of this challenging and beautiful countryside that is my home.

After the ceremony, we streamed out of the chapel and into the August sunshine. Each of our guests was holding a zinnia, daisy, or black-eyed Susan. We were all part of a glorious bouquet.

Because I field so many wedding questions for my advice column, I'm exposed mainly to the ugly, tacky, problematic side to this tricky celebration. Bridesmaids complain about the expense and effort required to participate.

Siblings stop speaking. Divorced parents won't sit next to each other. Bachelor parties in Vegas get out of hand. Wedding cakes previously agreed upon are the wrong flavor or the band is too loud. Everybody is sick of shelling out money for elaborate showers, destination weddings, and gifts. Marrying couples expect guests to fill "money trees" or pay for their honeymoons. Many of these problems are generated by the marrying couples, by planning too many events and expecting too much of their guests. Bruno and I circumvented all of these issues by throwing one party, telling people to skip the gifts, and asking our guests to simply show up and celebrate with us.

After we had greeted our guests, Bruno scooped me into his arms and carried me to his truck. We joined our guests at Maryhill Farm, and we gloried to the food, drink, and music under our big white tent. Massive round hay bales stood sentry in the pasture as we toasted one another and our guests. The huge, full, milky white harvest moon rose over our party, and we danced with our children until the band put away their instruments. Our bridesmaids stayed elsewhere that night, and Bruno and I returned to Pemberley to start our married life together.

So many of my important life events have played out like a version of "Things were going so well until THAT happened." This is so much a part of my story that I have come to expect it. But on my wedding day to Bruno, Hapless Amy stayed home. Pratfall Amy was otherwise engaged. Unhinged Amy took a powder. Showboating Amy, Selfish Amy, Judgy Amy, Cranky Amy, Loudmouth Amy, Obnoxious Amy, and Anxious Amy must have been attending an Amy support group somewhere, because they did not show up at my wedding. The Amy who did show up is the Amy I like the best: the hopping, happy, joyful middle-aged woman who never expected a perfect wedding, but got one anyway.

Chapter Thirteen

The Powdered Wife

When Bruno and I returned from our honeymoon (I wanted to go to Cooperstown; he took me to Italy—further proof that I had married well), I entered his home and the deep, broad, and complex realm of his family as a full-time member. Bruno and I were wildly in love, and now that matrimony had ended our voluntary chastity, we set about doing what newly together couples tend to do. However, we were both middle-aged and with an audience comprised not only of our own daughters, but also of both of our families and, it seemed, the entire population of our hometown.

I'm sure I'm not the only woman in the world to be in a newly sexual relationship while also going through perimenopause, but I certainly felt like it, as I shopped for birth control and menopause remedies at the same time. Although my doctor had described my eggs as "geriatric," I reflexively chose to try to protect my elderly eggs like an old hen facing life in a new coop. I hadn't shopped for birth control for many years, and my expectation that I would be able to find something—anything—at my local Walgreens came crashing down when I wandered over to the birth control aisle and saw that it had become a sex emporium during the several years I had spent regrowing my virginity. I saw shelf after shelf of what can only be described as "enhancement" products, highlighted by several rows of technical-sounding condoms that seemed more terrifying than useful. My antique diaphragm was meant to be paired with products that no longer seemed available. Or perhaps the condoms had simply pushed the spermicides onto another shelf, and I would find them snuggled up next to the tube socks.

I faced this dearth of options by appealing directly to the pharmacist, who located a dusty box of sponges in the storeroom. Ah, The Sponge! It was like seeing a treasured artifact from a previous life—like finding my letter sweater in an old trunk. As the pharmacist handed the box to me, promising that she would order more, she reminded me that I had gone to high school with her mom.

The other items in my basket that day were hair dye, which guaranteed "complete gray coverage," and an estrogen product that promised relief from "hot flashes, night sweats, stress, mood, and memory." I threw in a package of actual sponges for cleaning in an effort to camouflage my other purchases and to prove my life sponge-worthy on multiple fronts.

I was a newlywed. An over-the-hill, root-dyeing, hot-flash-suffering, slightly lumpy newlywed, but still—a bride. A wife. I gloried in my wifely status. All through our honeymoon in Italy, I declared to my new husband, "*Mi esposo*, please bring me *uno gelato, subito*!" as we strode hand in hand through the hill towns of Umbria. Bruno and I frequently glanced at our simple gold wedding bands. I signed my notes and texts to him "Wifey." He signed his "Husband." I was secure in and delighted by my spousal status. I hoped the stepparenting aspect of my new life would more or less take care of itself.

Like all prospective stepparents, I was swept into this challenging state on a tide of excitement and love. I buried my trepidation and declared to myself, "I've got this thing nailed! I am, after all . . . *me*."

But the thing about being a stepparent is that other people are involved, and they are children who were not raised by you. They were raised by others, and they have their own personalities, characters, rhythms, challenges, and secrets—as well as their own dynamic and ways of relating. You, the stepparent, are the interloper. You are the new kid at the lunch table, and you're asking everyone to make room so you can wiggle your way in.

When I entered the household, three of our five daughters were there to warily greet me: Angela and Michaela—both starting their senior year in high school—and Avila, in fifth grade. Clare, twenty, was away at Bryn Mawr. Emily, also twenty, was at William & Mary. She was the daughter I had raised and the only child whose middle name I knew.

The house I moved into is a sturdy Victorian farmhouse nestled between two hills, surrounded by 220 acres of forest and farmland. Sheep graze in the pasture across from the broad front porch. Bruno had sweetened the deal with his daughters before my arrival by renovating the kitchen and master bedroom and by screening in the porch. Not only can Bruno sling a hammer to make structural adjustments, but he also tends to drill straight to the heart of the matter when emotions get tricky. We were both confident in his ability to fix anything.

Bruno had been living alone with Avila, Michaela, and Angela for about five years before he and I met. After the divorce, everything eventually settled down and his three younger daughters lived full-time with him. He was a handsome, burly guy running his own construction company, and he was also a very involved dad, with a household of beautiful daughters. And, yes, from many angles this was every bit as adorable as it sounds. I could practically see the movie poster in my head.

I arrived with one wheelie bag and my adored orange tabby cat, Chester, transplanted the four miles from my house on Main Street. The family had an ignored barn/house cat named (sigh) Kitty and a young, bounding, and dopey black Lab named Calvin. Calvin kept after Chester until, about a week after we arrived, my tabby decided to pack his little hobo bag and take to the open road. Eventually I found Chester a mile away, heading toward the highway and the prospects of a better life, eating Hot Pockets scraps at the Dandy Mart. I stopped my car in the roadway and Chester looked up at me from the ditch. He looked very small. I knew there were foxes and coyotes about. "I'm sorry, little pal, but we live here now," I said to him. He hopped in through the car's open window and I took him back to the house.

I kept all of my personal possessions and clothing at my house on Main Street and spent our first months together bringing in clothes and my prodigious coat collection one item at a time, as I wore them. I also brought a few paintings, which I hung in the living room.

I felt like Mary Poppins, entering a household with one carpetbag, out of which I pulled everything I needed. I continued to use my house as an office. Every day when I went there to work, I would sit on my own couch, watch my television, bathe in my bathtub, and fix my lunch in my own kitchen. I was discovering that, unlike Mary Poppins, the contents of my carpetbag were not enough to sustain me. During uncertain times, I derived great comfort from being surrounded by my own things. I also spent some of this private time performing my middle-age ablutions: tweezing my eyebrows and chin with the aid of a magnifying mirror, bleaching my impressive mustache, dyeing my roots, and occasionally doing jumping jacks in my bathrobe while listening to the radio. As I grew older, I was amazed at how much maintenance it took just to look like myself. These were activities I didn't necessarily want my new stepdaughters to witness.

This ability to have some privacy eased my transition and spared our daughters the shock of the sudden arrival of another parent in their lives. Instead, I slipped in gradually.

Bruno had ideas for all of us from the get-go. He seemed to want an instant blending, as if he could add a portion of powdered wife, mix thoroughly, and create a family. I appreciated his enthusiasm, but I knew this would never work. One evening very early in my life in the household, Bruno declared to me, "Give Avila a hug!" Poor Avila stood there, looking miserable. My heart broke for her. I cannot imagine anything more awful for a young preteen than to have to submit to a hug from your brand-new stepmother. I declined the hug and instead offered her my patented "sidewinder"—a sort of sideways shoulder squeeze—and Avila looked relieved.

School started two weeks after I moved in, and I attended back-to-school nights, introduced myself to teachers (they'd all attended Ithaca schools, unlike Bruno and me), baked birthday cakes for our two September birthdays (Avila and Michaela), and went to soccer games and track meets. I enjoyed going to games, which was one parenting experience my own non-athletic daughter had never given to me. I was an enthusiastic sideline cheerleader, all the while hoping that eventually I'd be on the same team as these new daughters of mine.

I tried to give myself—and them—time. I didn't want to rush things, but instead tried to get to know the girls gradually, based on our shared experiences. This is the only way to know teenagers, because teens are wise and wary about people. I was raised by a mother who loved teenagers; she was a great listener with a high tolerance for complication. My relationships with Bruno's girls were complicated by a factor of ten, and my understanding of them happened in fits and starts. In addition to being my new stepdaughters, Angela and Avila were adopted. Both Bruno and I come from extended families with many adopted members, and my experience is that each adopted person reacts differently to questions of birth, family, and parents. Adding a stepparent to the relational mix is introducing yet another X factor into the complicated family diagram.

Bruno and I were attempting to blend cultures, as well as adjust to everyday differences in the way each of our families moved through the world. Actually, Bruno wasn't attempting to blend anything. He loved me, and he loved having me around, but he kept forgetting that the ladies in the household didn't know one another all that well.

Michaela was studious, determined, and ambitious. She ran cross-country, wrote for the school newspaper, and had flung herself into preparing her college applications. Avila was the adored youngest—affectionate and sweet, but shadowed by occasional bursts of anxiety. Exotic, gorgeous, and with a radiant smile, Angela never talked about how she felt. She rarely discussed her frustrations or even how her day was going, instead holding her feelings behind a quiet and stoic façade. Angela had extended family in the Dominican Republic, and although Bruno and the kids took annual trips there and Angela talked to her grandmother, aunts, and older siblings by phone (she was brought to the States after both of her parents died), I worried that she felt homesick. Occasionally she described complicated and colorful dreams, full of symbols and portent. Angela's deepest feelings seemed submerged and out of reach.

In the evenings when it was her turn to cook, Angela would put on a CD of Latin music and create wonderful meals of chicken, rice and beans, and plantains. Though she was always polite, her temperament seemed to range between stoic and miserably unhappy. Bruno insisted on trying to plow in and fix whatever was ailing Angela, but although she was completely fluent in English, her deeper emotions seemed somehow lost in translation. I could see that she was very attached to her two sisters and was especially tender and loving toward her youngest sister, Avila, painting her nails and letting her clomp around in her high heels.

Angela didn't always come home after school, preferring to stay with a girlfriend in Ithaca. At times she dodged phone calls regarding her whereabouts, and Bruno and I were unsure about how to react. As my first autumn with the family progressed into fall, I started wondering if Angela was basically trying to move out of our house in stages, much as I had moved in.

Bruno and I continued our romance, which now felt so different from our courtship. Marriage and family life seemed to be adding layer upon layer of depth to a relatively young relationship that was still growing and evolving. As a couple, we drafted along on Bruno's original intent, shared in our very first phone call, to "do everything differently this time." We simply tried to be intentional and kind to each other and to the girls. I extended this kindness to them in the ways I knew how, by not caring in the slightest whether or not they kept their rooms neat and by taking up some of the domestic slack in the household, cleaning up after supper and emptying the always-full dryer. I left piles of neatly folded clothing outside their bedroom doors and bouquets of wildflowers on their crowded bureaus.

Soon enough I realized that, to the girls, my most appealing qualities were that I had a driver's license and a car. Having another driver in the household meant that everybody got to go where they wanted to go and that there was an extra person to share the chore of picking up groceries. Driving them places and doing errands together helped us get to know each other better. We each revealed a little bit about ourselves through trolling sales at the mall and revealing our yogurt preferences. And we talked. There in the car, I'd hear about school, sports, college choices, and middle school milestones.

Bruno tended to deal with his parenting challenges by matter-of-factly tackling one little emergency at a time—always focused on putting out the fire, getting dinner on the table, and starting afresh the next day. Consequences didn't always seem consistent or balanced. Thus I arrived at the essence of the stepparent's eternal lament: I saw things from a different perspective because I had no history with these children and was blind to the nuances of their behavior. I tried to support Bruno, but sometimes I found myself advocating instead for our daughters (after all, I, too, had once been an adolescent girl surviving a divorce). At times I was tempted to pull out my metaphorical puppets in order to entertain and win their trust and convince these cool girls that I was a cool mom. Occasionally, when I was feeling particularly overwhelmed by the chaos or uncertainty of being a parent in a family of five children, I eyed my wheelie bag in the corner of our bedroom and fantasized about my own escape.

When there was a dispute, argument, or problem between our daughters, I mainly stepped into the background. I'd weigh in privately with Bruno after the fact, whispering to him up in our bedroom. Bruno and I also tried to confine our own disputes to the cab of his red pickup truck. Now, instead of riding out into the night to look at the moon, we stole away from the household to discuss private matters, business schedules, and parenting struggles.

I rarely corrected or expressed frustration with the girls directly and never tried to discipline any of these very good girls (although they said they could read my face like a book). I forced myself to wait instead of weighing in. My influence was chiefly filtered through Bruno. He was the father, and I became the father's backstop.

Keeping my big trap shut was one of the hardest things I have ever done. I hoped that one day I would attain full team status, but I didn't want to push this too fast. Our daughters had dozens of aunts and uncles, and Bruno's mother lived just five miles away. They had a lot of opinionated people telling them what to do.

I had read a number of stepparenting guides to research questions for my advice column, and they all said the same thing about being a stepparent to older children: The primary parent should remain in charge. The stepparent should be a friend. Friendship and parenting are sometimes in opposition, and friendship with adolescents is different than with fellow adults. I tried hard to anchor to the friendship values I hold close—to be supportive and respectful, to listen more than talk, and to be truthful but circumspect. In addition, I tried not to be too intimate, through sharing my own concerns or insecurities with kids who were too young to understand them (and in no position to care).

I didn't always succeed in my textbook parenting. Sometimes I caught myself monologuing about my own experiences. And I worried excessively about what my stepdaughters thought of me.

Our most effective form of mother-daughter bonding in the early days was to complain about and make fun of Bruno, as if he were the hapless dad in our new family's sitcom. Bruno encouraged this by behaving like a combination of Ward Cleaver and Ray Romano. His old-fashioned values and conservative worldview often translated into quaint lectures about sportsmanship, religion, the value of hard work, and the United States Constitution. These mini-lessons, while sincere and mainly valid, still made all of us laugh. Once I declared open season on their father's earnestness, the girls and I engaged in a gleeful household insurrection. But we really reached common ground when forced to listen to Bruno's daily recitations of his maladies.

Bruno's burly exterior conceals a delicate constitution and multiple physical sensitivities that he enjoys drawing attention to and describing in detail. His ailments range the gamut from invisible rashes and digestive problems to self-diagnosed maladies such as toe displacement and chest bubbles. He has a fear of earwigs, tendonitis, and mysterious lymph node swellings. He has an actual allergy to dust mites but an outsized suspicion that he is allergic to many other things. Generally, if anyone in the household complained of any ache, pain, or upset, Bruno would instantly one-up us. If I had a cold, Bruno developed imaginary bronchitis. If a daughter had cramps, he would commiserate by sharing his fear of angina. Many nights after supper he would beg one of us to walk on his back, crack his neck, or rub his tired feet. I offered to pay our daughters to take my turn.

Ganging up on Bruno was a unifying dynamic that helped us inch closer to one another. We banded together through shared eye-rolls and complaining about this man, whom we all loved, each very much in her own way. Bruno took the family ribbing with good humor; he said he didn't mind being the household's punch line, because he loved hearing laughter in the house, even if it was at his expense.

Blending our two families together involved much more than clearing closet space for my many coats, or convincing the cat to stay in his new home. We were all survivors, to varying degrees, of loss and displacement; we were all players in a new family drama.

As I started my new life with this family of daughters, I was aware, most often, of what it was like for me. I didn't consider too deeply what it was like for them. People often say that second marriages are the triumph of hope over experience. There around the kitchen table with my new family, we were all buoyed by hope. Experience would prove to be the greater teacher.

Chapter Fourteen

Real Housewives

I had only ever raised one child, and I had done so by myself. I had raised Emily to understand me. We shared a culture underscored by my own family's values and propped up and influenced by music, books, movies, and television. Bruno was raising his children in an approximation to the way he had been raised: cloistered and vaguely Amish but without the woodworking and pony carts. The family's cultural isolation was such that when I arrived in the household, they had no radio, one channel of broadcast TV, and no cable. Until wireless came into the house (enabling us to at least look up answers to deep questions such as, "Who is Renée Zellweger?"), the family's main cultural touchstones were a collection of movies on tape and DVD, including a few seasons of *Law & Order* and the entire *Gilmore Girls* series. One of their favorite movies was a slapstick Dominican film called *Sanky Panky*, which featured lots of characters hilariously pratfalling, mostly in Spanish. They would watch it as a family, crowded onto the couch, and howl with laughter.

Bruno bought a radio so I could listen to the news and prepare for my monthly appearances on *Wait Wait...Don't Tell Me!* He also offered to get a satellite dish installed so I could watch television (we didn't get cable that far out in the sticks). Aside from the unpleasant prospect of living in one of those beautiful Victorian homes in the countryside with a satellite receiver attached to the roof, I suggested a waiting period. The reason for my skepticism was because the previous Christmas (when Bruno and I had just started dating), I had given the family a DVD of *A Christmas Story*, Jean Shepherd's caustic, nostalgic tale of his midwestern family's fouled-up Christmas. Bruno and the girls watched the movie together and found it incomprehensible, mean-spirited, and unfunny. Before pouring 200 channels of television into this innocent family's heads, I wanted to conduct a basic media survey. Evenings spent playing chess in front of the fireplace instead of watching sitcoms together might be the only nightly entertainment this family was prepared for.

Bruno and the girls knew who Seinfeld was, but they couldn't identify Frasier Crane in any iteration. They had never seen the *Dick Van Dyke Show*, *The Andy Griffith Show*, *The Honeymooners*, or, it seemed, any sitcom—classic or otherwise—aside from *Friends* in syndication, which ran on the one channel coming into the house. The family had never watched a national or a local newscast at home or watched election returns together. I worried that they had never been group-disappointed by the anticlimax of the ball dropping in Times Square during a New Year's Rockin' Eve.

The family also had no knowledge of the long-running and classic television ads that littered our local landscape, with their earworm jingles—like the one for Sam Dell Dodge, or the ambulance-chasing law firm in Syracuse that you were supposed to call when you were in a car accident. They had never seen anyone get slimed on Nickelodeon. They didn't seem to know that some people swallow live bugs or zip-line across alligator-infested ponds for TV fame. They thought *Real Housewives* were women who stayed home and took care of the house. Although they knew what the real world was, they had no familiarity with *The Real World*.

After about a month, I tabulated my results and announced to Bruno that according to my data, unfortunately it was too late for these girls of ours. Throwing them into the vast and unfiltered television cesspool at this stage in their development would only ruin them and pickle their intellect forever. Not on my watch, mister.

Instead, I brought in a DVD of *Sense and Sensibility* with Emma Thompson and three different versions of *Pride and Prejudice*. Bruno recognized Colin Firth only as the dad named "Lord Henry Dashwood" (get the sly *Sense and Sensibility* reference there?) in the Amanda Bynes movie *What a Girl Wants*. In fact, Bruno had a disturbing familiarity with the entire Amanda Bynes oeuvre, left over from his tenure as a single father taking his daughters to movies at the mall. He quoted from a scene in *What a Girl Wants* more than once, until I asked him to please never do that again.

Soon enough, the girls cast me in the role they were most familiar with—that of Lorelai Gilmore, the quirky, fast-talking, noncooking single mother from the *Gilmore Girls*. True, they were onto something there, especially when it came to cooking. Each member of the family could whip up a delicious dinner for six in a half hour; when it was my turn, I spent the day food shopping and planning as if for a dinner party. I made massive, gooey, cheesy casseroles, fit for a Methodist potluck. Clare, a skilled and instinctive cook who relished pulling together holiday meals for forty, seemed especially flummoxed by my inability to get an entrée and two sides to appear at the same time. In the kitchen I suffer from a sort of mealtime Tourette's, where the presence of a spatula brings on the swears. Eventually I was relegated to chopping and salad assembling. Occasionally I was permitted to produce a stew or soup, dishes I could prepare in advance and leave simmering on the stove.

We ate dinner together every night, and the meal was preceded by the Catholic grace. I eventually learned the words to this prayer and joined in but declined to use the sign of the cross. For some reason, doing so felt like an affront to my Huguenot ancestors. Bruno liked to conduct current events seminars during dinner, as his own father had done, but these conversations were more like sermons. When he was finally spent and we had all stopped fake-yawning with the sheer torture of it all, the girls and I would talk about school, college applications, friends, and clothes. When we ran out of topics and things got quiet, I would pull out a vexing question I had received for my advice column and ask them how I should answer it.

Parents don't spend enough time asking their children questions—other than "How was school today?"—and listening to their answers. My work as an advice giver gave me a way in and fostered my growing relationship with these teens. Sharing tough questions sent in from readers provided great talking points for this thoughtful and diverse family group.

Over the years, I had heard from scores of parents, middle-school teachers, school counselors, and teachers of English as a second language that my column was used as a teaching tool and as a way for people to discuss real-world issues. Couples frequently reported reading my column aloud to one another, and after reading the question, guessing about what my advice would be before reading the answer.

At the dinner table I would open up my laptop and read a letter from a sixth grader wondering how to handle a tricky triangle with two frenemies. "So, Avila, what do you think I should say to her?" I'd ask, and she would dig deep and perhaps confess to a similar situation in her own life, before offering her advice. My hope was that this would help her to self-guide through her own tricky personal situations.

But real life doesn't always reveal itself as neatly as a question sent in to an advice columnist. I was about to be tested and challenged by this new family of mine. My own foolishness, hubris, and frailty would be exposed, and I would need to be forgiven.

Chapter Fifteen

All the Single Ladies

After dinner, while we cleaned the kitchen and put the dishes away, my stepdaughters would sometimes pop in one of the few CDs we had kicking around. My taste in music zigzags between Haydn, the soundtrack for *Seven Brides for Seven Brothers*, Frank Sinatra, Patsy Cline, Nancy Wilson, and Bob Wills & His Texas Playboys. I winced through Celine Dion and Mariah Carey until—bam!—Beyoncé kicked in the door to our kitchen. We crowded around the kitchen table and watched the "Single Ladies" video on YouTube, stumbling through frequent buffering sessions that had all of us frozen in place. Naturally, all of the girls instantly absorbed the dance through their pores, while I watched in wonder and then occasionally attempted to join in. My dancing to Beyoncé was, I assume, like watching Laura Petrie try to skateboard. Were these girls laughing with me, or *at* me? I wasn't sure.

I don't consider myself a particularly picky person. I have a fairly relaxed attitude toward housekeeping and other people's habits, but the girls adjusted to my nonnegotiable pet peeves, namely the sounds generated by chewing and the clipping of nails. Also, I refuse to touch anyone else's feet. Otherwise, they also quickly learned that I don't share well. Don't eat off my plate, don't wear my sweater, don't use my laptop, and if you want to slip on my boots to go out to get the mail, please ask first.

In this family, possessions flowed between sisters. This was a vestige of Bruno's upbringing in a family with thirteen children, where the brothers pulled their shared clothing out of a "community chest" at the top of the stairs. In the mornings when Bruno drove them to school in his pickup truck, the girls plugged hair dryers and curling irons into the truck's cigarette lighter attachment and did their before-school primping as they shared the tiny mirror visor. They also shared (and sometimes bickered over) nail polish, soccer cleats, T-shirts, and—I assume—opinions about their new stepmother's peccadillos.

Watching the girls interact was a reminder of my own experience growing up in a tribe of sisters. The dynamic between adolescent sisters is one of the universe's most beautiful and volatile chemical compounds. I felt loved and fiercely protected by my own sisters growing up, and yet I still remember being chased screaming through the house by one sister wielding a hairbrush like a machete while the other calmly threatened to call our mother at work to rat us both out. Jane always insisted that we all must get along. However, when she left the house, sometimes all hell broke loose. In my new household, I had to occasionally watch all hell break loose, knowing that I shouldn't (and probably couldn't) leap in to make peace. I asked my mother, "Remind me, how did you do it?"

"Damned if I know," she said.

Integrating into my new family was challenging and exhausting. I had led a quiet life raising Emily. It was far from a perfect life, but because I had created it, I almost always knew where I stood. In contrast, my life in Bruno's household during the early days felt like a continuous blind date at a Slovenian cocktail party. I was always exerting and on my best behavior, but I didn't yet understand the family language. Getting to know one person intimately is challenging. Knowing a household of individuals thoroughly seemed impossible.

At the end of my workday, I would drive the short distance from my house/office, stop by Jane's, and spend time with her as the dusk descended over her quiet house. My aunts Millie and Jean were usually with her when I arrived. I would visit with them and try to cook a little something that she might eat, and then I would gingerly say good night when her neighbor Deborah arrived to help get her to bed. I was entering a period of deep sadness over my mother's declining health, which I didn't know how to handle. After leaving her, I would drive to Pemberley, sit in the car in the driveway, and steel myself to have a second dinner with my new family.

My stepdaughters all kindly embraced my close relationship with my mother and asked about her during those periods when they realized that I was almost continuously worried about her. Michaela seemed especially interested in my mother, and her thoughtful curiosity about Jane was a kindness and a relief to me. Michaela was applying to colleges, and within a year she would leave the household; she seemed to be working extra hard to get to know me before her exit.

Jane thought they were all lovely; she engaged them by occasionally asking great questions and by watching and listening, but otherwise never expressed any opinion about them. I tried to push my stepdaughters toward my own family of sisters, aunts, and cousins, but my clan's politeness toward them did not feel like much of an embrace but more like they were waiting to see how things turned out before committing to new family members. (In fairness, they were dealing with their own busy families and were involved in Jane's care, just as I was.) It was as if my two families were running on parallel tracks, with me at the median. My new daughters were already part of a huge clan with almost a hundred first cousins. My far smaller family added another grandmother, two great-aunts, two aunts and uncles, and a dozen new cousins (most living locally) to the mix.

On our first Thanksgiving Day together, we attended three turkey dinners: first at the Freeville United Methodist Church feast, then at my cousin Nancy's house on Main Street, and then at Bruno's mother's house at Maryhill Farm. The night before, I had lain awake, trying to map out our movements to make sure that everyone would be seen and satisfied, timing out the baking of the casseroles and pies, and worrying about whether my stepchildren would like my own family enough to want to keep me in theirs.

I entered a period of frequent travel; my first book came out two months after our wedding, and I left town frequently for readings and other public appearances. Occasionally leaving the household for short periods of time was a blessing for this stepparent at the beginning of blending a family together—everybody let out their breath, relaxed, and regrouped. When I would return from these trips of three or four days, I sometimes wondered if the girls even realized I was gone; in my absence they would simply slip back into the pattern of many years that they had already established, dipping back into their own story of a single dad and his beautiful daughters, drying their hair on the way in to school.

Three months after moving into the household, I traveled to Chicago to visit my office at the *Trib* and to attend my monthly taping of the radio show. I was sitting on the couch in my apartment in Chicago, congratulating myself after the show ("I so funny! I so smart!"), when Bruno called. He told me he had some news. "Sure, lay it on me. I'm already sitting down," I told him.

"It's about Angela," he said. "She's pregnant."

I think of myself as someone who is resilient and flexible. I see myself as someone who rises to personal challenges. In truth, I am frequently none of these things. I was shocked by my reaction to this news, which I can only describe as free-floating, crippling, dark anxiety. *I can't do this,* I thought. And then I said it out loud a few times, to Bruno and to others.

Bruno and I tried to crowbar details out of Angela, but she was silent and frustratingly resistant to our efforts. Mainly, she acted like the eighteen-year-old person she was. I also acted like an eighteen-year-old, like a petulant teenager who'd had something snatched from her. I could not think of one thing more challenging than trying to fast-track into this family's life, until I was faced with the prospect of adding a baby to it.

This feeling went on for months. I went with Angela to a couple of prenatal visits, flipping the pages of *What to Expect When You're Expecting* in the doctor's waiting room. After her appointments, she would ride quietly in the car on the way home. Eventually, Angela engaged a couple of her girlfriends to go with her instead, and I kept some distance. There were no "what can we expect, now that you're expecting" discussions at the dinner table, and no plans emerged. When asked how she was feeling, Angela would only say that she was tired. Her other thoughts and feelings seemed quietly submerged. I told family members about the news. "How is she doing?" my mother asked. I told her she seemed well. "How are *you* doing?" she asked. "Me? I don't think I'm doing very well."

Bruno adjusted to this event the way he seems to adjust to everything: very quickly and with little worry or angst. This is someone who grew up with twelve siblings. He is authentically a "the more the merrier" kind of guy. Bruno often cheerfully repeated a phrase left over from his own crowded childhood: "That's life in a herd!" But I wasn't equipped to live in a herd. Tearfully I recalled our courting days, driving around the countryside in the snow, unaware of how challenging the journey might be, and innocent of the complications lying in wait around the next bend.

But also, Bruno had never given birth and raised a baby on his own. I had done this, and I was filled with dread and worry. I worried about the impact of this new child on our very young marriage. I fretted about the prospect of trying to raise a baby as we were also trying to raise its young mother and her sisters. I worried about trying to mentor a young mom, when I didn't know her very well, and barely had a handle on my own parenting. I fretted about cribs, onesies, diapers, and baby seats. My thoughts seemed to automatically settle only on the endless challenges of having a baby on board as I anxiously ruminated about every possible delicate complication of adding another child to our crowded household. At one point, when I stated point-blank that I wasn't ready for this, Bruno reminded me that I didn't have to be ready. I wasn't having a baby; Angela was, and ready or not, this was happening.

Chapter Sixteen

What the Dog Did

The undeniable reality of having a baby on the way is that—regardless of your own level of preparedness—that baby comes. I was hoping the gestation of my anxiety and negativity would be that of a chipmunk (one month), versus a giraffe (fifteen months), but it turned out to be very human-scaled.

In fact, my worries seemed to grow instead of fade as the months passed and we in the household waited for our May birthday.

Bruno's "the more the merrier" ethic weighed me down. I wanted for the "more" to genuinely be merrier, but often it was not. Mainly, "more" just felt like more—more people, more complications, more questions without any resolution, more failed attempts at connection, and more challenges I was unable to meet.

The turning point came courtesy of our dog. Calvin, being young, dumb, and an energetic runaway, tangled with a car down the road, and his leg was badly broken. Michaela, who was at that time dreaming of becoming a doctor, took charge of his care. The dog returned home after surgery hopped up on painkillers, with a massive stitched wound across his hind leg and his head encased in a plastic cone, which he removed whenever he felt like it. The instructions were to take him out several times a day, holding up his midsection in a sling so he wouldn't put any of his eighty-five-pound weight on his injured back leg. I took Calvin out when the kids were at school, and otherwise we all bickered over whose turn it was.

It was March. There were four inches of snow on the ground, topped by a crusty shield of ice. The spring rains had started; it had been raining sideways most of the day. Michaela was at the kitchen table, working on her calculus homework. I assumed she sensed the reason behind my presence in the kitchen ("Hey, have you taken Calvin out yet?") and therefore she deliberately didn't make eye contact—not that I blamed her. I put on my coat and boots but couldn't find Calvin's leash or sling, or Calvin. I pressed my face to the window and looked outside toward the darkened driveway. And there was Angela, seven months pregnant, wearing the coat she could no longer button and the strappy sandals she had worn to school that day in the snow. In her right hand she held up the sling around Calvin's body; in her left, she balanced an umbrella, which she inched over the dog's head while he pooped.

My heart cracked open in that moment, and I softened to the tenderness and kindness of this teenager, who after all was flailing about and really just trying to figure out how to grow into her own life—just as I was also trying to do.

Angela remained in high school and continued taking good care of herself. We hosted a huge baby shower at the house in April. Three weeks later, Angela went into labor while at the movies with two girlfriends. She calmly asked for her money back at the ticket counter, left the theater, walked down through the shopping mall, bought herself some pajamas for her confinement, and drove herself and her friends to the hospital after the movie let out. Angela's baby daughter, whom she named after her beloved Dominican grandmother, entered the world surrounded by excited teenagers. We laid her in a little Moses basket (the same one Emily had slept in as a baby) in Angela's bedroom, and the young mother and new baby got to know one another. I nicknamed the baby "Sparkle Pony," because she was sweet and sparkling and because seeing her beautiful face each morning chased away my anxiety and made me smile.

Five weeks later, Bruno, Avila, and I passed the sleeping baby back and forth in the gym when Angela and Michaela received their high school diplomas. We celebrated our first wedding anniversary with our baby grand-daughter, now three months old.

Sparkle grew. She was healthy, bright, and cuddly. Our domestic life became exponentially more chaotic. We got through months of interrupted nights, ear infection scares, and the occasional rash. We always seemed to be putting a car seat into or out of a car. We pulled a high chair up to the dining room table and took turns holding the baby while we cooked. Bruno's sister Ceci brought her kids' crib to us from her home in Philadelphia. I explained the difference between Ferberizing and cosleeping and made Angela stay downstairs during bedtime for a few nights while I sat on a chair outside the bedroom door, training Sparkle to soothe herself so Angela could sleep through the night.

Angela took the baby to our neighbor Lisa (who had also taken care of all of the sisters as young children) and started working a few hours a week at a local nursing home. After picking her up from the babysitter, Angela would hold Sparkle in the air in the kitchen while one of us pulled off the baby's puffy snowsuit. It was like unwrapping a beautiful present. We gave Sparkle a doll for Christmas, which Calvin quickly chewed the face off of. He dragged the faceless doll around with him and eventually pulled all of the baby's toys into his kennel, where he slept curled around them.

Michaela had sifted among her college acceptances and decided to go to St. Andrews University in Scotland. Although I was now sensing how very much I would miss her, I told her to fly, fly away. During a break from her own college, Emily went with Clare and Michaela to Scotland to look at the school. They stayed with my mother's antic friend Faye in Edinburgh, who I assumed taught them to smoke cigarettes and drink whiskey. They returned from the trip quite whiskey conversant, having inched closer toward a rela-tionship that for Emily was starting to seem sister-like. Emily was an only child, who (because she was raised by me) didn't like to share. And yet, now she was sharing me.

I settled into the role of cruise director. I planned trips to New York City to go to the theater, Christmastime weekend jaunts to see the Rockettes and window-shop, weeklong summertime trips to Block Island, and trips to Cooperstown for Bruno and me to attend the opera in the summer. Avila started saying things like, "Remember when we were on Block Island and Kirk [my best friend from childhood] cooked all those lobsters for us?" Avila also had a way of wordlessly taking jelly jars out of my hands to open them (I have weak hands) that made my eyes water with gratitude. We were starting to have memories together. I even turned up as a supporting player in one of Angela's vivid dreams, and I was flattered when she told me about it—even if I was a little unsure of the context.

I never knew how much I valued and needed my privacy until I didn't have it. The gregarious side of me powers through groups of people with competing agendas and their infernal complications. The other side of me wants to spend the afternoon in a darkened movie theater, alone. This impulse is impossible to carry out in a small town, where even if I could hide out from my families of birth or marriage, I would still inevitably have to make small talk with at least three sets of people along the way.

I coped with this by stealing away when I could, sometimes driving to a nearby town where nobody knew me, walking an unfamiliar Main Street and spending the afternoon in the town's library. Sometimes I told Bruno I had an afternoon conference call but went to the movies instead. When the weather and my work schedule permitted, I'd go to our nearby ski hill and spend the afternoon riding the chairlift with teenage snowboarders. Flying down a hill on my rented skis, I felt free in a way I needed to feel, before returning to a household where I was starting to feel almost too necessary.

After several months of delicate negotiations (more on this later), Jane moved to a nearby nursing home. Bruno's mother (still on the farm where he grew up) transitioned to a wheelchair. When my plane touched down after one business trip, I drove straight to the hospital from the airport. Bruno's mother was in the acute care ICU. After visiting her, I took the elevator three floors up to the other ICU to see my own mother. There were nasty diagnoses for various family members, crises for others, middle school lacrosse games for Avila (two concussions), blizzards on top of snowstorms, sideways spring rains. A baby learning to crawl. Calvin, limping now on his bad leg, broke his other hind leg. Again with the meds and the sling and the head cone. Emily and Clare each graduated from their colleges the same June weekend. Bruno and I split duties and each attended one ceremony. Emily, with her degree in English and a minor in music, moved into her old summer room in my Main Street house. While she figured out how to somehow turn her passion for reading and writing into a profession, she took a job at the Gap at the mall.

When Sparkle was a toddler, Angela took her to the Dominican Republic to see her extended family. We played "bye-bye" at the airport gate. Three weeks later, they returned home. Angela was glowing. She had gotten engaged to her boyfriend, Junior. At the time, we didn't know that Angela had a boyfriend, but we had become accustomed to Angela's preference for living her life outside of our sometimes bossy influence. Angela had figured out how to bring Junior to this country and pursue citizenship for him. I was warily happy for her—she was making a family of her own and excitedly planning her future.

Three months later, I was in Chicago, patting myself on the back after another taping of *Wait Wait* ("I so smart…"). Bruno called. Was I sitting down? Yes, I was. He told me that we were going to have another grandchild.

I would like to say that I handled this news entirely differently than I had two years earlier, that I had picked up so much wisdom and motherly (and grandmotherly) seasoning along the way that I now reacted with grace. And yet—no. Not so much. I was the same amount of anxious, the same amount of panicked, and felt the exact same amount of everything that I had two years before. Angela powered through this tough pregnancy, taking care of herself and Sparkle and spending her evenings filling out a foot-high stack of paperwork to bring her guy to America.

Unfortunately, because of a backlog at the INS, Junior didn't make it in time for the baby's birth. This time, it was just Angela and me in the hospital room on a chilly day just after Thanksgiving. "I can't do it," she said, wincing through her painful back labor. I gripped her hand. *I can't do it either,* I thought. And yet, she did and I did, too. We welcomed another daughter, "Sprout," to the family.

I spent my days working on my advice column in my house in Freeville while Emily was working at the mall. She was looking for a journalism job in Chicago, and I knew it was just a matter of time before I said good-bye to her again. In the afternoons I visited Jane in her nursing home and ate an early dinner with her. Then I drove back to Pemberley in the gloom of a winter dusk and sat in the driveway looking in through the lighted windows while I watched my beloved husband and house full of daughters glide, turn, and bump in the kitchen. Dog barking, cat on the counter, babies in their bouncy seats.

Oftentimes, navigating all of these varied relationships, with everyone's life so crowded with needs, incidents, and drama, overwhelmed me to overflowing. The health scares, the homework assignments, the frequently hospitalized elderly mothers, the middle school musicals, birthday parties, college departures, business worries, cell phone bills, the annual conversations over whether to get some chickens—sometimes I simply longed to know what would happen next. Even if it was a bad thing, I just wanted to know. After all, Calvin still had two healthy legs left to break.

Angela's fiancé, Junior, finally qualified for a visa, caught a plane north, and moved in with us. My first glimpse of my soon-to-be son-in-law was on a frosty and freezing January morning. Sparkle was a toddler, and Sprout was two months old. I had sent a wool cap and down jacket along with Bruno and Angela when they went to the airport to retrieve Junior on his first trip outside of the Dominican Republic. He was sitting at our kitchen table in the silvery dawn light, still wearing his cap and cooing over my cat, Chester, who was sitting on his lap. I realized in that moment that, although they claimed to like Chester, not one member of the household had ever voluntarily held my cuddly cat. Junior was starting off well.

Junior didn't speak English, and the only Spanish I could recall from my high school class was, "Esto es mi amigo, Ramon. Juego al tennis?"

I said, "Ummmmm...Que bonito. Bonita? Bonito. Shit."

I recovered. "Esto es Chester," I said, pointing to the cat.

"Allo, Chester," Junior said.

We pulled another chair up to the table. One month later on Valentine's Day, Angela and Junior were married in the living room at Maryhill Farm. I held Sprout while Sparkle shyly hugged my leg. Within a couple of months, Angela, Junior, and their children moved into one of Bruno's candy-colored rental houses a few minutes away.

With Angela and her family in another house and Michaela away at college, our house was suddenly emptied out, and Bruno and I were left with only Avila, now a high school junior. "Oh my God, you guys, stop staring at me," she said regularly at the dinner table. Alone among our girls, Avila truly seemed to see her father and me as a parental unit. I had first met Avila when she was a little girl, wincing her way through a hug. Now she was a confident young woman studying for the SATs. She flopped onto our bed on Saturday mornings and described her dreams of the night before. Avila was also the only one of our daughters to whom I had confided my secret ambition—to be a school bus driver. She held this knowledge close. One day when she got particularly good news at school, she called and left me a breathless, screechy, and hilarious message that I still have on my phone. I listen to it when I'm having a bad day.

Michaela graduated from college in the spring. I had missed her during her time away. In addition to enjoying her company, I suspected that she was the only family member who truly thought I was funny. I loved to sit with her in the kitchen during her visits home. Bruno and I took Clare and Avila to Scotland for her graduation, and along with Michaela we explored the Highlands in the rain and hiked the hills of Edinburgh. As Bruno drove through the Scottish countryside, the girls and I took turns yelling at him to drive on the left. One blustery day during this visit, Bruno and I climbed to the top of Arthur's Seat, the ancient volcanic cone in the middle of Edinburgh overlooking the North Sea. Bruno stood at the very top of the small mountain and bent down and extended his hand to me. I let him pull me up. We had come a very long way, and we traveled well together.

Michaela introduced us to her college friends at St. Andrews. "These are my parents, Bruno and Amy." Depending on the context, most of our daughters at some point had decided to shortcut through the verbal logjam of introducing us as "This is my father and stepmother." Whenever it happened, it always made me smile. I was not the mother of these young women, but I had become their parent.

Chapter Seventeen

We Abide

A couple of months ago, I had a lunch meeting with three *Tribune* executives to talk about my professional future.

At that meeting, we never actually got around to discussing me, because we ended up talking about our parents. Around the table we went, trading stories about where our folks were living, what ailments they suffered from, and what we were doing about it. Every single one of us was involved in the care of an elderly parent, a job made all the more challenging by the fact that we—a salesperson, an editor, a writer, and a financial analyst—were doing the caretaking. Woefully unprepared, each of us was up to our elbows in the heartrending task of taking care of someone who would never get better.

Two of us got teary during the lunch. One of us was stammering with frustration. And one seemed to have checked out.

"God," I said. "Look at us. Remember when all we used to do was talk about our kids?"

Those days of bragging about toilet training and Little League coaching and slipping our kids' awesome SAT scores into the conversation seemed like a lifetime ago, even though all of us still had children at home. But our kids didn't command the attention or grab the personal headlines anymore. We'd stopped worrying about their learner's permits and driving tests. Now it was all about how to get our folks to turn in their car keys. We were at the tail end of the baby boom generation, the middle-aged daughters and sons who waited to have kids because we were so concerned about getting everything just right. We built our careers in industries that no longer seem to exist, and now we tried to avoid downsizing as we struggled to pay our mortgages and our kids' tuition bills.

Those of us whose youngest child has just left for college enjoy exactly 3.5 weeks of freedom before our parents start to depend on us. Someone falls and breaks a hip, and then the other joints start to go.

Caretaking seems an inadequate word to describe the whole-life transformation of dealing with an aging and ill parent. For me, the transformation started slowly but gained momentum over time, until caring for my mother and worrying about her seemed to take over my life. Jane had rheumatoid arthritis, a chronic and painful illness that did its damage gradually but inexorably. She had always managed her health, and her life, very much on her own.

When I first moved back to Freeville, my caretaking mainly involved watching. Watching and waiting and wondering what to do. It was a short walk down Main Street to Jane's old house. I would work on my advice column during the early day and visit my mother in the afternoons. She was using a cane, but she was still driving her black Jetta on what seemed like twelve very short errands a day. I'd look out my front window and see her rolling through town, the top of her head barely visible through the windshield.

My sisters and I started worrying about her. We'd call each other and gossip about her dangerously glacial driving and talk about how her hands were getting worse. After I noticed that my mother had tried to open a can of plum tomatoes in her kitchen by attacking it with a ball-peen hammer, she confessed to me that her preferred method of opening jars and cans was to drive them to the gas station on the corner (a hundred yards away) and hand them out the car window to Jimmy Whyte or one of the mechanics. They'd loosen the lid and hand it back. "It takes a village!" she offered gamely, repeating for the umpteenth time a phrase that I had come to loathe. And yet, it really did take a village. Freeville has a population of 520 people, and at one time or another every single one of them seemed to have a hand in my mother's welfare. We all wondered how long she could hang on in her house on Mill Street.

The last five years of Jane's life were a gradual slide into entropy, punctuated by occasional terrifying emergencies. The Year of the Cane morphed into the Walker Year, which turned into the Era of the Wheelchair. Jane's beloved Jetta eventually sat idle in the driveway, collecting leaves and snow and coatings of pollen as the seasons changed. At one point when Jane expressed a (terrifying) determination to drive her car again, Rachel dealt with it by saying to her, "I'll tell you what. If you can open the car door, get in, and close the door by yourself, then go for it." Needless to say, she didn't.

Getting Jane to move out of the house where she had lived by herself for thirty years took months of strategizing, subterfuge, and frustrated coercion on the part of my two sisters and me. She was the human equivalent of Chinese handcuffs: The harder we tried to persuade her to move, the tighter she held on. Somehow, the physically weaker our mother became, the more she was able to exert her ancient powers of passive aggression to control everyone around her. Her primary weapons were a raised eyebrow and a pursed lip. She told me once that she had spent the entire summer of her eighth year practicing raising one eyebrow like Hedy Lamarr. Seventy years later, she ruthlessly employed this technique to send her daughters scurrying away from the topic of moving somewhere safer. We visited nursing facilities, secretly put her name on waiting lists, and kept in touch with nursing home directors. When I would get a call that there was an "opening," I knew what that meant. Someone had died, and we had twenty-four hours to grab the slot.

Rheumatoid arthritis had attacked all of her joints, pulling her fingers and toes sideways. After multiple surgeries to replace a knee, a shoulder, and other smaller joints in her hands and feet, she became extremely frail and disabled. The Life Alert button my sister Anne got for her, and which she wore around her wrist, did in fact save her life, several times.

The times Jane pressed her "I've fallen and I can't get up" button, she was never found lying decorously on the floor, arm outstretched like in the ad. Instead, she was injured, sometimes seriously and always bloodily, because when she fell, she tended to hit her head on one of the sharp-edged heirlooms populating her small house.

One time I showed her a full-page advertisement for one of those fancy assisted-living places that dangle the promise of what an aged person's life would be like. The people in the ads look like they're my age; they seem to play a lot of golf. There is always a man AND a woman in these ads, and they're always thin and fit. They look like they're only one dose of Viagra away from playing a round of golf, if you know what I mean. So I showed my mother this ad, which said, *Maturity is wonderful. Growing older is exciting!*

I looked at her. "What do you think, Mom? Is growing older exciting?"

"It is the way I do it," she said wryly.

Late at night during her many hospitalizations, my sisters and I would meet in the parking lot between visiting shifts and stand in the snow and cry. You know how all the articles about caregiving talk about having regular family meetings and developing a family plan? Our family plan involved lots of standing in the parking lot, venting our despair.

Our caretaking was pieced together in loose shifts—Rachel in the mornings, a paid caregiver through the day, and my mother's two older sisters, Jean and Millie (both in their eighties), in the late afternoons. My sister Anne drove two hours from her home on the weekends. When I stopped in each day around supper time, I would see my elderly aunts, clutching their teacups, helpless to do much other than wipe down a counter or fix a sandwich for their youngest and much more frail sister. Her old friend and neighbor Deborah, a retired nurse, came in the evenings and left at midnight.

Being with my mother during this stage of her life created weird parallels and muscle memories of my own experiences as a mother. Trying to take care of her brought back the old feeling of being completely frazzled and on the verge of a tantrum (often, my own), left over from my daughter's childhood. It was a strange bookend experience of dealing with equipment, ailments, doctor's appointments, and somebody else's bodily functions.

As the youngest of my mother's four children, I am the yippy terrier at the end of her leash. My position in the family seems to have imprinted upon me a chronic need to please, which, when coupled with some basic competency issues, sometimes made me more of a menace than a true helpmate to her. I am someone who forgets the roll of stamps at the post office window and drives away from the gas pump with the nozzle still attached to the tank. My most dangerous characteristic is my tendency to try to be helpful. The worst true statement that can be made about me is that I mean well.

I'm fairly certain that if polled, my two older sisters would have voted me most likely to run over myself with my own car. And yet, there I was, a forty-eight-year-old refugee from my successful career as an advice-giver, a professional know-it-all who actually knew very little about anything that seemed to matter to someone nearing the end of her life, where all of life's questions seemed to boil down to this: How can I stay?

That's me standing on the sidewalk outside the doctor's office, pushing my hair out of my eyes and trying to lock the car as the wheelchair (with my mother in it) started rolling through a parking lot because I'd forgotten to lock the wheels. All I could do was yell, "Hang on, Mom!" while I ran after her.

So much of my caretaking was devoted to trying to help Jane maintain her dignity. She kept hers, while I seemed to lose mine. In fact, her dignity didn't even seem to be in play. She rarely complained about anything and continued to deflect every challenge with little verbal sideswipes. My coping mechanism was to *lose it*, usually in the supermarket while hunting for a favorite food that my mother probably wouldn't eat. In her elder years, Jane had become finicky, like a cat. My sisters and I turned ourselves inside out trying to find her favorite foods. When Clark's Shurfine Food Mart stopped carrying Sara Lee coffee cake, I drove into Ithaca and frantically scanned the freezer sections of the massive Wegmans supermarket. When I finally found it, I bought several packages and e-mailed my sisters to let them know that I had cornered the local supply.

Much of Jane's adult life had been one of satisfied solitude. She seemed to love living alone, happily in charge of only herself. Her bills got paid on time, her home was beautiful, and her gardens were exceptional. While she always seemed to welcome company, she was just as happy to say good-bye at the end of a visit. Over the years, my sisters and I had learned to keep our visits short, especially when our kids were in tow. My mother always preferred teenagers. "Toddlers," she said, "give me a pain." As her health declined, her little living room always had someone extra in it: the paid caregivers, the visiting nurse, or a neighbor stopping by. Yet I knew what she really wanted was to be left alone.

Decades ago when I was an associate producer at NBC, I worked on an awful news magazine show that eventually morphed into the truly awful show *Dateline*. My mother came to New York City on the bus for a short visit, and I pulled out the stops to entertain her. We went to the ballet, and then the next day we went to the Plaza for lunch and to the Oak Room for drinks. Jane didn't drink, but at the Oak Room she ordered a whiskey sour. I proudly brought her into my office at 30 Rockefeller Center, past the Depression Era murals in the grand black granite lobby and up the Art Deco elevator to my office. My mother and I were in the same movie that day—I was Tippi Hedren and she was Bette Davis, belted securely into her favorite trench coat. My (then) husband and I had just announced that we were moving from New York City to London. Jane, who never expressed an opinion on any matter she considered "personal," had taken a characteristically completely neutral and noncommittal stance.

There in the doorway to my office we ran into Connie Chung, the glamorous anchorwoman who hosted our program. I introduced them.

"JANE!" Connie exclaimed. "We're losing our girl! She's moving to London!" Wearing the same intense expression that she would later use on Newt Gingrich's poor mother, Connie reached down and took my mother's face in her hands: "How do we feel?! We feel happy. We feel sad. We feel happy-sad. Happy-sad, happy-sad." Connie seemed capable of yin-yanging this concept into infinity.

My mother was small. Unprepossessing. She was not used to being touched and emoted over by a willowy Anchor Goddess. The one eyebrow went up. "Yes, that about describes it," she said.

Happy-sad. Happy-sad. I pitched assisted-living places to Jane with the enthusiasm of Connie Chung. She batted them right back at me, saying, "I'm fine here."

"But you're not fine here," I said.

"You're doing too much. Just go about your own business and I'll be fine," she said.

My sisters and I tried to pull together and work as a team, but mainly we each played out a version of our distinct temperaments, using our mother as a foil. No one wanted to actually BE in charge (a terrifying responsibility for three women with jobs and children), so we traded off seizing control and then—just before a sisterly eruption—stalked off, slinked off, or merely refused to appear at the house for a while. Then the next sister would step up. We didn't fight in front of our mother, and we didn't really fight much with each other, except there was sometimes an underlying air of tension and unexpressed judgment as we silently gauged one another's competence, which was often found wanting. Then one sister would call another to complain about the third. A week later, the dynamic in the sister triangle would shift, as we more or less took turns sulking on the porch. Sometimes we gave each other a break and complained about other people.

Our accommodations to try to keep Jane in her house ranged from structural to emotional. When climbing the stairs became impossible, we brought her iron bed from her unheated bedroom upstairs and set it up in front of the fireplace in the living room. When she became too frail to climb into the high bed, Bruno hacksawed the legs down. Various ramps were built. Instead of installing standard hospital handrails (which were too big for her hands to grip), Bruno cleverly attached one-inch metal piping alongside her bed and along the walls of her room and the kitchen; the pipe turned corners and changed elevation and eventually lined much of the interior of the house. It reminded me of the interlocking "Windows Pipes" of the first screen saver on my very first desktop computer.

We got proficient at delivering basic medical care. A chronic wound infection in her foot required IV antibiotics and daily dressing changes for several months. We strung up the IV bag over the curlicues on a 1930s brass floor lamp next to her comfortable chair. Jane said that her living room, crowded with furniture, two unruly house cats, and now medical equipment, was starting to look like a George Booth cartoon. My brother-in-law Tim and I took turns attaching her to the IV bag, inspecting and cleaning her wound, and changing her dressing. I can barely make a sandwich without inflicting injury, but I got good at this chore. I was Julianna Margulies flicking the air bubble from the IV line. *Tap tap tap.* I'd snap the plastic tubing and hold it up to the window to check for air bubbles. "Stat!" I commanded before attaching it to her port. Jane looked up at me: "Are we having fun?"

"No. It's just what we say. In the healing profession."

My mother had always been prickly about her personal space—she wasn't a hugger or a holder of hands—but I shelved my aversion to foot-touching because now she let me bathe her feet and clip her nails. I rubbed lotion into her sideways-slanted fingers. I brought her out onto her porch in the sunshine, where she let me wash and comb her hair.

The tasks were so unrelenting and sometimes so strange. The caregiving both upended and reinforced the pecking order in our family, because we were trying not only to take care of our mother, but to please her as well. She raised us using a technique I would call "conditional approval." Rachel once described this as sort of a "points" system. Like, everybody starts out with all the points, but you lose them as you go. Even though I never remember Jane actually disapproving of anything I ever did, throughout my entire life, here's the thing: I wanted to keep ALL my points.

Embroiled in the family dynamic playing out in Jane's kitchen, I had flashbacks to our childhood summertime gymnastics shows after supper out on the lawn. As the youngest, I had to yell, "LOOK AT ME" the loudest. And in some ways, I was still doing it. I can still feel the sense of righteous satisfaction when my sister and I both brought oranges for our mother—and she ate mine. BAM! I win! Points preserved!

Even though we developed a basic schedule of multiple people providing care for Jane in her home, there were gaps, and I lived in a state of constant anxiety that Jane would fall through one. As she became more disabled and less able to move safely through her house, she reported having vivid hallucinatory experiences that felt completely real. One morning she told me she was awake all night and didn't dare move in her bed because she was convinced that my father, Buck, was lying next to her.

"Oh, did you like that?" I asked in my most annoyingly clinical voice.

She shot me a look. "Ugh. No. I did NOT like that."

And another time: "At six o'clock this morning, I went out to the mailbox, and I saw that [a neighbor] had run over the cat," she told me.

"Well, the cat is here. And…um…you can't walk," I said, offering an unfortunate backhanded reassurance. "Sounds like a very vivid dream."

"I know that's true, I know you're right, but even now it doesn't feel like it was a dream. It feels real—like a memory," she told me.

Neighbors helped. Dennis, who lived up the road, appeared out of nowhere and plowed a path over the yard and right up to the front door so we could bypass the longer route to the driveway with the wheelchair. Others popped in, fed the cats, and brought supper. The local pharmacy delivered her medications and supplies. The guy who read all the utility meters in town caught up with me at Clark's Shurfine Food Mart. He told me that he had driven his truck past her house and didn't see any of our cars there, so he stopped and pretended to read the gas meter outside the house while he looked in a window to make sure she was all right. (She was.)

My only relief during this time was to talk to friends who were also facing these depleting duties. I was drawn to my friends' efforts and capers with their elderly parents, partly because they were not my own.

My friend Gay drove from Washington, DC, eight hours each way to Pittsburgh every weekend to be with her mother so that her sister could have a break. She took her mother in her wheelchair to Atlantic City whenever possible so her mom could play the slots. Nancy's mother, who had only shown mild signs of forgetfulness, left the house one morning to drive to the hairdresser around the corner and ended up driving around Washington's Beltway for thirteen hours before she finally exited. The Maryland County sheriff had to lay out rumble strips to blow out her tires to get her to stop. Several years before that, Nancy's elderly and ill father had left the house without telling anyone. He took a cab to the airport and somehow ended up kicked off a cruise ship in Bermuda.

My friend Jean's father owned a factory in New Jersey. He was wealthy, successful, and in charge of everything. He was always nattily dressed in a suit with a bow tie. Jean had four children of her own and left her newborn baby at home while she nursed her mother in her dying months when her father couldn't handle it—running back and forth from her own home in suburban New Jersey to her parents' place. Her husband, Jim, picked up the slack and raised the kids by himself during this almost yearlong daily odyssey. After her mother's death and when her father's dementia emerged and worsened, Jean resumed her daily trips back and forth, while trying to convince her father and her brothers that he was too ill to live on his own.

One night at ten o'clock, Jean's father called her. He wanted her to bring him an envelope. His instruction was to bring him one white business-sized envelope. Jean weighed her options, the way you do dozens of times a day when you're trying to balance the scales between the loads you carry. Someone else's needs and your own needs. Your parents versus your toddlers. Jean decided that she wasn't going to get in her car and take her dad the envelope. Not this time. This one time she was going to draw a boundary.

Jean didn't bring her father the envelope. And then she stayed awake all night, worrying about not bringing him the envelope. "I mean, it's only an envelope!" she said to me guiltily.

I know all about that envelope. Only in my case, it was a can of cat food. One tiny, eighty-nine-cent can of cat food. This was the thing I got out of bed for and got in my car to take to my mother late one night. That was the thing that tipped the balance and forced me to say, "Is this really working for us?"

So I called Jean. "How's your dad?" I asked. Jean always had a story. And it was always just that much more surreal than my own.

A few months after the Night of the Envelope, Jean's eighty-nine-year-old father ended up wandering around New York City at two in the morning. Some police officers helped to get him back to his home in New Jersey. After that, he was moved to a facility that couldn't handle this once mild-mannered man's outbursts. Jean was then forced into the heartbreaking decision to commit her father to a hospital's psych ward until she could find a place for him. Jean's brother, who didn't believe their father had dementia, then discharged him from the hospital and took him to a high-rise hotel. Long story short, when the elderly man got up at night to wander and his son ran after him, both men ended up locked outside the hotel room, naked and hiding in a stairwell.

He was moved to several different homes and facilities until the family finally found one that could handle him. He lived there until his death. At the reception after her father's funeral, Jean gave every guest one of her father's bow ties. He had hundreds of them. It was a sweet and tangible reminder of the man he had been, before things got so sad.

My cousin Jan, who moved into my house on Main Street with her husband, Roger, gently nursed him through his final illness this year. Jan sent out text messages every day updating family members on Roger's condition. At the end of each message, she wrote, *We abide.*

We abide. To abide means to stand with someone, to suffer alongside someone. But it also means to live somewhere, and for me, abiding meant to live in that tender and tenuous place of knowing but not knowing. Knowing what would happen but not how it would happen. Knowing it would all end, but not what that ending would be like or how it would feel.

One winter night, a year before my mother's death, after a series of harrowing emergency trips to the hospital—always through the snow—I sat with her. Everyone else had gone home. Her living room felt cold and gloomy. I said out loud what we all knew: "We can't do this anymore." I told her the only way we could get through the rest of the winter was if she would move and stay elsewhere—at least until spring, when she could come back home if she wanted. As I said this to my mother, I knew it was a lie, but the director of the private nursing facility at the edge of Cornell's campus had just called to say they had an opening. I had twenty-four hours.

After so much time spent trying unsuccessfully to persuade and pressure my mother to somehow spontaneously decide to give up her independence and leave her home, finally I became brave enough to take responsibility for making a decision that broke her heart. "This is happening," I said. And then I abided with her. I stayed with her through her disappointment and uncertainty. I assured her that we would be with her every step of the way, so she wouldn't be alone. She bravely accepted her reality.

Jane's care would be paid for from the proceeds of my just-published book. She wouldn't have to sell the house. I promised her that everything would stay the same and that I would try to bring her home again. She accepted my promise, even though we both suspected it was one I would never be able to keep.

Chapter Eighteen

Heroic Measures

The day in February when Jane died was like all of the other days that winter: The temperature hovered near zero, and the wind sliced through you in sudden gusts. That was the year it started snowing in early November, and snow fell every day until May. Not crushing blizzards with school closings and power outages, but daily fresh blankets of snow layered one on top of the other.

Each morning I could hear the whine of snowblowers up and down Main Street as neighbors dug out and then dug out again.

By February, the drifts and snow piles were impressive mini-mountains. The massive bulldozed snow mound in the parking lot at the mall was three stories high. It didn't disappear until June.

I dwell on this, sometimes, because when my mother died, the end was such a confusing combination of grotesque and gentle that experiencing it was like being buried beneath layer upon layer of snow, which when it falls is weightless and beautiful, while what it is covering is its own dense, heavy, and frozen heart.

She made it through Christmas, sitting in her chair in her pretty private room on the second floor of the nursing facility where she spent the last year of her life. Her bed was placed against a large window; the view outside was of a huge maple tree and a quiet street on the edge of Cornell University's campus. The nursing home was housed in a restored Victorian mansion scattered among the other private homes and mansions of the university's "Greek Row."

All winter long, waves of glossy-haired sorority girls paraded on the sidewalk below my mother's window on their way to "rush" gatherings. They were all bare legs and UGG boots and tended to move in large and liquid groups—prancing like Lipizzaners, clapping their hands together, and huddling in clusters for warmth. The previous fall, we watched through her window as teams of shirtless boys played volleyball on the grass. They were members of Alpha Zeta, the university's agricultural fraternity—raw-boned and muscular Adonis types who reminded me of the farm boys I'd gone to high school with three decades earlier.

After my father left and our dairy farm failed in the 1970s, my mother went to work at Cornell, floating through various departments before settling in as a typist at the College of Engineering. She did this for seven years, and then, encouraged by her bosses, she applied to and was accepted at the university as a full-time undergraduate. She was forty-eight years old. She went on to receive her MFA at Cornell and taught, briefly, in the English department, the same place where she had once xeroxed lesson plans and syllabi for professors.

Later on, after her death, a university administrator made a special point of letting me know that she would always see Jane as a hapless, frumpy, amusingly incompetent secretary, giving me some insight into the downside of my mother's late-life experience in academia. By leaving the ranks of the staff, getting an education, and becoming a professional, she must have been uncomfortable evidence that, if a single mother and ex-wife of a down-on-his-luck dairy farmer from Freeville can do it, then the professors strolling the ivy-draped campus might not be quite so special as they thought. My mother later went on to a successful fifteen-year career teaching writing at Ithaca College, and she came to deeply appreciate the students and faculty of the lesser-known local college, who treated her like one of their own, until her twenty-year-long battle with rheumatoid arthritis forced her to retire when she was seventy.

Despite her somewhat complicated relationship to the university, living in the nursing home in a big old house on the edge of campus felt right. For someone who was older than many of her professors when she went to Cornell as a commuter student and who had never lived in a dorm or had a roommate, my mother's presence in what we jokingly called "on-campus housing" at the end of her life was symmetrical.

We moved her into the room in the big Victorian house in January, along with her portable wheelchair, books, television, some ancestral paintings, and her cat, Sophie—delivering her to the care of professionals, whom she quickly befriended, although she never mixed with the other residents. She took her meals on a tray in her room and occasionally went downstairs to have coffee on the home's enclosed porch. My sisters and I closed and padlocked the front door of her house on Mill Street. The late-night Life Alert calls stopped, the village's volunteer fire department EMTs turned their attention elsewhere, and we all breathed a sigh.

Our visiting shifts at the nursing home coincided with what we had established when she was still home: Rachel in the morning, my aunts in the late afternoon, and me for supper. Anne drove from Rochester every Saturday.

My mother's family and friends rallied around her. They colonized her room, and many late afternoons when I went to have supper with her, there was at least one other person there. Often, her nieces were laughing with her about a movie they had watched, a friend was trading campus gossip, or her sisters were talking about what Mika Brzezinski had said that morning on MSNBC. (Old people fall into two camps: Fox or MSNBC. She was in the latter.)

Winter finally ended. I took her for drives, and, twice, we visited her old house on Mill Street. In advance I took the padlock off, turned on the heat, and put on a pot of coffee. I was nervous about what it would feel like to be with her in the old house again, but I wanted to reassure her that it was just as we had left it. Sure enough, there was her bed, the walker, the pipes attached to the walls. We sat and drank coffee together, talking about cleaning and organizing projects we needed to do. I told her that we could stay at the house as long as she wanted. She looked out through the ancient wavy glass of the front window toward the Japanese lilac tree. Dusk was starting to fall. "I feel like I'd better get back to Ithaca," she said. I got her coat and wheelchair, unplugged the coffeepot, and put the padlock back on the door.

Through the summer, when Cornell's campus was made quiet by the absence of students, we kept the big window next to Jane's bed open. The leaves of the maple tree just outside twirled in prisms of sunlight. We went wherever a wheelchair could go.

Autumn slid in, and the students came back to school. The volleyball-playing bros took off their shirts, and the girls gamboled down the sidewalk in shiny-haired packs. On Labor Day, I had arranged to pick Jane up to go to the movies. When I arrived, she was being brought out strapped to a gurney. I followed the ambulance to the hospital, and my sisters and I spent the night with her in the ER, along with drunk and disorderly partying college students. I was too nervous about her frailty to take her out after that.

For our mother's last Christmas, my sisters and I organized a family musical for her and the other residents of the home. I hired a pianist, we chose favorite Christmas songs, and her grandchildren and her daughters—the old Gene Pool Choir—sang for her. Bruno, Michaela, and Avila came, and Angela brought Sparkle, who slept quietly on her lap. Some of the other residents were wheeled in and a fire was blazing in the big stone fireplace. Jane's eyes were closed. I knelt down next to her. I knew she didn't want it to end.

Jane stopped eating. My sisters and I frantically tried to find food that would appeal to her. One day I brought her a small cup of beef stew I had made—a throwback to the hearty meals of my childhood. She thanked me, and then she said that the smell of it made her feel sick. She asked me to take it away. Heartbroken, I ate it alone in my car, sitting in the parking lot of the nursing home.

On Christmas Eve, some of her grandchildren gathered in her room. She drank a sip of champagne. Shortly after that, she asked us to tell even her closest friends that she didn't want any more visits. This drawing-in is fairly common with people who are dying, but we didn't know that she was so near the end. We did as she asked.

The medical director presented us with a "do not resuscitate" form to fill out. I assumed this was the standard option for anyone facing medical treatment in a hospital or nearing the end of life. Even though my sister Anne had walked Jane through filling out an advanced directive a couple years before, the DNR kept coming back at us—offered up on clipboards in the emergency room, the ICU, the doctor's office, and the nursing home. Every time it was offered, Jane's answer was the same: Heroic measures, please. Where do I initial?

This time, the medical director explained that if she collapsed or stopped breathing, chest compression would likely break her ribs. She described the violent CPR procedures EMTs would be required to perform. Jane looked up at us. Her voice was little more than a whisper: "Heroic measures WILL be taken," she said. I laughed. The DNR dance had become a joke between us. It wasn't that she was in denial, I decided. She just wanted to stay.

A few days later, Emily and I asked Jane if she was up for a caper. She laughed and agreed, and we took her to the movies. My mother was the original movie fiend; she had the encyclopedic knowledge of a savant and the heart of a fan. We picked her up at night. She hadn't been out after dark in many months. Somehow, with the help of an aide, we got her and her wheelchair into the car and drove through the snow to a downtown theater. We watched *The King's Speech*. I kept glancing over at her to make sure she was still okay. As fitting an end as it might have been, I did not want my mother to die at the movies. Afterward, she asked if we could drive around through the backstreets of Ithaca and past the frozen waterfall at the edge of town. Emily reached forward from the backseat and helped to prop her up so she could see out the window. A cinematic and gentle snowfall was powdering the dark, thick, and frozen air. It was beautiful, and she knew she would never see any of it again.

Since Jane raised my sisters and me to stay comfortably off topic, our time together at the end of her life was spent stoically sharing small talk. She never discussed her death, even after a hospice aide started coming. She only ever made one acknowledgment of what was ahead: "I told Rachel she could have the carriages in the barn," she told me. The two old vehicles were remnants of her grandfather's life as Freeville's doctor in the 1900s. My sisters and I loved these big ancient museum pieces. We would sit on their scratchy horse-hair seats as children and pretend we were making horse-drawn house calls. I didn't know if some long-ago agreement existed between Jane and Rachel about the carriages, and I couldn't imagine where Rachel would put them, but our mother's one directive seemed reasonable. More importantly, it told me that Jane was trying her best to face what was coming, without talking about it.

I called Brad, our local funeral director. I wanted to know if there was room in our family plot. Brad pulled down an old leather-bound ledger, dating from the mid-1800s, and found our family's page. Although the funeral home had computerized its records, he said he still used the old book to record and map out the cemetery plots. "There's room," he said. "We can put her next to her parents." Then he gave me his cell number and said, "I want you to call me whenever this happens. I will come myself and take care of her."

I asked Bruno if he would make a casket for her. I knew he had made his father's, a simple box crafted of rough pine with rope handles. When he asked me what we wanted Jane's casket to look like, I told him to make a polished oak box with plain brass handles—just like the Stickley furniture that had been passed down through our family.

My relationship with Bruno had progressed in reverse proportion to my mother's fading. During our courtship, I would leave her side and leap into his truck. We would drive out through the countryside, lower the windows, and look at the moon. I had never felt such exhilaration; maybe the fact that it was leavened with my dawning grief made it such a happy sadness. When we decided to get married, a mere five months after our first kiss, we visited Jane, still living in her house, and held hands as Bruno asked her permission to marry me. She was taken aback by this old-fashioned gesture and looked at me. "Amy doesn't have to ask my permission for anything," she said.

"Ma, I love him something awful," I replied, giving her a line from *Moonstruck* to draft upon.

She laughed. The eyebrow shot up, and she continued our movie reference: "Well, that's too bad...but okay."

Bruno and I shared a life marked by emergencies, middle-of-the-night phone calls, pacing outside the ICU, and impromptu conferences in the car or the hospital parking lot. Aside from my sisters, my husband was the only person who understood my desperation to get my mother to stay.

I left Jane's bedside and drove several miles out of town to the carpentry shop where Bruno was making her casket. The wind had picked up; it was starting to howl. In my mind I always associate a certain type of winter howler with *Little House on the Prairie* and the fierce winter of 1880 described in the book *The Long Winter*. I scored this particular squall as a 3 out of 5 on the Laura Ingalls Wilder Scale and mentally asked myself my standard question: "Pa, do we have to rechink the logs in the cabin with rags tonight to try to keep the blizzard out?" (If the answer is no, and it always is, one does not complain out loud.) All the same, this was a coat-flapping, hat-losing, scarf-spinning subzero blast. It was 6:00 p.m. and already dark. Up the country road, I saw the carpentry shop with its lights on. Bruno's truck was parked near the front door. I sat in the car for a minute, trying to prepare.

Inside the shop it was warm, and the air smelled of sawdust. Bruno was working with Ben, a cabinetmaker who regularly made kitchen cabinets for the houses Bruno built. The two men stood back and let me circle the box, which was sitting on sawhorses. It was entirely plain: quarter sawn oak, dovetailed corners. A lid to be placed on top and fastened down with pegs. I felt honored by the labor of these two men, crafting a simple box for an old woman who was about to die. I told them she would love it. Weirdly, that seemed very important.

The day before Jane died, Aunts Jean and Millie spent most of the morning with her. I arrived in her room and saw Rachel at her side and our two dear aunts sitting, huddled together at the foot of her bed. For once, these sisters who had been engaged in a lifelong conversation were silent.

Mom perked up. "Do you hear that?"

"Um, no, Mom, hear what?"

"All night long, I heard a choir singing."

"Oh." Rachel and I looked at each other. "What were they singing?"

"Songs from the thirties."

"Like…Fred Waring and the Pennsylvanians?" I asked her, referencing the cheesy pop chorus from that era that we used to laugh about.

"Yes, sort of," she said. We told her that even though we couldn't hear it, we were happy that she could.

She asked us to look out her window to see if there was a glee club practicing in the snow. We looked outside, past the bare limbs of the giant maple tree. It was quiet.

"Is it the morphine?" I silently mouthed to Rachel.

She nodded in return. "Must be."

Rachel went home to check in with her kids after school. I called and asked her to come back. "Grab a book so I can read to Mom," I told her.

Periodically, especially through her times in the hospital, we read aloud to her. I enjoyed doing it. Our mother was a great reader and writer. She had the refined and literary taste of the intellectual she had become. During one long stint in the ICU, I read James Joyce's *Dubliners*. We finished with the peerless, melancholy story "The Dead," with its beautiful meditation on love and the passage of time. And, of course, the elegiac setting in snowy Dublin. I also read my entire memoir aloud to her, as I was writing it. ("Make it funnier," she always said.)

An hour later, Rachel came back waving *A Passage to India*. "I don't know what I was thinking—I just grabbed it off the shelf," she said. She sat down and handed the book to me, and I began to read.

I struggled with the pronunciation of the Indian setting and characters, which I was trying to express using what I thought was a vague Indian dialect (when I'd read *Dubliners*, an awkward Irish accent kept creeping in). Then I would try to switch to something Englishy for the British characters, but the characters, place names, and accents quickly got confused.

I was definitely making E. M. Forster funnier.

Jane's eyes were closed. Was she sleeping?

I bumbled along until I came to this description of the sky over the landscape of Chandrapore:

The sky too has its changes…Clouds map it up at times, but it is normally a dome of blending tints, and the main tint blue. By day the blue will pale down into white where it touches the white of the land, after sunset it has a new circumference—orange, melting upwards into tenderest purple. But the core of blue persists, and so it is by night. Then the stars hang like lamps from the immense vault.

"Oh, I love that," she whispered. "I know just what that looks like."

Our mother was an aficionado of skies, clouds, and the beautiful celestial blanket that draped over our farm at the edge of the village. She claimed to even love the (unlovable) gray, bleak, lowery skies of winter. I pictured her when she was healthier, out on her porch in springtime, looking at the sky and listening to the pulsing song of the peepers on the creek as she smoked her one cigarette.

This is the last thing I remember her saying.

Where do we go? If you don't believe in a heaven populated with angels, Jesus guiding flocks of children, overseen by a benevolent god sitting on a massive throne, what else do we have? My mother, although a lifelong Methodist, didn't seem to believe in these things. She kept her own counsel about her most private thoughts and beliefs. And yet, Jane seemed to be headed somewhere. She was passing on.

The next day, the day of her death, Rachel and I sat with her again. She took some sips of water. She ate one blueberry. It didn't feel like a vigil to me, but more like keeping her company. We'd done that my whole life: at the kitchen table with cups of coffee, taking drives out into the countryside, weeding her garden together.

Rachel left, and Jane and I were alone. She was asleep. I turned on the television. Turner Classic Movies had launched their "30 days of Oscar" programming. I kept the sound very low, sat in a chair next to her as she slept, and opened my laptop to work on my advice column. *Citizen Kane. The Philadelphia Story. Sullivan's Travels.* It felt like a minor miracle that these movies my mother had taught me to love were running through her room on a glorious loop. And if Charles Foster Kane and C. K. Dexter Haven and Veronica Lake accompanied my mother wherever she was headed, then all the better.

At six o'clock that evening, Bruno called me. He said he was sitting in his truck down in the parking lot with a cup of coffee for me. I left quietly and hurried down the stairs to see him. I ran out through the snow. I had just climbed into his truck when Dan, my mother's favorite aide, came to the door and waved me back in. "She's gone," he said. He had been hovering outside the room and ducked in as soon as I had left. He told me later that people often wait until a loved one has left the room to die.

We called Brad, the undertaker. I called my sisters. While we were waiting for Brad to arrive, Dan brought in a bottle of wine and we poured three glasses. Bruno, he, and I sipped it while we sat with my mother's body. I felt a strange sense of exhilaration. An almost giddy sort of happiness. Heroic measures had been taken. I thought that through the years of accelerated caretaking and leave-taking that we had granted our mother a good and gentle death. I thought that because I had been so present with her and had accepted the reality of it, I had somehow pre-grieved my mother's passing. But as it turned out, I was wrong about that.

Chapter Nineteen

The Fallacy of Closure

Immediately after my mother's death, my primary feeling was one of relief. I felt genuine relief that she had died so peacefully and that I had been with her. Our good-bye to her was, I thought, beautiful and dignified—there in the little Freeville church, underneath the gauzy Methodist portrait of Jesus and alongside the stained glass window bearing my family's name. In the crowded sanctuary, my cousin Roger officiated (as at my wedding, he traveled from his church to be with us) and we sang the old hymns my mother loved. The Gene Pool Choir, auxiliary chapter (made up of her grandchildren), sang. This was the place where my grandmother had once been the organist and where my sisters and I had learned to read music.

My beloved aunt Lena had died five years before, and we buried her from this same sanctuary. It seemed like only yesterday that the family had gathered to say good-bye to her. When I was eulogizing my mother, I concentrated on trying to describe her life before she had gotten so ill. At so many funerals, grieving family members tell the story surrounding their loved one's death. I wanted to remember Jane as a younger woman—how much fun she was, how remarkable and accomplished she was. I also described her need to wallpaper every room of the house, the way she knit tiny, scratchy black turtleneck sweaters for all the babies in the family, and her long and beautiful chestnut-brown hair.

After the eulogy, Aunt Millie rose slowly and said, quietly, of her sisters: "We used to be four, and then we were three, and now we are two."

After the service, my mother's pallbearers—her grandsons Jack and Sam, my old friend Kirk, and her three sons-in-law: Bruno, Tim, and Brian—carried her casket out of the church through the snow. It was February and bitter cold. The air itself seemed made of frost, and snowflakes were suspended in it. They seemed to be dancing but not falling. My sisters and I and our daughters and our elderly aunts and their daughters—a slow parade of women—followed the casket silently. The ladies of the church hosted a luncheon in the church hall, as they always did. As her body was taken away in the hearse, we ate casseroles and cold cuts. One after another, people spontaneously walked to a microphone and talked about my mother. Several read letters she had written to them. Kirk read a funny, wry letter she had sent to him twenty-five years before. It seemed that Jane was one of the coolest people any of us had ever met.

Over the three years before my mother's death, I had been sucked into what felt like an increasingly surreal lifestyle where my days were bookended by the presence of babies in our crowded household and the constant and changing needs of someone nearing the end of her life. After her death, I was relieved that I could finally stop commuting to her nursing home in Ithaca, creeping along the snowy roads, eating dinner with her at 5:00 p.m., and then worrying my way home in the winter dark to stop at the store and then eat dinner again with everyone else. Trying to be on my best behavior—to be a great mother, grandmother, and daughter—left me exhausted and on edge. My best behavior, it turned out, wasn't so great. Even my readers noticed it. I received more than one "Amy, what's your problem?" query, wondering why I was ill tempered in response to a letter. "I'm writing my column from the ICU," or "I was up half the night with an infant," I wanted to whimper.

But I didn't. I simply tried harder to be the wiser, nicer, less complicated version of myself—the version of me that smiled from the headshot that appeared over my newspaper column. Over time, I could hardly remember, let alone maintain, that version of myself.

During this period of intensive caregiving, my trips to Chicago were my only respite. Up until then, I had always hated to fly, but now I relished the experience of being taken away, gazing down on the landscape from 30,000 feet. I looked forward to spending time alone in my quiet Chicago apartment, even though the minute I arrived I started to worry about the situation at home. I would spend the day of a *Wait Wait* taping exhaustedly trying to arrive at anything—anything at all—that I thought I could be funny about. Before the show started, I would duck into the ladies' room, heave a quick sob or two, look into the mirror, and hate my haircut. Then I'd walk onstage, smiling and waving to the crowd.

Bruno was kind and supportive, but I barely noticed. His own mother's health was failing, too, and he raced back and forth to his mother's farm or the hospital, just as I did. He coped with stress by working harder and extending himself even further, and aside from occasional skirmishes with the kids or his siblings, I never saw him crack. But then again, he didn't do the vacuuming. He didn't do the Christmas shopping, or talk to his daughters about their outfits, or change his granddaughter's diapers, or read to his mother before tucking her in at night, the way I did with mine. Also, honestly, Bruno has bigger and broader shoulders than I do. His ability to carry the world upon them was simply greater than mine, and while I benefitted from it and appreciated his capacities, sometimes it also just . . . pissed me off. I wanted Bruno to be more flawed and frail, like me. I wanted him to be angry, or teary, or so distracted that he paid for the groceries and then drove off, leaving them sitting in the cart at the store, the way I kept doing. I thought that if Bruno had been more like me, then I wouldn't feel quite so alone.

Jane's death was of a kind that people claim is really a blessing. When people do that, I suppose they're trying to acknowledge that it was simply and inevitably time for that person to die. But for the grieving person, the alternative to death is not a static state of suffering, but life. Selfishly, I wanted my mother back. Her death didn't feel like a blessing; it felt like a shame. But still, it happened.

Initially, I was convinced that I had already grieved Jane's passing. I had seen pre-grieving before, with friends who buried their aged parents and seemed to move on. I assumed they had done their grief work ahead of time. One colleague whose father died flew home, buried his dad, put the family home on the market, and returned to work the following week. Back at the office, I expressed my condolences, and he replied, "Well, what are you going to do? It's not like it was a surprise. He was old." I don't assume that my colleague didn't grieve for his father, but he definitely seemed able to move on.

The good news for me, I believed, was that I had been so present with my mother. My sisters and I had done everything we could think to do. I had few regrets about my own choices concerning her. I'd always thought that regret, guilt, and shame fueled grief. Jane was old and then she died, and now she was gone, and it was over.

I had a dim memory of those early months of being with Bruno when we first fell in love—of me leaping over snowbanks to jump into his truck. Singing softly into his ear. Ice-skating and skiing and reveling in the antic joy I found in simply being alive on the planet and in his presence. I wanted to be that person again, and not the empty shell that I seemed to have become during the final year of my mother's life.

Unfortunately, the lifting sense of relief that I felt just after her death turned out to be temporary. For weeks after her funeral, I kept driving back to the nursing home. It was like my car knew the route, and every day in the late afternoon it simply took me there. Sometimes I would sit alone in the driveway. Some days I would go in and have a cup of coffee with the staff. There in the presence of old people at twilight, I felt at home.

At night I would lie awake and think about Jane's body and the home-spun flour-sack quilt I had brought to the funeral home to wrap her in. I worried about the beautiful coffin Bruno had made. The funeral home had stored her body in its coffin in a vault at the cemetery until the ground thawed for burial in the spring. Awake at night, I thought of her there, in some weird limbo storage state before her final rest. Irrationally, I wondered if the quilt she was wrapped in would keep her warm enough.

I stopped attending services at the Freeville United Methodist Church because I felt overwhelmed by memories of my mother's funeral and of her pallbearers carrying her casket through the snow. I stopped singing altogether, but I also couldn't bear to even listen to music—especially music I associated with her. Jane went through phases of compulsive listening to artists such as the Beatles, Aretha Franklin, and Stevie Wonder, and even spent several months during my teen years playing Jethro Tull's *Aqualung* over and over on her stereo. Because her taste was extremely broad, the music I now couldn't bear to hear included just about everything from Brahms to Beyoncé. I couldn't drive past her house on Mill Street, now dark, depressing, and padlocked tight. Because of the financial support I had provided during the last years of her life, my siblings generously turned our mutual inheritance of her house and property over to me. I had inherited the house, but I didn't want it. Nor could I face the idea of parting with it.

During one blizzard-blown night, I stood, paralyzed and weeping in the middle of the bedroom Bruno and I shared. My mother's funeral had been the month before.

The windows in our old house rattled with the force of the wind. Bruno, a mighty oak who nevertheless also seemed able to bend with the blizzards, tenderly asked me what was wrong.

I looked at him. "What's wrong? It's like the universe said to the advice columnist, 'Advice *this*, bitch,'" I replied bitterly.

I told millions of people each day how to respond to the challenges in their own lives. And yet, I was out of answers. I had no words left. I had outrun my own ability to fake it. My husband embraced me. I was like a bundle of twigs. "Please, Amy, be gentle with yourself," he said.

That sounds awesome. But I don't know how to do that. I don't even know what that means.

I withdrew from friends. I only wanted to talk to my friend Gay, whose mother was dead; my friend Nancy, whose mother was dead; my friend Jean, whose mother was dead; or my friend Kirk, whose mother was also dead.

Stopping for food at Clark's, I fell into my high school friend Kim's arms because her mother, too, was dead. I did not want to talk to Bruno about my grief. His mother was still alive. My sisters each withdrew into their own orbits. They didn't seem to want to talk about it either.

One night, I called my aunt Millie. I think of Millie as the family's philosopher. Her thoughts are not fixed in any particular direction, but she sees things from multiple perspectives, sometimes all at once. I was standing outside Pemberley, delaying my entrance into our usual dinnertime circus.

I asked my aunt, "Where do you think we go when we die?"

She said, "I'm not sure, Amy, but I know that the universe is made of matter, and we are made of matter. When I look up at the stars, I think we somehow end up there among them, as dust—or whatever." I panned my gaze up to the spectacular star-struck sky. Oh. Yes.

In my family (on my father's side), depression is our special malady. Our clan boasts ties to both Meriwether Lewis and Emily Dickinson, and while I'm not saying that either the great explorer who killed himself or the wonderful poet who stayed in her room was depressed, the amateur diagnostician in me says it's a distinct possibility. Regardless of the fates of our more notable ancestors, depression seems to snake down through the Dickinson family tree like a DNA strand, skipping over this person but landing on that. There's the ancestor who took his life, the one who spent decades drinking in his room, and the one who as a child simply stopped speaking. Or my father, who drank in roadside taverns, cheated on his wives, and then abandoned his various families. (Was he depressed or just a jerk? I'm not sure.) Add to that a cultural and familial reluctance to disclose negative feelings, coupled with an expectation that we all have a responsibility to take care of ourselves, and we were each left to cope privately with what ailed us.

In my family, talking about your health smacks of "complaining." My mother declared all of her health problems to be too boring to discuss. My aunt Jean has coped with heart disease, requiring two balloon angioplasties. Well into her eighties, she drove herself to and from the hospital, watched the surgeon perform the procedure on a monitor, and described it as "no big deal." My mother also drove herself to the local clinic after having a heart attack. After she was airlifted from the clinic to a hospital for surgery, she said that aside from the inability to catch her breath or use her left hand to steer the car during the ten-mile trip, she was fine. Plus, she didn't want to bother anyone.

Considering such stoicism, concern about one's feelings seems neurotic. And admitting to having serious problems is risky because your emotions will be argued over and either validated lovingly, dismissed entirely, or joked about until your feelings flee the scene.

Since about the age of twenty, much of my conscious life has been devoted to trying to answer the two essential questions of anyone's life: "Who am I?" and "What do I want?" Whenever the consequential flow of my life seems challenged—or interrupted by change, hardship, triumph, or storms within or without—I return to these questions and struggle to answer them. Although the questions stay the same, the answers are elusive and ever-changing.

Several months after my mother's death, I asked the therapist I see about six times a year in Chicago why I still felt so sad. As usual, I was looking for a complicated answer—one I felt might match the magnitude of my emptiness. She briefly reviewed my particular challenges in childhood: poverty, instability, abandonment. She explained that coping with these challenges might have made others harder to bear. "And...your mother died and you miss her. You are grieving." Oh. Yes.

The answer to "Who am I?" was now "sad person." "What do I want?" Less of that, please. I asked my therapist if she thought I was depressed, and she answered, "Well, why wouldn't you be?" I wondered if I should take medication, and she said that was an option and we could talk about it. She suggested that for now I try breathing and meditation exercises, and she walked me through them. I've never taken medication for any reason (except for self-medicating, of course, with food, occasional cigarettes, and wine). I decided to wait to have that conversation, but I did stop at the donut shop on the ground floor of her building after I left.

Given this wise validation, I stopped trying so hard to suppress my sadness and paper over my depression. Instead I decided to admit it, name it, and see if I could learn to live within it. It turns out that grief isn't something that can be hurried. You can't move through it faster than it moves through you.

I learned to stop trying to feel better. I think this is the gentleness that my husband was trying to urge me toward. I finally allowed myself to give in to my own grief, cloaking myself in it and walking around with it, while still finding ways to be in the world, do my job, and relate to people. The world is full of people in trouble. I have only to dive into my "Ask Amy" mailbox to realize that. I had always thought that one of my strengths was that I never judged people's problems—with their tricky wedding dynamics, uncooperative kids, or rude in-laws—as being somehow less consequential than my own. But now I found myself struggling to stay open to the reality of the human condition, even in its pettiness. Our troubles might be different, but we all wanted to feel better.

During this period, I realized that, for me, the whole "closure" concept was useless. I don't know who started the closure movement, but many people mentioned to me that the funeral, the eventual burial, the setting of the grave marker, the six-month anniversary, the year anniversary were turning points that would bring acceptance and closure. However, the ticket for a grieving person isn't to try to close the book on something, but to find ways to cope with the way you feel about it.

Things I've tried in order to feel better include, but are not limited to, donuts, yoga, ukulele, walking, meditation, prayer, therapy, drinking, denial, talking, solitude, knitting, poetry, spiritualism, singing, romance, jogging, journaling, Netflix, and church.

Every single thing I've tried has worked, although sometimes only briefly. But in order for me to coexist with my own grief, I had to strip it down to the simple fact that I loved my mother, and now she was gone and I missed her. It was what it was. I didn't know where she went, but I missed having her in this world.

Over time, I learned to manage my sadness by simply accepting it as being an unavoidable aspect of who I was in that moment. I stopped comparing my sadness to that of other people. I found myself more able to face hard things that I had avoided—not by stuffing things down or sucking it up and getting on with it but by knowing and accepting that these things would be hard. I learned to ask myself, "Can I do this today?"

I set up a secret bargain and reward system. If I could face a hard thing, I would reward myself with an easier thing.

I started with my mother's house, now forlorn, dark, and empty of her. One day two months after she died, I steadied myself, unlocked the padlock, and entered it. The house was freezing and musty. Right after Jane's death, Rachel, Anne, and I divided up her paintings and furniture and they took the things they wanted to their homes. I had invited them several times to meet me at the house to clean it out, but they declined. The house now belonged to me; they reminded me that it was my privilege and responsibility to do with it whatever I wanted.

The place looked like a family of bears had ransacked the set of *Antiques Roadshow*. Leftover furniture was randomly strewn around. Jane's bed was still downstairs in front of the fireplace, made up and expectant, but random medical supplies were tossed on the quilt. The piping system Bruno had installed for my mother's handgrips crawled along the wall and down the side of her bed. Her wheelchair and a walker were in the bathroom, as were a toothbrush, a heel of soap, a used washcloth, and her collection of threadbare differently colored towels that always drove me crazy (I was always giving my mother new towels, and they were always unused, stacked neatly, and presumably waiting for special occasions).

My sisters and I had not gone through any bureaus, desks, cupboards, closets, or the pantry. The refrigerator contained a half quart of milk turned to cheese. We had not touched any of her clothes, books, photos, letters, or personal items. We hadn't taken anything at all from the upstairs of the house. No one had set foot on the narrow staircase leading upstairs for three years.

That first day, all I could do was walk through the downstairs. I felt my breath quickening, and then I exited. I sat in my car and tried to breathe deeply, remembering the lesson from my meditation class. My reward that day was the satisfaction of knowing that I had done something I didn't believe I was able to do. I also stopped at Dunkin' Donuts on the way home.

I started visiting the house in the afternoons. I cleaned out the coffeepot and took one of my mother's old Woolworth's mugs off the shelf. I dragged a wicker porch chair into the otherwise empty kitchen, turned on her gas-fired potbellied stove, and sat, drinking coffee and looking out her window, pondering the same gentle view of the barn and the field beyond that we used to look at together from her kitchen table. I did nothing else.

Spring came. In my mother's back garden, the hellebore pushed up through the crusty snow. The ancient gnarled lilac bloomed purple. The days lengthened and the trillium pushed out their delicate triangular blossoms. The peony bushes, the iris, the clematis, and then the beach rose. Surely spring would bring its symbolic awakening. It did not. I only opened the back door to the kitchen in order to let the breeze into the musty house.

Sitting alone in my mother's old kitchen, two phrases came back to me, over and over.

One was from my reading on Buddhism: *All things must pass.*

And one is from the movie *Tootsie*: *I'm going to feel this way until I don't feel this way anymore.*

Chapter Twenty

The Rising Tide of Things

Like just about everyone I know, I am almost constantly concerned with what to do with all the stuff that litters my life. This is the perennial preoccupation of baby boomers like me, who have spent half of our lives accumulating things, only to spend the last half of our lives trying to rid ourselves of our things.

Assuming that I spent my adulthood up to the age of forty acquiring possessions, my basic assessment is that I have had, generously speaking, about fifteen years to play with my stuff. This means that I have enjoyed more seasons with *The Simpsons* than I have with my possessions. Most people my age seem fated to spend our empty nest years literally emptying our nests, as we sort, toss, and sell, in an ongoing project that will last more or less until we either winnow our possessions down to nothing or finally go mad from mothball fumes and mouse droppings.

Recently I had a random encounter in a supermarket parking lot with a woman I had gone to high school with. I hadn't seen Pam in almost thirty years but I recognized her immediately and we stood outside in the fluorescent glow of the store, catching up. Like me, Pam had recently been through the loss of a parent, and like me, she was dealing with an extra household of stuff. She motioned to her small pickup truck, which was overflowing with boxes and chairs and black garbage bags. "There it is," she said mournfully. "All of my father's things."

Jane wasn't a collector or a hoarder of twist ties or plastic yogurt containers or newspapers, like some people her age. But she was the keeper of over 200 years of family possessions—books, paintings, quilts, letters, documents, and photos—and she did seem to have a strange fondness for chairs. Her small house contained dozens of chairs: spindly chairs, which had been carried on covered wagons; sturdy Stickley chairs, which had been passed along from my grandparents' generation; and chairs she had purchased simply because she thought they were cute.

Jane had wonderful taste, and she loved her things. Until almost the end of her life, she rearranged her rooms in a way that was often surprising. The dining room became the living room, the little bedroom was transformed into an office, and then she changed them back again. When I was a teenager, I went out on a date with a guy who picked me up at our farm. My mother was wallpapering the living room in a deep red. One week later, he returned, and she was wallpapering the room in a light green. "Wait…last week, wasn't this…?" he asked.

"Don't even go there," I told him.

This place was the home Jane lived in for thirty years and loved until the end of her life. This was the place inherited from her neighbor John, which was fated to her from childhood. And now it was in my hands.

After Jane's death, I spent many months visiting her house each day, sitting among the heirloom flotsam and spindly chairs and missing her. Without her there, the house, which I had always loved, was just a big box with a lot of stuff in it. Every day I would tell myself, "Today, I will just fill one bag." But I was so overwhelmed by the prospect of any task that I did nothing but sit.

I finally told Bruno I was spending time in the house in a state of acute sadness and paralysis. His let's-get-this-thing-done quality is great in a contractor, but it's not so great for someone like me, whose forward motion can sometimes only be measured in baby steps. Bruno has a way of behaving that he sees as urgently encouraging but that can feel pushy. I've never felt ready for anything, and I hate to be pushed. Stand me on the high diving board and dare me to jump, and I will hold my nose and gently bump up and down and pace back and forth and go halfway down the ladder and then come back up. I'll play to the crowd and take a poll and call my lifeline. I will eventually jump, but it will be ugly, disordered, and painful to watch. But if you push me, I'll push back, and you'll be the one taking the dive.

I derived some comfort from my afternoon coffee time in my mother's house, but like the house itself, I was inert. Houses, like people, start to die if they're neglected, and I didn't want my mother's beautiful old farmhouse to end up dilapidated like so many others in the area, with their great bones and mossy, sagging roofs.

One day, eight months after Jane's death, Bruno met me at her house. I had finally confessed to him that I didn't know what to do with it. It was un-insulated, with ancient wiring from the 1920s, and the roof looked bad. "If you tell me to sell it, I'll sell it," I told him—and I meant it. My mother was attached to the house, and I was attached to her, but the more time I spent in her house without her in it, the more I realized that it was just a house. I would rather sell it to someone who would love it as she had than continue to sit in her cold kitchen, paralyzed and weeping.

Bruno walked through the place, poking the woodwork and walls with his mechanical pencil, trying to find the furnace (it was in the cellar) and the entrance to the cellar (through a trapdoor cut into the kitchen floor). I trusted his judgment and was completely resigned to his answer. Unloading the house would be one less thing for me to manage, even though the concept of "managing" was a reach, because truthfully I wasn't able to manage anything at all.

Bruno rendered his verdict: "This house is a gem, and you're a gem. I would like to fix it for you."

Immediately I started looking at the old place differently. Suddenly it seemed to have potential. Bruno decided not to do anything too structurally dramatic: to only renovate the downstairs and to leave the exterior of the house exactly as it was.

With a plan for renovation, I started the process of going through my mother's possessions. This was a horrible, weepy task, made much worse by my effort to do it alone.

I was just pushing things around, not organizing and not getting rid of anything but moving things from place to place. I would get up a good head of steam until the sight of a pair of my mother's shoes would be so over-whelming I would have to sit down and catch my breath.

My dear Emily finally took pity on me. She was living in my house on Main Street, working at the mall while she looked for a job, which would take her back to Chicago. Over a period of several weeks, we met at Jane's house and played music or a movie as we attacked separate rooms with our garbage bags. Then we would drive our gatherings to the Salvation Army or to the church for donation. Doing this with someone else made all the difference.

Freeville has a sort of sharing economy where possessions seem to float among households. I have had the strange sensation after donating cloth-ing to our church's biannual giveaway of looking out my window and see-ing a neighbor wearing one of my coats. Recently, when our neighbor Dick Blackmon died, I was reminded that I possessed two folding army cots that Dick told me had been his and his wife Edie's beds right after they got mar-ried. When I contemplate those canvas cots, I envision not only the times Emily and I took summertime naps on them in our backyard, but also their grander history as the starter marital bed for a couple who were together for almost seventy years.

Emily and I managed to create some order by toting the broken-down chairs and box upon box of random things up the dark and steep staircase into the second floor of the house. These boxes, jammed with small heir-looms of lace collars and chipped teapots, ancient postcards, shell-encrusted saucers, and marbles rolling loose at the bottom, were set aside and stacked in uneven groupings while we tried to determine which were tchotchkes and which were treasures. We labeled these boxes "Trouble Boxes," because, much like a junk drawer, the contents seemed to expand in volume and com-plexity once the lid was closed. Opening a Trouble Box would lead to hours of aimless sifting as I touched, pondered, and worried over each little object, until I finally gave up, replaced the lid, and left it for later.

Emptying out a large hutch, Emily discovered a stuffed manila envelope labeled "Amy." She called out to me, "Mom, you need to see this." I was in the kitchen, jamming tea towels into a bag. When I walked into the living room, my daughter was holding a thick foot-long ponytail of chestnut-brown human hair. The ponytail dangled in the sunlight. *Gross,* I thought, until I realized it was my hair. Then I thought, *Oh, cool.* In the envelope was a note, which I had typed on *New Yorker* stationery in 1983 (at the time I was the receptionist for the magazine):

Dear Mom,

I finally cut my hair! No more ponytail. My long hair is now in a chin-length bob. The haircutter wanted me to donate it so someone could make a wig out of it, but I wanted to send it to you. If you ever want to make a wig out of it, let me know. I'll sell it to you for a good price.

Love,
Amy

Emily also found a copy of the following letter, written by my mother, typed out on her trusty Selectric and sent to me after she had visited me in Washington, DC, a year after my graduation from college. It alludes to an incident between us that is now long forgotten:

March 1982

Dear Amy,

I just got your letter and thank you. We had a misunderstanding and that's not a bad thing to happen occasionally since that's the way, or one way, we learn about other people and ourselves. We have so few it seems more important than it is.

Since coming home from Washington the tail pipe has fallen off my car, it only starts when it feels like it, and the turn signals have stopped working except for odd times when I don't need them. Various people have said to me, "You drove to Washington in THAT?" Well yes, I did. And back as well.

Last night I couldn't sleep all night and got up at 3 a.m. to take a hot bath and watch "Daisy Kenyon" with Joan Crawford, which lasted until 5. Easter didn't really dawn here. At 5:30 a.m. the power went out due to 30 mph winds and they couldn't hold the sunrise service and breakfast at church because with both the sun AND the power out, what are you gonna do? You can't roller skate in a buffalo herd.

Yesterday [a neighbor] asked me to, yes, his latest wedding next Friday night, which will be at his house, where he will be married by Jack Miller, Justice of the Peace. I can actually kill two birds with one stone because I owe Jack $25 for a speeding ticket which I haven't paid so I can pay him off right after the wedding.

I have just purchased Mahler's Fifth Symphony, which is on the record player right now. I just love it. It was the background music for "Death in Venice," which I just saw. It was perfect in the movie because there was practically no dialogue and the music was just outstanding for that story. Besides, supposedly, the incident behind the book was written by Thomas Mann about Mahler's infatuation with a young boy on a train. Aren't artists mean. I have read the Mann lectures you gave me. That's a nice little book I will always enjoy having. It sits right next to my Selectric.

I must go because I feel like I'm going to fall over since I didn't get any sleep whatsoever last night. Until next time…

Love,
Mummie

Emily also found an old, yellowed newspaper clipping from 1973. It was a picture of Bruno, from when he was a football star at Dryden High School.

My mother had clipped and saved it in 1973 and at some point had put it into the Amy envelope. Jane wasn't one of those people who are always clipping things out of newspapers and magazines. In fact, going through her house, this clipping was one of only a very few that Emily and I found. Why did my mother take scissors to our newspaper in 1973 and clip out a picture of the man I would marry thirty-five years later? I have no idea. But the clipping seemed a portent, a message sent through time, to tell me that my past and present fates were somehow braiding together.

Chapter Twenty-One

Does It Spark Joy?

There is a book that promises a pathway for people to tunnel their way out when they are buried beneath their stuff. It is called *the life-changing magic of tidying up*, by Japanese tidying expert Marie Kondo (the title of the book, which is all in lowercase, suggests that uppercase letters themselves are quite untidy).

Flummoxed and feeling overwhelmed by the tide of acquired possessions in which I was drowning, I purchased the book, like millions of other people, and dove into its tidying secrets. The author describes her lonely childhood, when she, at the age of five, first started her campaign to make the world tidier. As I read this biographical account of her life and the evolution of her extreme tidying technique, it occurred to me that what Marie Kondo was really describing was her own lifelong struggle with obsessive-compulsive disorder. She describes skipping recess at school, where, instead of playing outside with her peers, she spent her time rearranging the books in her classroom. Garbage bags were her best and constant companions as she tamped down her anxiety by filling them in her quest for tidy perfection. After she had perfected her own space ("perfection" is an important concept for her), she moved on to her friends' rooms and the storage lockers at school. Marie Kondo strikes me as a very strange person. I do not want to be like her. I also do not want to be like the ruthless and tidy monsters who follow her technique and roll their socks and stack their clothes sideways in drawers and who throw so much away.

The one useful takeaway for me from this book was the question the author suggests everyone ask themselves when looking to release the grip of possessions: "Does it spark joy?" Going through my mother's things, I was able to apply this question, but I was surprised at how often an item sparked not joy but extreme sadness. Finding Jane's briefcase, placed in a drawer beneath her typewriter, made me light-headed with grief. Both items were tangible reminders of how hard my mother had worked and how important working was to her. Jane typed her way into college and a career as a professor. During my visits over the years, whenever I saw her leather briefcase full of student papers, I felt tremendous pride in what she had done. I decided to keep both things, but I also promised myself that I would somehow box and bag my sadness and that each day I would take at least one box or bag for donation (unlike Marie Kondo, who seems to pitch a lot away, I'm not big on sending things to the landfill).

My old friend Kirk traveled from Maine to help me sell some of my mother's collection of bureaus, chairs, plant stands, bone-china cups and saucers, pails, baskets, picture frames, and assorted tinware. Kirk and Jane were close friends; the three of us shared a taste and sensibility about things, and we also loved and cherished stuff. He and I often laughed over Jane's aphorism, *My stuff never lets me down.* (People, she implied, often did.) Kirk helped me to sort, tag, and price items for a yard sale. We had some business at our sale during the day and then left unsold furniture by the side of the road.

In Freeville, you can set something by the side of the road in the morning, and it will be gone by the afternoon. I had furnished much of my Main Street house with (almost) perfectly good used furniture I'd found roadside. I liked the idea that my things were landing in others' homes. But there was one category of my and my mother's possessions that stumped me: spindly chairs that were broken and couldn't be repaired and other pieces of furniture that I simply didn't like but couldn't seem to part with. This included a small pine chest with a broken bottom drawer that my former husband and

I bought at an antique store in 1985. I had taken this pine chest from house to house as I had moved to London and back, and then around the country with my many moves. The chest had started to develop a burdensome emotional stink. I felt it was too old and fine to give away, leave by the side of the road, or take to the dump. Emily wasn't interested in having it. I didn't want to spend money repairing it, and I didn't want to see it anymore. I wanted to lose it, along with all of my painful associations of early married life with my ex-husband, which the chest seemed to unleash. It most definitely did not spark joy.

My confusion over what to do with the pine chest led to a decision that some people might find distasteful but that worked for me. This is how I dealt with the never-ending suck of continuously rearranging the broken deck chairs on my emotional *Titanic*:

I decided to burn some shit in the yard.

I live in a place where many people heat their homes with wood, so outdoor burning is an acceptable practice. I looked up the local statute and learned that in Freeville, burning is permitted but must be confined to a fire pit. Coincidentally, our daughter Clare had given me a small portable metal fire pit for Christmas. I decided that I would start the New Year with a personal burn.

New Year's Day was cold and snowy. Perfect. I wanted my burn to be at a time when my neighbors' windows would be closed so the smoke didn't bother anyone. I started the fire with a tiny bit of newspaper (featuring my advice column—I liked that symbolism) and a twig-style plant stand that had started life as a tripod but was now a bipod.

I watched the plant stand go up in smoke until it was no more. Knowing that it wouldn't languish in the dump or outside a hoarder's trailer made me feel good. I moved on to my mother's collection of broken chairs. One by one, I fed them into the flames and stood in the snow, enjoying both the heat from the flame and the feeling of lightness that accompanied it. Soon enough I started to feel a Marie Kondo–like need to rid myself of other things.

Throughout the winter, I conducted burns—of broken bookshelves and two-legged stools, sprung baskets, the stripped frames of once-wicker tables, and a heavy twig-style porch chair that I had given to my mother but was so uncomfortable to sit on it actually inspired contempt. Yes—I burned the small pine chest. I burned extra copies of the programs from my mother's funeral, along with the cardboard box they came in. I burned duplicate photographs of arty still lifes that I had taken in college and copies of *Farm Life* magazine from the 1950s.

When I was done, I spread the ashes on the winter-dormant bed of my mother's back garden. I was free. I was tempted to also burn Marie Kondo's book, but even I cannot burn a book. Instead, I donated it to the library's book sale. I imagine the book changing hands and continuing to inspire or disgust people until it, too, lands in a garbage bag and is finally discarded forever by someone for whom it does not spark joy.

Inspired now by my ability to sort, toss, and burn, I started emptying my house on Main Street, readying it to turn over to my cousins Jan and Roger. Roger's cancer had forced his retirement from the ministry at his large church near Rochester. Moving to Freeville, with Jan living next door to her mother, Millie, would enable the family to pull close.

Leaving the sweet house where Emily and I had lived and renting it to another family member let me detach from it with more joy than sadness. If you are someone, like me, who gets deeply attached to people and to things, letting go is a heartrending process. I remembered my ex-husband, Andy, who left me so suddenly, telling me that it was best to rip off the bandage quickly. This was best for him, no doubt, but for me, detaching is a serious and sad business. I don't know if I'll ever master it.

Bruno took almost a year to renovate my mother's house on Mill Street. The job progressed in fits and starts as he pulled workers off of the project to work on other (higher profit margin) jobs. The delays gave me time to adjust to the house's transformation. I had managed to completely empty the bottom floor of the house, but now the two small bedrooms on the second floor were crowded with bins, boxes, and hundreds of books stacked in teetering towers.

Bruno redesigned the small kitchen in back of the house and installed a window over the sink, which faced the barn and the old outhouse. He raised the very low ceiling in one room, exposing the original rough beams. He insulated the plank house and installed new wiring and a new furnace, as well as new windows in half of the house (I decided to keep the old windows, wavy and painted shut, along the front). He put in a new tub and sink and installed a window in the once-dark bathroom. In the evenings, after work was done, I walked to the house from my place on Main Street, and Bruno and I met to go over his progress. The floors—ancient chestnut in one room, wide-planked pine in all the others—gleamed with polish. The windows were newly trimmed in a stately style. Bruno had described the house as a gem, and when he was finished, it did look gemlike, unique and lovely.

I once described for Bruno Virginia Woolf's essay "A Room of One's Own," which so perfectly describes the artist's need for independence, space, and privacy. It also expresses my desire to have a place that is all my own and that others need to knock upon the door to enter. My husband grew up in the most crowded household imaginable; he is happiest when all of our daughters and granddaughters are with us and we have to put an extra leaf into our oak dining table. Given his need to be surrounded by people, it was an act of extreme generosity to make a house for me that is so inviting, and very much my own. As I set up my office and placed my mother's old wicker chair in its rightful spot in the kitchen, I assured Bruno that I loved the home he and I shared—and now if I ever went missing, he would know the first place to look.

Chapter Twenty-Two

Imperfect Pitch

In the eight years since moving back home to Freeville, Bruno and I have grieved the deaths of eight close family members. Some of these losses have been long and lingering, some heartbreakingly sudden and tragic. We have experienced four of these deaths in February, which, although the shortest month, seems to be the longest and heaviest for us.

The state of grieving implies loss—the loss of any future with a loved one, but also a myriad of other losses. Grieving unmoored me and made me lose my place in the world. If I was no longer Jane's daughter, Lena and Harvey's niece, Roger's cousin, or Auntie Amy to my niece and nephew who had also passed away, I wasn't sure who I was. I missed my mother dreadfully. She was the person who might have made these other losses easier to bear.

I have read about how grief is different for everyone, and I've reminded readers of this when fielding questions about grief and loss for my advice column. I have advised readers to give themselves time, and, echoing my husband's advice to me, I have urged grieving readers to be gentle toward themselves and to others. But while dispensing my own compassionate advice to readers, I have often at the same time felt quite hollow and discon-nected. I have been surprised at how long it has taken me to recover. My therapist's counsel was to simply allow myself to feel, instead of trying to power through and somehow force my sadness to go away. This simple advice and permission was profound for someone like me. My normal practice was to qualify every tough moment by being ashamed for my self-absorption, while reflexively reminding myself of how lucky I am. I am free. I'm not a refugee fleeing from war or hunger. I'm healthy. I have a loving family and good friends. But these qualifications seemed like hollow platitudes, so I gave up trying to pretend to be perfectly well adjusted or to convince myself that I was lucky. And what I realized, very gradually, was that even when I tried to force sadness away, it still perched on my shoulder. When I tried too hard to move on, I became paralyzed. Every time I denied myself the gentleness or compassion I needed, I turned in anger toward someone else. And so I let the gray veil drop, hoping that a breeze would come and catch it, lift it, make it billow and fly away. I waited.

For me, time *has* helped to close the wounds opened by loss. The turning of the seasons in our harsh and beautiful countryside reminds me of the temporal nature of life and of how the natural world dies and renews and eventually replaces itself. Some mornings, I take my coffee to Willow Glen Cemetery. While there, I do not talk to my lost loved ones; there is no cinematic outpouring or lamentation over the graves of my dearly departed. I just sit there sipping my coffee, staring out at the view, and imagining them in the ground. I think of these lines from the Book of Ruth: "Do not urge me to leave you or turn back from following you, for where you go, I must go. Where you lodge, I will lodge. Your people will be my people, and your God, my God. Where you die, I will die, and there I will be buried."

My mother told me that she wanted these words on her tombstone: *Life is a memory*. But there was no room for this inscription on the grave marker I chose to sit atop her grave. When I met with Brad, the undertaker, to choose her marker, he suggested a flat stone matching those for her parents, grandparents, and other ancestors laid to rest around our family's large memorial stone. All of these bear only a first name, carved in simple block letters. I agreed with his choice but had my mother's stone chiseled, not in block letters, but in a Courier typeface. This was a nod to her years when she had supported her family as a typist and an inside reference to the font on the daisy wheel of her treasured blue IBM Selectric.

Several months later, when the stone marker was placed on her grave, the cemetery workers put it facing in the wrong direction. Where all of the other family markers were facing in toward the memorial, Jane's was facing outward. It was distinctly and most definitely upside down, and when I first saw it, I laughed. My mother always went her own way.

The strangest and most unexpected ancillary loss I experienced in grief was the turning away from music. Immediately after Jane's funeral, I found myself unable to listen to or make music. Muzak playing on a sound system at a store was tolerable. I could also listen impassively to the radio, if somebody else had turned it on (I never did). What I couldn't seem to tolerate was live music. When that occurred, I simply had to leave.

It wasn't until I felt its absence so keenly that I realized that music—both listening to it and experiencing the pleasure of making it—had been an emotional gyroscope throughout my entire life. Those times when I was most lonely and searching, such as after my father's departure and during my most homesick days in adulthood, I compensated by singing my way through it. At Georgetown, I sang with three choirs simultaneously. After college, I worked as a lounge singer in a small, run-down hotel bar on M Street, singing Gershwin and Rodgers and Hart standards for $50 a night. The pianist and I split the modest tips left in the brandy snifter on the piano. I remember standing at a pay phone on the street and calling my mother after one gig. I thanked her for stacking the playlist of my childhood sound track with show tunes and standards, because now I was making a living from them.

To be bereft is to experience a lack, an absence and a mournful emptiness. I assume that my strong association with my mother's love of music tipped some unknown internal organ stop to "mute" once she was gone. I couldn't attend a concert or go to church, and if I had to attend one of our unfortunately regular funeral services, I sat quietly and simply let the tears stream down my face.

Bruno's mother died in the summertime, about eighteen months after my own mother's death. Marnie was ninety-three and, after her own series of injuries and health emergencies, she had spent most of the summer fading away. That last day, Marnie was lying in her bed at Maryhill Farm, with many of her twelve surviving children gathered at her bedside. Bruno wanted me in the room with his mother and brothers and sisters, but I tried to stand near the back, closer to the door. As my mother-in-law's breathing became more labored, several in the room asked for a song. The only musical members of Bruno's family seemed to be on the road, as they were making their way to her bedside, and suddenly I felt the group turn expectantly toward me.

My mind...was a blank. I tried to flip through my mental Rolodex of remembered hymns and sacred songs to sing for this very religious and devout person. I had nothing. Nothing at all. Marnie had been important to me, and her children were *very* important to me. I tried to coax that dormant performance gene into life in order to lead the group. Suddenly, I was relieved to feel a song start to bubble up from within. But the song that surfaced on that strange day was the title song from *Oklahoma!* I pushed "Oklahoma!" down, but it wouldn't stay there.

I remained mute and sweating. While someone else started an off-key version of "Amazing Grace" and the group joined in, I slipped out of the room.

It wasn't until three years after my mother's death that I was finally able to attend a local concert of live music. The towns around Freeville host summertime community choruses and bands. It's a no-audition situation right out of *The Music Man*, where people rifle deep in their coat closets for the clarinet they played in high school, show up for one evening a week of rehearsal, and then squeeze out a few songs in a concert six weeks later. Emily and I had both performed with the community chorus when she was young, when my sister Rachel directed it for a few summers.

Bruno and I sat together in the high school auditorium for that summer's concert, holding hands while our neighbors sang "Buffalo Gals" and played "The Washington Post March." I was expecting the now-familiar "flight" sensation, where my heart raced and my breath quickened, and I wanted to jump out of my skin. But this time I didn't want to flee. I wanted to stay.

And I wanted to feel it. I promised myself that I would try harder to bring music back into my life, in order to feel the way I used to feel, back when I felt like myself.

Last summer, I persuaded myself to join the chorus. Rehearsals were held in the heat-conducting linoleum-clad basement of the Methodist church in nearby Dryden. The air was thick with summer heat and the unmistakable scent left by the honey wagons, spreading manure on nearby fields. There were almost eighty of us: farmers and retired people, office workers from Cornell, and schoolteachers. The age range was eight to ninety. I sat next to Mrs. Streeter, who'd taught typing in my high school fifty years ago. "We altos have to stick together, Amy," she said, patting the seat. *Damn straight, Mrs. Streeter.*

The chorus was led by Jen, a local middle school music teacher. Jen had chosen a perfect program, with a balance of challenging new music and old-timey crowd-pleasers. She got us warmed up and blasted us through rehearsals quickly and expertly. She taught a little bit of theory and vocal technique. I hadn't sung a note in three years, but I could feel the old tumblers moving and shifting. Out in the parking lot after rehearsals, standing and talking about the program with my neighbors, I felt the old antic joy rising.

Over the course of the summer, I let myself fall in love with music again, but now I noticed a change. After a lifetime of being entranced by the sound of my own voice, I was now focused on how it felt to blend my voice along with others'. I was no longer the best singer in the choir—not by a long shot. Those slots were taken by younger and more practiced singers. But I no longer needed to be heard. I dropped the snobbish need for excellence I had assumed over the years. What felt good to me was the experience itself: coming together with other people, all of us showing up at a church basement, bravely baring our musical inadequacies and rusty pipes. My happiness was enhanced by standing next to Mrs. Streeter, the robust ninety-year-old alto.

One evening at rehearsal, I asked our director why music makes us feel the way we do, why it seems to rearrange our cells. She explained the physics of cymatic vibrations. Membranes vibrate and matter assumes new shapes when sound waves hit. I didn't only *feel* like my cells were rearranging themselves when I was making or listening to music—it was actually happening. That's why music was so healing and life-changing, and why its absence was such a genuine loss, compounding all my other losses.

Our concert was held on a stifling August night at the high school auditorium—the same place where forty years before, I had been a lead in *Oklahoma!* and *Bye Bye Birdie.* During our program, we sang a challenging new piece, commissioned to celebrate the twentieth year of the chorus. The band played its annual performance of "The Washington Post March," while the audience clapped along. We also sang "Buffalo Gals" as a crowd-pleasing male-versus-female duel. I didn't faint, weep, or want to run away.

A month after that summertime concert, I returned to the Freeville United Methodist Church on a Wednesday night for choir practice. I had passed the church several times a day on my trips down Main Street, but I hadn't entered it since the most recent funeral I had attended there, two years before. There were ten of us at rehearsal. Every other person had been singing with the choir for years, and I knew them all, personally and musically. The church had a brand-new minister and a new choir director, and I liked the symmetry of starting afresh with others.

I hadn't put on one of the polyester gray robes and sung regularly with the choir for twenty years, but I knew how things would go; we would charge our way through the hymns and that week's anthem. Some of us would struggle with nerves during our short solos. Some of us would spend the rest of our lives searching for, but never quite finding, the note. We would sing at two services on Christmas and Easter, remember each other's birthdays, and pass around homemade fudge.

At my first rehearsal, I grabbed an old leftover three-ring binder to hold my sheet music from a pile scattered on the table in the choir room. When I opened the notebook, I noticed a small mailing label stuck to its upper right-hand corner. My binder had once belonged to Mrs. Ayers, my very first music teacher and the person who taught me to read music. Mrs. Ayers, like Jane, was now gone, but I decided that this was a sign that it was time for me to do my best to put their music back into the world, in the hopes that it would continue to bring me back, too.

Our new choir director is Steve—the son of two Salvation Army musicians. Steve grew up playing piano in the Army (Salvation), but after our first rehearsal, he told me that he had gone through a lengthy break with his faith. He was also going through a divorce. Like me, Steve seemed to be sad and just a little bit broken but trying to tiptoe toward something.

Our new minister's name is Paul. Pastor Paul is young and green, while our church congregation is old and crusty. In his bounding enthusiasm, Paul reminds me of a Saint Bernard puppy. Paul's first service (and my first with the choir) was conducted out of order. The church bulletin seemed to have been printed inside out. The (mainly) elderly congregation tried to keep up as Paul jumped from one part of the service to another, leaping back and forth through the bulletin, apologizing as he went. Paul did something extraordinary that first Sunday, when he told the small congregation, "I love you." He had yet to learn our names, but he was claiming to love us. In my fifty years of dipping in and out of this church, I had never heard a pastor make such an extravagant declaration to our buttoned-up congregation. On the spot, I decided to love him right back.

During the "Joys and Concerns" and announcement portion of the service, my neighbors stood and shared their news and testimony. Sue—now bald from chemo—rose from her pew and announced how her treatments were going. She optimistically talked about her recovery and asked for continued prayers. Paula, who had shaved her own head in solidarity with her friend, raised an "Hallelujah!" Melissa rose and spoke about the youth ministry's overnight sleep-in. Melanie said she could use an extra hand for the food giveaway, because the biweekly distribution of canned goods and restaurant donations had become so popular. Someone asked Keith (a weather forecaster) if we were going to have another cold winter (yes). Mike had agreed to replace the church kitchen's old and rotting floor; work would be starting soon. The Eagle Scouts were volunteering to rebuild a part of the church's old stone foundation for a service project. The Harvest Festival and community yard sale were coming up.

Finally, Aunt Millie stood up and said, "It's nice to see Amy back in the choir."

Listening to this recitation, I was reminded of how life in my little town goes along, even when I am not there to witness it. Since childhood, my family and neighbors have indulged my comings and goings, offering up prayers for my frequent departures and welcoming me back after my sometimes-lengthy absences. My own life seemed to have had more verses than the old Charles Wesley hymns that soaked up so much of our choir time. This congregation remained steadfastly willing to supply the chorus to my life's song. Through the joys and concerns of their own lives, they had done me the favor of staying fundamentally the same.

I have sung my way back into the communion of casseroles and chicken barbeque at the Freeville United Methodist Church. In the months since my first tentative return, Pastor Paul has managed to shake off his butterflies and has become an inspiring leader. Church attendance is creeping up. Our choir director, Steve, has gained in strength and confidence and may some-day date again.

Last week Steve played the old wooden pump organ, which had traveled from the church, to our farm during my childhood, and now back to the church. The organ's asthmatic dynamics and wheezy sound had not changed in the forty-five years since my mother played her favorite Burt Bacharach song over and over at night, during a tough time in her life.

In my years away, I had forgotten how filled with music the Methodist service is. Some Sundays, I'll look out from the choir and see that Bruno has skipped his Catholic Mass and is sitting in a pew. He likes to hear me sing with the choir, and he joins right in, enthusiastically bellowing the old hymns. This reminds me (yet again) that I married very well. When my step-daughters visit the church, they always remark on how loudly the relatively few of us carry on with our rafter-raising. I remind them that you don't need to read music, know any music, or commit to any particular point of view, philosophy, or spiritual belief to sing these ancient songs. You just have to close your eyes, let the music rearrange you from the inside, and hear what happens.

Chapter Twenty-Three

Counting Sheep

I don't sleep well. I do not enjoy being an insomniac, and so I don't like to dwell on how little sleep fuels my day, although it feels like it is usually somewhere between forty-five minutes and four hours. There are people who traffic in their sleeplessness—they get four hours a night and then run marathons. I'm not like that. Most of the time, I'm pretty tired.

I have married, however, into a family of braggy sleep-getters—a group of near-narcoleptic wonders who can fall asleep in full daylight while waiting for a traffic light to turn green or catch a quick nap, head down, at the kitchen table while supper is simmering on the stove. Frequently my mornings will start with one or more family members reporting on how exhausted they are because they only got nine hours of sleep. Avila, especially, although a teenager, seems to have the sleep schedule of a toddler—preferring a solid eight or nine at night and, if possible, a good long nap after she gets home from school.

Bruno falls asleep instantly. The moment he shuts his eyes, his muscles twitch, starting from his head and shoulders and moving down his body, all the way to his feet. They twitch once and then relax, one at a time, into slumber. It is as if a factory whistle has sounded and the assembly line is shutting down, section by section. The workers grab their lunch pails and stream toward the exit after their shift, shutting off the lights with a *thunk* as they go. The last person out slams the factory door with a thud, and the deep snore commences.

I live with sheep grazing outside my bedroom window. They lazily cluster in the pasture we lend to our neighbor Brian, who has the world's most alluring résumé because he is—yes—a shepherd. At night I listen to Brian's flock lowing and murmuring to one another until they fade with the passage of the stars into a soft silence. I listen to the sheep and the occasional coyote barking in the distance, and then I listen to the silence.

You might think that having sheep at the ready would be all the better for a chronic insomniac; I could count them as they bound one by one over an imaginary fence. Yet if you live in proximity to sheep, the last thing you want to do is picture them jumping over a fence at night. That's because they do, occasionally, jump fences. The last time this happened, I had gone downstairs for my morning coffee. You know that feeling that you're being watched, but you can't put your finger on the source? I raised my heavy-lidded eyes to the kitchen window and—*BAM*—there were many pairs of eyes, blinking in concert like a *Wallace and Gromit* cartoon, as the entire flock stood calmly in my flower garden, four feet from the window. I herded them myself that morning.

The secret to herding sheep is to walk slowly toward them with your arms outstretched, waving your arms in a downward scooping motion. You are not flapping—please! If you flap, the sheep will scatter, and you deserve whatever happens next. No, you circle and scoop, circle and scoop. (A soft wave is okay.) I learned this herding technique by doing it (and also, I think, from *Wallace and Gromit*). Brian, the shepherd, has a dog to help him. Also he sometimes uses swearing.

Along with my inability to sleep at night, I am also unable to nap during the daytime. What happens is that I lie stiffly on our stiff Stickley couch, hyper-aware of the sun shining and the birds flying outside the window. When I close my eyes in the daytime, I play a home movie on the inside of my eyelids. My movie is of a little girl on a swing set, flying back and forth against the sky. She kicks her legs and arches her back to pump higher and higher as she is silhouetted against the clouds. The girl is me, and the person pushing is my mother. The girl is also my daughter, and the person pushing her is me. I watch the swing rhythmically pulse, and this lets me rest, although I don't seem to sleep.

Most nights I wake up two or three times, and when I'm awake, I tend to stay that way for up to an hour. Lately I am awash with nighttime thoughts of my mother. I remember what she was like, and I think about what I am like. During Jane's life, I was often aware of how different we were. I didn't physically resemble her very closely, favoring more my father's side of the family. My mother was introverted and shy until she knew you. She was a listener. There was a special quality and depth to her attentiveness. I often felt she paid better attention—or a better kind of attention—to me than I did to myself.

I've inherited my father's low forehead, heavy eyebrows, and movie star minky hair. Like Buck, I have moved around a lot. I also seem to have come into possession of my old man's loud assholiness. I got Buck's jackass gene. I like to hold forth, to tell people what's what. I have a case of chronic verbal jazz hands. These are qualities right at home straddling a barstool in a roadhouse, which is where my father used them to some effect. My being a gasbagging know-it-all is certainly useful in my career as an advice columnist. But, when I was younger, there was a louder and more persistent edge to my personality, and now when I look back, I simply don't like that about myself. I wish I had spent less time showing off and more time showing up.

I hold my mother partially responsible for my occasional unbridled displays because of something that happened when I was eight. I had been very entertaining at the supper table that night. I was into impersonations, and that night I had done Gomer Pyle, my third-grade teacher, and Carol Burnett's Tarzan yell. I could feel the disgust of my three older siblings, who left the room, but I pressed on. I finally went upstairs to change my clothes for bed, and as I headed back down the stairs, I heard my parents talking. About me.

"Do you think she's all right?" I heard my father ask. Buck's voice had a reasonable tone, and I had never heard him be reasonable, so I knew it was important. I couldn't see him from behind the door, but based on his inflection, I could imagine him drawing his index finger in a circular motion next to his temple—the universal symbol for "cuckoo." I imagined the ride to school on the special short bus where they put the special kids who went into the special ed classes. I had always wanted to be special, but not in that way.

"Oh..." Jane sighed. "I think she's funny. I really do."

Just as an unkind remark from a teacher can scar you for life, this overheard comment from my mother forever cemented my belief that she was on my side, no matter what. Jane sometimes appreciated—but mostly tolerated—my social boisterousness. But there were times, especially at a crowded table closer to the end of her life, when she would shut me down with a look that said: "For the love of God, STOP!"

I have trained myself to modulate my behavior publicly, but it's like I've merely pulled a curtain on my vaudeville act. At night my thoughts race and gambol backstage. They put on puppet shows and cabaret acts and tap dance for quarters on street corners. They do standup sets and declare, *"Thank you, thank you very much! We'll be here all week, and for the rest of my life!"*

When I was a child, I fought sleep every night by imagining what it would be like to die. At the age of seven, I saw my dear grandmother in her casket, and after that I dreaded and feared death. At night, I would lie awake imagining how it would happen and how terrible it would be for me to die. Some nights, I distracted myself purposely from my death thoughts by thinking about what it would be like to be a member of the Cowsills family singers or fantasize about having Davy Jones and Peter Tork pull me onstage to sing with them. But not even the Monkees could keep me from my fatalist rumination for long.

There were many nights as a child when I couldn't bear my own thoughts anymore, and I would head down the creaky stairs to sit with my mother. I did not want to be the big baby in the flannel nightgown crying to my mommy at night, and yet—night after night—when nothing else worked, I would leave my bed, make my way to the staircase, and sit on the top step, tucking my legs and feet under my nightgown for warmth. I breathed my hot breath down through the neck hole of my nightgown to create a little body furnace while I tried to calm myself.

I would sit on the stairs in my flannel cocoon and listen to Johnny Carson's muffled voice on the TV in the living room. Sometimes, say, if Buddy Hackett was on, I might eventually be jollied back to bed, but most nights I would sit on the top step, quaking and dreading my compulsion to go down the stairs. Some nights, this death thing was riding piggyback, and I simply had to have help shaking it off.

Getting to my mother in the living room was a torturous journey in failed self-control. I would slide on my bottom, stair after stair, counting to a hundred on each step, thinking that I might eventually calm down and be able to go back to bed by myself. Eventually, I would find myself on the bottommost step, and so I would slowly, accidentally-on-purpose poke the door at the base of the stairs open with my feet.

Jane's perch was on the couch, directly at the foot of the stairs. Strangely, she always seemed happy to see me. I found this surprising. I was usually pretty sick of me by the end of the day; I could not imagine that my mother would want a visitation. Buck was never around at that time of night. As a child, I figured he was in bed because he always got up early for the morning milking, but now I realize that he wasn't there because most nights he went out.

Jane would get some toilet paper for me to blow my nose, turn down the TV, and let me sit super-close to her on the couch. She always asked me what was wrong, but I could never bring myself to tell her. "I remember when I was your age, I would get afraid that my parents would die and leave me. Is that it?" she asked me one night. I lied and said it was. I didn't have the courage to tell her that in my late-night heart of hearts, it was every man for himself. I wasn't worried about her death, but about my own.

Jane told me about her own remedy for sleeplessness. In her head, she recited the names of Franklin Roosevelt's wartime cabinet. Did I want to try that? No—I didn't.

One night on the couch she told me about a story she saw in *Life* magazine. When I was a kid, I was obsessed with *Life*. I liked to write letters to the editors, commenting on articles I had seen there, and urging them to send a team of their award-winning photographers to cover breaking stories in Freeville. I always wrote my name, followed by my age: "Amy Dickinson, age 9," figuring that the editors would find it charming and precocious to hear from an avid reader my age. I never had a letter published in *Life*—not even the one I wrote praising their Kent State coverage—but other ambitious youngsters did, and I hated them for it.

On this night, Jane said she had seen an amazing story in *Life* at the doctor's office about how babies grow in their mother's bodies. She told me there were pictures showing babies floating inside their mothers before they were born, tiny pre-birth babies sucking their thumbs and waiting to come out. "Are you interested in that? Next time we go to the library, we can get out a book about it," she said.

I was *not* interested in that. I was thinking about bones and skin and caskets. But I said yes and that I was feeling better. Then I asked if I could watch a little bit of Carson with her, and she said okay.

When I was twelve and Buck left so abruptly, essentially going out one night and not returning, my insomnia kicked into full gear. It got so bad that one day Jane kept me out of school and took me to the doctor. I only saw Dr. Ferger once a year for my physical. He was kindly and "old" (probably fifty), and he had soft, giant doctor hands. Jane took me into his office and then went out to the waiting room where the magazines were. I pictured her thumbing through that feature on babies in the womb. Dr. Ferger told me, "I hear you're not sleeping lately." I nodded, and added that sometimes I also had headaches (I didn't, but I wanted to give him something he could work with). He said, "Well, I understand that you've been going through some things at home."

Dr. Ferger's knowledge of my family's situation felt shocking and gossipy. His office was a full four miles away from our house. Although his kids went to school with us and I was the third generation of our family to be his patient, I was hoping our embarrassing situation had been contained. I felt as if *Life* magazine had, in fact, dispatched a team to Freeville, only they were covering the wrong story. They were covering my Kent State.

I felt the tears come and the snot run, all on a tide of acute embarrassment.

"No, I don't think that's it," I said as Dr. Ferger handed me a tissue.

"Oh. Okay, maybe not," he said, and pushed himself backward across the room on his metal wheelie stool, to where his desk was. "I think I have something that will help you." He took out a small white envelope and he wrote on the front: *Amy, for sleep.* Then he tipped a jar and counted out six white pills, which he put into the envelope. He licked the small flap on the envelope shut. "Here are some tablets," he said. "Take one before bed. And remember, you're going to be fine."

I felt important, receiving medication for my condition. And yet I also knew it was a placebo. I thought, *I'm dumb, but I'm not stupid. No doctor would give sleeping pills to a kid, especially Dr. Ferger, who obviously thinks this is all in my head, which it probably is.*

I continued to lie awake at night, worrying now not only about my death, but also about my life. I felt the door to my childhood starting to close. I no longer snuck down the stairs at night to visit my mother, who was now ensconced in a sadness over my father's departure that no amount of Buddy Hackett could remedy. I flattened out the empty pill envelope and put it on my windowsill, next to my geranium. Jane said I looked better and that the medication must have worked. I lied and said that it had.

In the solitude of my adult insomnia, I no longer obsess about my death. Mainly I listen to the sound of my mistakes and regrets. I think about what I might have said, done, or written that I might need to clean up the next day. I perform a mental version of my Methodist confession, strategizing about those things I have done, and fretting about those I have left undone.

I think about my e-mail correspondence, like the one today with a young woman who wondered if she was in an abusive relationship. The subject line of her e-mail read: *Is my BF abusive?* After describing a relationship that was not only abusive, but alarmingly so, I responded to her privately (not in my published column) and told her to please, *please* call the National Domestic Violence Hotline. I gave her the website link and phone number. I asked her to get back to me afterward. She e-mailed me back, saying, "My boyfriend doesn't punch me. He only chokes me. One time he threw me down. I thought my hip was broken, but it's only a bruised tailbone. I've got it better than a lot of people. He only does this when he's angry. I really love him…"

I told her that she deserved much better than this. I told her that this wasn't normal and that this wasn't what a healthy relationship was supposed to be like. I told her to tell a friend or a family member. I asked her to keep in touch with me. Throughout the day as we corresponded back and forth, she became more and more defensive of her partner's behavior, before cutting off the communication altogether.

A few months ago, I expressed a similar concern and alarm toward someone I knew who was in a volatile and violent relationship. After the police left her house, I told her how worried I was and urged her to call the hotline and speak to a counselor. She did not speak to a counselor, she did stay in the relationship, and the only thing she changed was that she stopped speaking to me. I ended up calling the National Domestic Violence Hotline myself. The young counselor on the other end of the phone line listened to me choke out the story and then said that she couldn't do anything for me, just as I couldn't do anything for the woman who wrote to me or the woman I knew who stopped speaking to me. In my dark night heart of hearts, I know—indeed—that it IS every man for himself.

That's what I think about at night. I try to mentally prepare for being one day closer to the next thing that might happen—the midnight phone call from the nursing home, the knock on the door from the state trooper.

But as I lie awake, nothing happens. The only insight delivered to me during these wakeful hours is the breadth of my powerlessness. I no longer shiver with the thought of my own death, because I'm convinced I've already experienced something that is likely worse: to close the casket on a loved one and be left behind to remember and grieve.

But perhaps my insomnia has also delivered a gift, in that I have gained a deep appreciation for the blessings of my waking life, which is real and raw and rich with incident. I have been granted and cursed with the privilege of awareness. I know I will both witness and tangle with the deepest part of the night, until the night is done and the sky turns platinum with the dawn. And when the sheep are lowing good morning, I know I will rise to greet them.

Chapter Twenty-Four

How to Use a Saw

1. Identify the Problem

There is a tree in the corner of my mother's yard. Unlike most of the other trees there, this one seems to have no history. It is not the sycamore my sisters and I planted after I came back from five years living in London. It isn't the ancient Japanese lilac that overhangs the driveway with its sweet and dripping blossoms, nor the towering maple that dwarfs the house and that itself replaced the gargantuan and graceful elm that was a local landmark before it died of Dutch elm disease. No, this tree just seemed to appear. It has undistinguished leaves and a strange trunk that is really four trunks that meet at the ground. It looks like a giant weed that got ahead of itself, and now this weed is twenty-five feet tall.

Half of the tree came down last week in a storm. Two of the trunks snapped off at the root and landed in the yard. The mess was large enough that it was like, "Whoa!" when I pulled into the driveway.

I went into the barn and found the pruning saw. This is a small saw that I bought for $7 at the hardware store last week. I was there looking for plants and lightbulbs, but I came out with cat litter and a saw. I looked at it, hanging from a peg in the saw department, and I thought, *I'm going to use this thing to saw the legs off of something.*

One of Jane's primary modes of home decorating was to saw the legs off of things. You'd go upstairs to bed at night, and in the morning when you came back downstairs, the kitchen table had become a coffee table. Growing up, we got used to it.

2. Choose a Good Angle

I was outside surveying the tree damage when my neighbor Mike stopped by to gaze at the Japanese lilac, which is in full glorious bloom and sending out a very strong honeysuckle scent that drifts down Mill Street.

Mike lives just down the road, occupying the house and farming the land that was once our dairy farm. Mike and his family live in the house I lived in during my childhood, before we lost everything.

Mike seems to know a lot about a lot of things. He keeps sheep on his place, and you have to know a lot in order to manage sheep. Sheep can be tricky. Sheep test a person's ability to handle sudden humiliation, because, like all livestock, they don't pay attention to what people want. Sheep move through the pasture in woolly barnyard cliques. They don't give a damn. They look cuddly from a distance but nasty, matted, and muddy up close. They have pointy hooves and spindly legs, improbably holding up ottoman-shaped bodies. Basically, as animals, sheep make no sense. They seem both untamable and illogical. It takes a wise and humble person to be a shepherd.

I asked Mike, "Hey, what kind of tree is this?"

Mike ambled over. "I call that a junk tree," he said. "They just sort of show up. Some people like them because they grow so fast, but they tend to fall over once they get big. Why?" Mike hesitated, suspicious, like this was a tree quiz. "What do YOU call it?"

"Yeah, I call it a junk tree, too," I said. "I'm going to saw it up."

"You'd better get yourself a chain saw. That's a bigger mess than you think," he said.

Oh no, I thought. *I will be sawing this tree myself, mister. You'll see.*

3. There Will Be Swearing

I've had a rough few days. Yesterday I got an e-mail from a reader who said my responses lately to advice questions were mean and grouchy. Of course I responded to her in an exceedingly grouchy way, and then she replied that her husband had just died. I tried to take it all back, but I couldn't make it right. Another reader wrote in: "Amy, you are a retart (sic) who doesn't know anything about relationships." Spelling aside, I knew what he was getting at, and I worried that he was right.

Also, our youngest is getting ready to graduate high school, and, just like all of our other girls at this stage, she is not going quietly. Lately there have been yelling sessions and door slamming. I've mainly tried to hide out in the bedroom, only catching snippets through the walls as she nails Bruno for being a concerned and protective parent who won't let her spend the remaining weeks of her childhood ramming around all night in the car. I had done this dance with Jane when I was a teen. Knowing this doesn't help.

Essentially, each daughter as she leaves home seems to want to renovate her father by trying to saw his legs off. Tomorrow morning I might go downstairs and see that Bruno has been reduced to the dad equivalent of a coffee table. Something you rest your feet upon.

People helpfully offer up the wisdom that kids have to push you away before they leave home. I've pointed this out myself—endlessly—responding to questions in my advice column. But like most life experiences, knowing about it does little to mitigate experiencing it.

4. Don't Hurt Yourself

Sometimes everything seems like a metaphor. I catch myself thinking that every experience is really about something else. Yard work is especially metaphor-rich, because even if a rose IS sometimes just a rose, quite often it is something else, too.

Last summer I had an epiphany about my family while weeding. I was yanking up bishop's weed, which is an exceedingly invasive plant. The roots of this weed are all connected belowground, and they are tricky and elastic, so they snap off when you try to pull them out. You don't get the visceral satisfaction of pulling up bishop's weed and bringing up its roots. You end up standing there holding a fistful of stems. The elasticity of the plant's root system is a brilliantly designed protective survival mechanism. No matter how many stems you manage to pull up, they will sprout again and spread. Don't make me draw you a diagram. This is how my family works.

5. If You Saw Too Fast, Your Blade Will Get Stuck

I haven't spent much time sawing things, but, like its cousin the hammer, a saw suggests how to use it by not offering many options. You draw the blade back and forth, just like a child actor in an episode of *The Waltons*. Going after a six-inch-diameter tree trunk with a pruning saw is like trying to cut steak with a cheese grater. I knew that, but I tried it anyway.

I stood in the kitchen, saw in hand, and pondered the mess in the yard from inside my mother's house. The weather had just become warm enough to leave the inside door open. The kitchen was still a jumble of boxes filled with her belongings, my own stuff, and random assortments of things that seemed like cast-offs from a Victorian-era yard sale: tallow candles, tiny ink bottles with quill pens, enough dish towels and doilies to dry all the dishes and host all the teapots in a small city, and odd-shaped lace thingies too lovely to throw away.

I promised Jane I would keep her house just as it was, and I have broken that promise. My mother's house is now my house. I just need to swallow that lump in my throat to be able to say it out loud. For now, the peculiar squeak and slap of the old screen door—so familiar from the thousands of times I've heard it—keeps me pinned in place.

Every sawing project starts with the first cut. I made a careful draw against the grain of the tree trunk. Then I caught a groove. The sun came out. I drew the blade faster and faster. Sawdust started to sprinkle down onto the cute shoes I brought back from my most recent trip to Chicago. Sweat trickled down the back of my no-iron shirt. I looked like a mom on her way to Target for guest towels, but on this day I was a lumberjack (and, like the old Monty Python song said, it was okay).

I started thinking about my father. Buck rambled from marriage to marriage, and when he was about seventy years old, he paused between relationships to work as an apple picker and tree trimmer at an orchard in Nova Scotia. At least, that's what he said he was doing. He lied about many things, but I chose to believe this particular story. I always enjoyed the vision of my old man scrambling up a tree. In his way, he has led something of a hair-raising life, in that he always had a tendency to saw off the branch he was standing upon. Now he languishes at a nursing home in Pennsylvania. Lately he won't get out of his wheelchair, even though the aides there tell me he can walk. I'm the only one of his children to visit him, and that's not saying much. I know I'm doing the minimum.

I sawed about three inches into the trunk when I faltered. My saw refused to go farther. I started to worry that a passerby would stop and try to help me. I am married to someone who drives a pickup truck, has arms like mighty oaks, is in possession of a chain saw, and loves to rescue people. But I have always resisted rescue, especially when I really need it. I know this is a legacy of the rugged individualism both my parents drummed into me, but I also know I've wasted a lot of time standing in the middle of a mess and saying, "Back off. I've got this."

6. When You're Not Making Any Progress, You Have to Come at It from Another Angle

I left my saw dangling in its cut and went into the house for a glass of water. Lately I've been trying to switch from coffee to water, but I don't like water. I like coffee. And Diet Coke. My friend Megan recently told me, "Diet

Coke is the worst thing you can do," but I know there are many, many worse things I can—and do—do. Just yesterday I ate a whole box of Easter Peeps I found in a cupboard. They sat there like a little conjoined flock behind their cellophane wrapper, taunting me with their tiny black dot eyes. I had a fleeting thought of wondering how long they had been there. Perhaps Easter 2005? I ate one. And then I ate the rest of them. It turns out that Peeps, like fine wine and Helen Mirren, age very well.

I have also lied and cheated. I have been a thief. When I was fourteen, I shoplifted a small item from the Woolworths store in downtown Ithaca. My mother left her job as a typist at Cornell and drove downtown to get me where I was being sequestered at the store's security office.

I had been caught attempting to steal the plastic insert from a billfold. I hadn't stolen the wallet itself, but only its plastic innards—those slots where you might keep your school photo or your license. This was a highly ironic choice, since I had neither a wallet nor money to put into a wallet, nor photos or a license to put in the plastic slots.

I was humiliated. I was upset and embarrassed. I remember thinking, *Why? Why? What is wrong with me? How bad am I? Will I ever get away with anything?* Jane was not a disciplinarian. Her only weapon was her disappointment, which she wielded like a broadsword. I was not afraid of her; her disappointment, however, was terrifying.

Jane walked me to the car, comforting me the whole way. Then she took the rest of the day off and took me out for ice cream at a Friendly's near the mall. We sat in one of the orange plastic booths under the unforgiving fluorescent light.

"Amy," she said, "this is not the worst thing you will ever do. But it's the dumbest." She then promised not to tell my sisters or anyone else.

I dried my eyes and ate my sundae. My mother got her purse to pay. Just before we left the restaurant, I said to her, "Mom, did you know you have these like jowl things under your chin? If you have jowls, does that mean I'm going to get them, too?"

"Thank you muchly. I really appreciate it," she said.

"Oh, anytime," I said. "Just trying to be helpful."

I have an unfortunate, and perverse, tendency to sometimes react to another person's compassion by snapping back unkindly. It is my own shame speaking, and I hate that about myself.

That's the sort of thing I think about as I rattle around my mother's place, which she made and which I have inherited. Sometimes our families deserve better than they get.

7. Don't Saw off More Than You Can Lift and Carry by Yourself

I returned to the tree and jimmied the saw from the cut. I went around to the other side of the tree and started from the opposite direction. The great thing about using a saw is that you can actually see that you're doing something as you're doing it. Most of my efforts at work and home offer less-obvious results.

I spent an entire afternoon attacking the junk tree with my pruning saw, feeling that righteous feeling that writers feel when they're actually doing real work, instead of sitting at their desks, ruminating and checking Facebook. I asked myself, as I often do, *Is this the best use of my time?* Even though the answer was no, I did it anyway.

As dusk was starting to descend, Bruno pulled up in his truck. My phone was in the house, so his calls had gone unanswered. I was standing in the middle of the yard, surrounded by the branches of the downed tree, holding my saw—which compared with the size of the job, looked like a nail file. Bruno wordlessly reached into the back of his truck, pulled out a chain saw and goggles, and walked toward me. He's a good man. Our love affair, which sprouted so suddenly and grew so quickly, now has deep, strong roots.

"Shall I ...?" he asked.

"Definitely. Have at it." I went into the house to grab us two beers so that I could sit on the porch and watch my husband finish what I had started.

Chapter Twenty-Five

Next of Kin

Last year, as I was visiting my father in the nursing home in Pennsylvania, I was beckoned into the director's office for the dreaded bill-paying conversation. Any caper involving Buck ends in an inevitable blizzard of unpaid bills. To know him is to be stiffed by him, and I consider it a minor triumph that I have never lent him money.

As the only one of his children who will risk much direct contact with him, I have coached myself on ways to have some relationship with my father, without taking responsibility for him. On the four-hour drive from Freeville to central Pennsylvania, I had reviewed my strategy for how to dodge the inevitable mess. I'd agreed to be the point person for the nursing home, and in several meetings with the facility's manager, I had consented that they should work with Buck to try sorting out his tangled finances, in order to pay the bills for his care. His holdings, such as they were, included a hundred-acre farm on an island in the middle of Lake Huron in Canada and a decrepit farm in Pennsylvania. Both properties were littered with unpaid-for vehicles, tax liens, pissed-off neighbors, and women he had promised to marry.

The nursing home director said he had a question for me. I braced myself. Would I be presented with an invoice?

"So tell me, because I'm curious," the director said. "Was your father good-looking? I mean, back in the day?"

His question surprised me. I thought back to my image of Buck as the rangy, raven-haired farmer of my childhood.

"Um, yes," I said. "He was. Movie-star handsome, in his way. Why?"

The director explained that my father, now physically a shadow of what he had once been, behaved like a guy who had basically learned to skate along on his looks.

I nodded. "Sell everything," I said. "And keep an eye on the nurses."

For much of my life I have been afraid of my handsome father. He was physically strong, for one thing, and because he was volatile and unpredictable, when I was a child he seemed capable of violence. Watching him manhandle our livestock was like witnessing someone always on the verge of losing control. He would push and shove our cows and sometimes beat their backs with a wooden cane when they started heading the wrong way in the barn. Buck could hoist a 150-pound calf into the back of a pickup truck and walk into the barn balancing 85-pound bales of hay from each hand. He had bulging forearms, like Popeye.

My mother always claimed that Buck's most lethal weapon was his big mouth, and as I grew older, I decided this was probably true. About half of my encounters with him over the years had ended with me telling him to stop saying something he was in the midst of saying. He made mean-spirited comments about my mother and her family, my siblings, and other members of his own extended family. His working theory seemed to be that as long as he wasn't trashing you to your face, you shouldn't have a problem. But listening to someone unfairly put down people you love is sort of like watching someone beat a defenseless Holstein. You know that the person doing it could do it to you if they felt like it.

Buck mainly chose to keep his distance from his children, and that came as a relief to me. As the child of a troublemaker, I possess some of the characteristics common to children of addicts or alcoholics: I am protective of myself and of others. I'm a worrier. Over the years, my fear of Buck seems to have morphed into an anxiety that I am somehow like him. I've made many life choices trying to prove to myself how very unlike my father I am, all the while worrying that I will turn out to have had his disease all along. Every time I act like a jerk at a party, telling someone loudly what's for, or going on for too long about myself, I think, *Oh no, I've inherited the jackass gene.* I've compensated for our poor father-daughter relationship by using Buck's instability as a way to proactively highlight my own relative success. It's easy to feel like a winner when compared to someone who once sank everything into speculating on sugar beets.

When I was ten years old, Buck announced his decision to devote all of our arable land to the magical sugar beet (promoted as the cash crop of the future by a seed salesman he'd probably met in a bar). Buck's scheme to switch from growing corn to sugar beets, like so many of his ideas, sounded like a disaster in advance, was a disaster in the making, and had completely predictable consequences. Well into the growing season, when no sugar beet plants were visible, my sisters and I were sent into the field with a picture of a sugar beet plant in hopes of finding a hidden pocket of beets somewhere within the weeds. In the fifty acres our father had devoted to this crop, not one sugar beet plant germinated. Buck did not become the Sugar Beet Baron of Upstate New York. His field of dreams grew into a field of weeds, and that winter we had no corn for the cows.

Given my sporadic contact with Buck, my knowledge of him was confined to him reporting on his latest scheme and then waiting several months to find out how things had turned out. There was the 50,000-gallon tank he purchased with the idea to fill it with oil (this is how he would beat the Arabs at their own game), the plan to turn his farm into a hunting camp, the idea to corner the local market on honey, and the latest woman he planned to marry. To me, none of my father's various life plans ever seemed plausible or even possible. He could pitch something as if it were the best idea in the world, and even during the rapid-fire recitation, I'd think, *Oh no, this will not end well.*

Because he combined a sense of daring with poor choices and perennial bad luck, Buck has led an anecdote-rich life. My friend Elizabeth used to prompt me to rattle off the names of Buck's wives: Jane, Joan, Jeanne, Jean, and Pat. He's the only father among my friends dragged into court (at the age of seventy-two) for shooting a bear. Well into old age, he continued to behave as if he were invincible, and as far as I could tell, he was.

Seven years ago, Bruno and I were having a little Fourth of July picnic on our porch. Jane was there, shielded from the summer breeze with a lap robe over her wheelchair. Her two sisters, Millie and Jean, were also with us. Rachel, Tim, and their children were on the way. My cell phone rang. It was Rachel. "Watch out; Dad's coming your way," she said. He had stopped by her house in Freeville, and she had a feeling he was now driving the six miles toward the house where Bruno and I lived with our children. Buck had a habit of doing "drive-bys," where about twice a year he would simply show up, unannounced. He'd stay for a half hour or so, talk incessantly about himself, and then leave as suddenly as he had arrived. Rachel was waving a warning flag. I said I'd text her when the coast was clear.

I didn't particularly want my father to see my mother on that day. There was no bad blood left between them, and on the very few occasions over the years they had seen one another, they were always cordial. But I didn't want him to see how much her health had declined. I knew that if he saw her in her wheelchair, he would say something ruinous. Something along the lines of, "Jesus Christ, Jane, what the hell happened to you?"

I saw a vintage powder-blue Mustang convertible pull up our quiet country road and turn into the long driveway. Bruno and I excused ourselves from our company and met him in the driveway. Buck bounded out of the car. "Hey ho, kid," he shouted. As usual, I was wondering if my father remembered my name. This was not a function of his age (he was seventy-eight), but more my experience of a lifetime of his sporadic attention. I knew for certain that Buck didn't know my middle name, or my birthday, or where I had gone to college. He did not acknowledge the existence of my daughter or stepdaughters. He only seemed certain about what I did for a living, because this gave him currency at roadhouses and diners, where he spun hangover lies and engaged in braggy big talk about his youngest daughter's career. My column appeared in his local newspaper and other newspapers along his tangled travel routes, and he could therefore prove my bona fides as a chip off of the old blockhead.

Buck's hearing had declined, and every encounter was high decibel. Bruno and he shook hands, and we hollered our greetings. "What's up, Dad?" I asked. This is the sort of open-ended question that could bring on virtually any answer, ranging from a recitation on the scourge of honeybee mites (at that time he was working as a beehive inspector) to "I just got married."

"Well, I'm moving," Buck said. The year before, his most recent wife, Pat, had died after a long illness. Two of the four women my father had married since he'd abandoned my mother in 1973 had died on him (as he put it). Though he operated on the "cut and run" end of the relationship spectrum, and I don't assume he had remained faithful to any of his wives, he seemed to have cared tenderly for both women through their final illnesses.

My sisters and I attended Pat's funeral in Pennsylvania, and at the post-funeral luncheon at the church, my father turned to me and shouted, "WELL, NOW I'M RICH!" Pat had property and an insurance settlement of some kind, which she had somehow managed to protect during their marriage of several years. Pat had squirreled away her money, and now it was Buck's. On hearing this, I reflexively glanced around the crowded church dining room, pushed my paper plate of Jell-O salad a little bit closer to my father, and attempted to shush him. He told me the amount of money he thought he would be receiving, which was indeed a windfall—especially for someone like Buck, who lived his life like a character in a George Strait song and who seldom planned beyond his most recent payday.

There in the church I asked him what he was going to do. He said, "Well, the first thing is, I think I'm going to buy a kayak." I pictured my elderly father being swept down the Allegheny River and wondered who among his children would be called upon to identify his bloated body. I feared it might be me.

I told him the money could be gone very quickly if he wasn't careful. I urged him to visit a financial planner, which I knew he would never do.

In my father's world, planners and advisors are for people who don't know what they're doing. Uncertainty, like monogamy, was a concept he had never embraced.

In the year since Pat's funeral, Buck seemed to have fought off her other relatives and gotten ahold of and spent his inheritance, hence the cherry Mustang and the plan to move on.

"Wow, Dad, where are you moving to?" I asked him. He reached into the car and pulled out a large folding map of the northern United States and Canada. He pointed to a large blob in the middle of enormous Lake Huron—his gnarled finger landed on an island called Manitoulin. He said he had bought a farm and had decided to raise sheep there. I was surprised that my father was moving to Canada. Throughout my life, he had made it very clear that he didn't like foreigners.

Buck pulled out some snapshots of his new property. It was pretty, with rolling hills and giant round hay bales, the sort of landscape he was always drawn to.

Manitoulin Island, he explained, is the largest island with freshwater lakes in the world. Some of these lakes on Manitoulin Island are so large that the lakes also *have islands on them*. One of these islands, within a lake on Manitoulin Island, is the largest island in a lake, *on* an island in a lake in the world. I tried to follow this world-within-worlds concept, which sounded more like a marijuana fever dream than a geographic reality. He pulled out a close-up map of Manitoulin and pointed it out.

I asked Buck when he was moving, and he told me he was shoving off and leaving Pennsylvania for Canada the next day. "Whoa, so soon?" I asked.

"Well, I've got my goose and my cat all packed up, and I'm ready to go," he said.

My father is the world's most ardent cat man. I didn't even ask about the goose. There are some questions you don't really want the answer to.

"What, Dad, no woman?" I asked him. I'd never known Buck to stay unattached for long.

"Naaaaah," my father replied in his distinctively nasal Upstate drawl. "I'll get one out there."

And then Buck drove away. In the time it takes to pour fresh glasses of iced tea, Bruno and I had returned to our guests on the porch.

Once Buck moved to Canada, his drive-bys were curtailed, and aside from the occasional note or one-sentence postcard from him (sample: "The geese are flying overhead"), I had no idea how he was doing. However, my cousin Tom spent several months living with Buck on Manitoulin Island, and Tom reported back the predictable details. Buck slept on a rollaway bed next to the smoky woodstove in the basement of his small, dirty, and cluttered house. He ate cornflakes for breakfast and a can of tomato soup for lunch. He shopped from the expired food section of the local supermarket. He had two tractors, a truck, an ATV, and a wood splitter. He spent a lot of time cutting and splitting wood. He had three cats, all named "Kitty." He corresponded by mail with several women, whose names he got from the classifieds section of farming magazines. Occasionally he left the island and traveled great distances to meet them.

It was about four years after our meeting in the driveway until I saw Buck again. He was lying broken and near death in a hospital in Buffalo, after a strange one-car accident that happened in the middle of the night along a state road near Buffalo. The state police found his license (expired) and managed to get hold of Rachel. The police told her Buck's body had been found down an embankment, when a passerby noticed a pickup truck toppled over on the icy roadway at 3:00 a.m. The police couldn't estimate how long he had been there. It was February, and the temperature was 10 degrees. The truck Buck was driving was registered in someone else's name and didn't appear to belong to him.

Buck wasn't expected to survive. My sisters and I exchanged tentative phone calls about what to do. None of us seemed to want to claim him. Anne, a master of detail and paperwork, immediately set about trying to figure out what had happened. The last any of us knew, he was farming sheep in Canada. Anne managed to locate a neighbor of his on Manitoulin, who said that our father had a habit of taking off and leaving his livestock to fend for themselves. The neighbor said my father's neglect bordered on criminal and that several of his sheep had died in the field. Anne arranged with the neighbor to get the sheep fed. She contacted a funeral home.

I said I would go to see him.

Buck was in an acute care ICU in a very large and busy metropolitan hospital. I drove the three hours from Freeville, fretting the whole way about what I would find when I got there. In my whole life, encompassing my childhood and the various random encounters I'd had with him over the years, I had never actually wanted to see him. I especially didn't want to see him now. I sat in the hospital's large parking lot, knowing that I could turn around and drive back home and still get some residual credit for giving the tiniest crap about my father. Bruno was urging me to do "the right thing" but wisely refused to say what the right thing was.

I forced myself to enter the hospital, walk through the chaos of the emergency department, and up to the ICU. All the while I was thinking that I could turn around and leave, able now to truthfully say that I had "visited" without actually doing so.

Down every hospital hallway, I told myself that I could turn around and go back home. This is how I force myself to do things I don't want to do. Most people give themselves pep talks to urge themselves forward, but I'm the opposite. When I'm faced with a terrible task, I tell myself over and over that I can quit anytime I want to. I guess I'm like my old man in that way. And yet, unlike him, I'm not much of a quitter. Ultimately, I almost always decide to press on.

My siblings and I all seemed to share a fear that we would somehow end up responsible for Buck. It seemed the final ironic injustice that our mother, who had been so steadfastly in our corner and who had lived so well, would die first, while our father, who had been such a perennial problem as he careened through life, remained healthy and vigorous into old age. During one meeting with my sisters, we each shared our private fear that Buck would land on our doorstep. Each of us had worked up an imaginary scenario where he would show up at our house and we would have to take him in. Knowing that he sometimes traveled with a goose in tow made this prospect even less appealing. Yet I knew that this was unlikely. Depending on his children didn't fit with how he seemed to move through the world. In old age, especially, Buck seemed like an old cowpoke whose wanderings were a way of life.

The ICU was quiet, like a library. I was led toward the glassed-in room where my father lay. I double-checked the name to make sure it was him because the body in the bed did not resemble him—or really anyone. His head was bandaged and swollen, almost twice its normal size. His face was black and blue. A trach tube was attached to his neck. He was in an induced coma and had been for several days.

I sat in a chair just outside his room, looking in. The nurse told me I could go into the room, but I said no, I was already close enough. His injuries were extensive: He had several broken ribs, a back injury, and swelling in his frontal and temporal lobes. The doctor said, "He's a fighter." I had to agree that this was one of his defining characteristics. I asked to see a social worker.

The social worker was in her mid-twenties. She asked, "Are you his next of kin?"

"Um, I'm his daughter. But I'm not sure if I'm his next of kin," I said.

She asked me if he was married, and I told her that I wasn't sure; I didn't think so, but it was entirely possible. "There's, um, some estrangement. But he does have children," I said.

She then told me that two older women had been to the hospital over the last few days, each claiming to be engaged or related to him. "Yes, that sounds about right; you can expect more of that," I told her. I contained my amazement that my father continued to find women who wanted him, and yet I knew that his practice was to lead with his imaginary assets and brag about his property, and insinuate or flat-out lie about his wealth. Perhaps this made him attractive.

Buck survived his car accident. He was in a coma for three weeks and then graduated from one level of care to the next over the following two months. I visited him most weeks, and the visits got easier. I moved my chair closer and closer to his bed. I was genuinely happy when he recognized me and when they finally removed the trach tube so he could talk. He had no memory of what had happened and wasn't able to say why he was on the road near Buffalo at 3:00 a.m. driving someone else's vehicle.

After my hospital visits, I would call my sisters and my aunt Anne to fill them in on his condition. Aunt Anne is my father's older sister. She was one of my mother's oldest friends. After Buck left our family, she maintained her close relationship with us. Watching my mother and her former sister-in-law maintain their close and generous friendship taught me a lot about how people could pull close (and stay close), if they wanted to. Like me, my aunt seemed mystified by Buck and was not able to explain him to me over the years, but at least she could commiserate. We periodically warned each other not to give him money.

After two months, my father was ready to leave the hospital. He was too impaired now to live on his own, and I found a nursing home near his former home in Pennsylvania that would take him. When I talked to the home's manager on the phone, she said with a knowing sigh, "Oh yes, I know Buck." She had been his neighbor. Even though she probably knew better, she agreed to take him on.

My father has lived in the nursing home for two years. Despite a lifetime of smoking, drinking, and overall terrible choices, his impressive vigor has kept him going. He has engaged in a stripped-down version of his familiar dynamic with people—getting into nasty and foul-mouthed disputes with at least one resident, making petty and sometimes cruel statements about others, and ingratiating himself to the female aides.

I drive to Pennsylvania about once a month to see him. Sometimes Bruno or Rachel comes with me, and a couple of times my aunt Anne has met me there. We have brief awkward meetings and engage in shouted chitchat with my father, who is usually in a wheelchair. Buck has cycled through bouts of teary depression, where he can't seem to explain how he feels, or why. His doctor affirmed this and told me that depression can come on after a head injury. During one visit, I sought out one of his favorite aides, who walked me down the hall and explained her theory. She said that as he slowly recovered from his brain injury, he was now trapped into thinking about his life. "He can't just jump into his truck and drive off," she said. "He's feeling things. He's feeling all the feels."

I am no longer afraid of my father. I don't dread my contact with him. I pull up close in order to shout into his ear. I hold his hand, and when he is in bed, I sometimes stroke his wispy hair into place. When he's feeling up to it, we go out onto the home's porch and look out at the steep hill that rises up and fills the view at the edge of town. Recently, Bruno and I wheeled him a short distance to the town's park, with its stocked lake. We sat in the sunshine and watched people pull trout from it. Buck always thought this rough countryside was God's country, and he still seems to love it.

My father never asks about his farm on the island in Canada or about his sheep, goose, or cats. He doesn't talk about his other property and scattered possessions. They're all gone now. Now that the lie of wealth can no longer be maintained, the women, too, have vanished. When I asked him recently if he liked where he was living, he said, "Well, I just don't give a damn." Searching for signs of depression, I asked him, "Wait, Dad, are you saying you don't give a damn because you just don't care?"

"No, I'm saying I don't give a damn because I know I will never leave here, and I'm happy enough. It's going to end someday," he said.

Gradually and incrementally, I seem to have accepted the position as my father's next of kin. I have made peace with his regrettable choices and ruinous actions. I no longer blame Buck for being himself. I don't know if I would call it forgiveness, exactly, but more a letting go of my own bitterness, in being the daughter of someone so hell-bent on disruption. Now that his life is nearing its end, I miss his antic energy and refusal to settle down.

My childhood happened so long ago. I am no longer the girl trying to outrun my father's failures but a middle-aged woman stroking the hand of a man who has nothing left. I have spent the bulk of my life missing my father. Now, at the end of his life, I know my father in a new way. The menace of his early years has faded. Every thoughtless, disruptive, and unkind thing he could do has already been done. He and I are shackled to the knowledge that it's going to end someday. The only burden I shoulder now is my knowledge that, when that day comes, I know that I will miss him.

Chapter Twenty-Six

Strangers Tend to Tell Me Things

I was putting gas in my car the other day, standing there at the gas pump and silently counting "One, one thousand, two, one thousand," which is the only way I can seem to cope with this, my least favorite chore. I usually close my eyes while I'm pumping, playing a little game against the ticking numbers of the gallon indicator. I tell myself, *Just pump until ten gallons and stop.* And when I reach ten gallons, I'll say, *Well, you've come this far, you might as well fill it.*

I had finally reached a full tank and was replacing the nozzle when a car pulled up across from me on the other side of the gas pump. A woman got out. She looked vaguely familiar, but when you're pumping gas, everyone looks vaguely familiar. Pumping gas unites the whole of humanity into one big washed-out blob. It's the great zombie leveler.

I was finishing my transaction when the woman spoke to me. She reminded me that we had met that one time at the farmers' market in Ithaca. Did I remember? (I did not.) "Oh...," I said. I never voluntarily cross the threshold of Ithaca's famed farmers' market, which is a crowded outdoor weekend market of organic goods, homemade soap, candles, and wearable art, housed under a large and fancy pavilion.

On Saturday mornings the hippie farmers come down from the hills, peddling their panpipes and goat cheese and batik tablecloths. They carry their babies in crossover slings. I love a hippie family (who doesn't?), but it's the adjunct professors at the farmers' market who give me a pain. They are the ones who stroll from booth to booth, holding up the line while they grill the proprietor about the locally sourced honey: *Are the bees from here? Do they feast on the nectar of buttercups? Is this a free-range hive? And the drones—are they encouraged to form a lasting relationship with the queen? This plastic bear the honey comes in seems a little gender-specific. I brought my own Mason jar. Can you fill it?*

I buy my produce from my neighbors, my soap from the supermarket, and I try to stay as far away as possible from wearable art. I get a rash just thinking about it. But once in a while, one of my daughters will drag me down to the farmers' market, where I spend all of my time trying to find a slice of pizza with real cheese on it and then grumpily wait in the car.

I did not recognize the woman at the gas pump and she didn't introduce herself to me, so I will call her Barbara (she looked like a Barbara). At the start of this encounter, I did what I usually do when I am greeted by someone I don't know. I faked it and said, "So, how are you doing these days?"

Barbara said, "Well, I'm sure you heard about Kurt and me." (I hadn't, and couldn't place him either.)

"No," I said.

She then told me about her husband's infidelity. Barbara supplied lots of details about her husband's behavior, the other woman's behavior, the woman's physical appearance, and even the breed and comportment of the woman's dog (not to put too fine a point on it, but that woman's dog was a real bitch). Barbara had already crossed over the hump of hurt and the river of denial and was now in the pissed-off phase of life after infidelity. Their children were torn but forming alliances, resulting in what sounded like a very uncomfortable standoff.

This sounded awful. As someone who had survived infidelity, I could still feel the emotional muscle memory of betrayal. I also remembered the almost manic need to tell the story. Sharing our problems with a stranger might be a naked bid for sympathy, or it might be an expression of a simpler and more elemental need to describe our lives, in a bid for connection. Right after my first husband left me, I was sitting in the dentist's chair for a root canal. As the dentist's probe mistakenly hit my tooth's nerve, I jumped and shrieked.

"Oh no, what happened?" the dentist asked.

"My husband cheated on me!" I cried.

"Well, I can't do anything about that," he said, offering me a tissue. "But I can totally fix this tooth."

I feared Barbara might ask me for something, because sometimes when people run into me, they either tell me their stories and seem to expect advice in return, or they flat-out ask in advance for advice, then tell their story, and then don't listen to my response (sort of the way you might ask your vet about your dog's heartworm at a cocktail party but then forget to pay attention to his answer).

I was praying for another vehicle to arrive at the gas pump, which would force me back into my car and permit me to drive away. But it was an extremely slow day for gas guzzling. After forty-five minutes of standing at the pump listening to the sad infidelity story, I realized with some relief that I had nothing practical to offer Barbara, and so I simply listened. I waited for her to finish, and then I told her I was so sorry this was happening. I told her I would be thinking about her and hoping for the best for all of them. And then I drove away, feeling heart-heavy over this unburdening.

This happens to me quite frequently, individuals offering a personal unburdening to me. As challenging as this can be, I prefer it to the other sort of encounter, which is heavy with expectation.

During my first year of writing the "Ask Amy" column, I became aware of a growing phenomenon at my office at the *Chicago Tribune*. A colleague would come in, close the door, unleash a personal problem, and then wait for me to help them solve it. This seemed to happen about once a week, and I did my best to be polite and helpful. I had even spoken with the referring therapist at Northwestern Hospital—just down Michigan Avenue from the *Trib* building—and he encouraged me to offer his contact information to colleagues who might want it.

One time, just before Christmas, I arrived to work early and noticed my coworker, whom I'll call "Gage," seated just outside my office. Gage and I were sort-of newsroom friends; we joked around and occasionally ate lunch together in the break room. Basically, Gage and I were break room buddies. This was the third or fourth time I had arrived at work to the sight of Gage, waiting for me to start my workday as his personal advice-giver. As I opened the door, he followed me in and plopped down in the chair across from my desk. As I was taking off my coat, Gage started babbling away about his romantic involvement with a newsroom intern. Gage was single and she was single, and I didn't care at all about any of it—or them, in particular. But Gage was now torn between two interns, and he wanted me to help make his choice for him.

I demurred, "Mmmm, Gage, I think you need to stay away from the interns. Otherwise, no. I've got nothing for you."

"But I'm here for advice!" he commanded.

That was when I realized that he saw me as a shortcut between one of his petty problems and an answer he didn't want to bother to arrive at on his own.

Here was my advice: "Gage, shut up." I then suggested that if he wanted me to solve his problems, he should write me an "Ask Amy" question and take his chances to see if I decided to publish it.

That felt sooooo good.

One morning, one of my coworkers closed my office door and told me about an ethical dilemma that was intensely intimate, essentially unsolvable, and quite heartbreaking, at least to me. As she spoke, I immediately realized that after this revelation, she would probably never speak to me again. I got the distinct sensation that she had violated her own privacy, and I knew she would regret it. We weren't friends, and although she seemed like a nice person, she was just someone I passed in the hallway and occasionally saw in meetings. I'd never had a personal conversation with her on any level. There was no relationship or context to carry us over her disclosure, nor did we have the anonymity provided by my advice column to hide behind. I tried hard not to offer any point of view at all, knowing that if I did, I would regret it.

My colleague was passing off a true ethical dilemma as a Hobson's choice, and after she was done telling me about it (and after I offered the therapist's referral phone number), she backed out of my office and went back to hers. I've often wondered what ultimately happened with this woman's dilemma, but I will never know, because in the ten years since her disclosure, she has indeed managed never to speak to me again.

Right after that, I called the referring therapist at Northwestern on my own behalf. My therapist does what skilled therapists do: She helps me to unspool the events of my own life and decode my problems, in order to arrive at a deeper understanding and sensible solutions. Sometimes we discuss the burdens unique to the advice-giver, of being the repository of so many sad stories. We talk about the pressure I have felt to somehow behave perfectly and the perception that I should always know what to do, despite the fact that I lead a distinctly imperfect life and make my share of bad choices. I'm smarter on paper, and I always maintain that if other people approached their own problems the way I approach their problems—with research and reflection and a time-consuming weighing of options—they wouldn't need me at all.

When I first started writing the "Ask Amy" column, Ann Landers's former editor at the *Tribune* gave me a gift when he told me a quote from the late, great advice-giver. When asked if she felt burdened by the volume of personal problems that landed on her desk, Ann Landers replied that she didn't let it bother her. "These problems aren't my problems. I've got my own problems," she said sagely.

Sometimes, though, the fact that people tell me things means that I can enjoy a moment of connection that feels real and where I leave the encounter with much more than I offered. This happened recently when Bruno and I were guests at the very fancy Gridiron Club dinner in Washington. The Gridiron dinner is a quirky annual Washington tradition, where members of the press and members of the political ruling class meet to lampoon each other, in a strictly off-the-record evening of songs and jokes. I pulled my one formal dress out of the closet, and we rented a tuxedo for Bruno for this famous white-tie event.

President Obama and many of his cabinet members were seated along a raised dais at the dinner, while the 700 or so guests were seated at long tables in the hotel ballroom. I was excitedly wearing my ding-dong dress. I call it the ding-dong dress because its skirt sways back and forth like a bell when I sway back and forth—which is something I tend to do after enjoying the cocktail hour and the free-flowing wine at these fancy events. Bruno, who had never worn white tie before (and who has?), was looking extremely handsome and even more awesomely Ed Harris than usual.

In between food courses, guests mingle and table-hop. Aside from the president and many important Washington officials, there are other celebrities and rich and powerful types in the room, and they seem happy to shake hands with the hoi polloi. I had already met President Obama at a previous Gridiron dinner nine years back when he was the freshman senator from Illinois. He did me the huge favor of saying, in front of the publisher and CEO of the *Tribune*, that he and Michelle couldn't start the day without reading my column over breakfast. I think I still owe him five bucks for that.

While Bruno and I were eating and chatting with our tablemates, I furtively scanned the room, looking for the people I most wanted to meet between courses. I skipped over Wolf Blitzer but put Madeleine Albright on the short list. I waved hello to Andrea Mitchell and Gayle King. But once I got a bead on *him*, I knew what my first stop would be. After the first course was cleared, I beelined across the room to meet Hank Aaron. I think I knocked over Chris Wallace on the way as I crowded in to shake the hand of my childhood hero. I told Mr. Aaron I had written him a letter when I was twelve years old, when he surpassed Babe Ruth's home run record. His letter in reply is one of my greatest treasures. Just clasping his giant hand made me happy to be alive.

Emboldened by my success with Hammerin' Hank, and perhaps also by that third glass of wine, after the next course I pulled Bruno over to meet Jeff Bezos, founder of Amazon.com and the new owner of the *Washington Post*. I introduced myself, and we started to talk. Mr. Bezos very politely said he read and appreciated my work, which is carried in the newspaper he owns. He asked me how I know what to say when I answer letters in the column. I answered him the way I usually do when I'm asked that question—saying that I had actually experienced many of the things people write in to me about and that I often used my own experiences as insight when I pondered how to answer. I told him I was from a small place and that the problems I had wrestled with in my own life were human scale and very real.

Jeff Bezos then told me that his mother had given birth to him while she was still in high school in New Mexico and that his grandparents were incredibly influential in his life because he spent his summers on their ranch in Texas while his young mother went to school and worked. I said I was also raised by a single mom and was a single mother myself and that Bruno and I were now the parents of five daughters and were trying hard to help raise our young granddaughters. Jeff Bezos's grandparents had been his great champions, and he encouraged and reminded me that what Bruno and I were trying to do in our personal lives—to have a strong marriage, and do good work, and to take care of our families—was probably as important as anything else any of us would accomplish. I don't know Jeff Bezos; I doubt I'll ever see him again. But an important feeling of human connectedness happens when people describe their lives and respond with compassion. Ding-dong. I can still feel it.

Jazzed by my warm feelings toward Mr. Bezos, I scanned the room again and saw Dear Abby—Jeanne Phillips—seated at a nearby table. Jeanne is the daughter of Pauline Phillips, the original Dear Abby, who was the twin sister of Eppie Lederer, also known as Ann Landers. During the roughly forty years when Abby and Ann wrote competing syndicated advice columns, the two columnist sisters had often been reported to be feuding or not speaking. I have always assumed the reality is probably more complicated and nuanced than the legend. But, sure enough, when I first started writing the "Ask Amy" column (replacing the Ann Landers column in many newspapers), Ann Landers's daughter, Margo Howard (also an advice columnist), had come after me in interviews in a way that made me feel like I had wandered into a dysfunctional family business. Because of Margo Howard's attitude toward me, I have—naturally—avoided any contact with or comparisons to her cousin Jeanne Phillips, of Dear Abby. And yet there she was, sitting two tables away. I recognized Dear Abby from the headshot that runs over her column, exactly the way people recognize me.

"I'ma let you do this one on your own," Bruno said, giving me a little push.

I gingerly approached Jeanne, who was enjoying her dessert. I seriously wondered how—or even if—she would respond to me. Syndication is a competitive business: something I had learned during my first months on the job, when I was roundly snubbed by two other columnists at an industry event. When I first started the "Ask Amy" column, I pictured a sort of Algonquin Round Table, where other advice-givers would occasionally get drunk together, give one another awesome advice, and go dancing at the Copacabana. After my snubbing, I returned alone to my hotel room and called my mother. I told her I was disappointed that the other kids on the playground weren't playing nice.

"They're not your friends; they're your competitors," Jane said.

It's called show business, not show friends.

I scooted down and introduced myself to Jeanne. Would I be snubbed? Would I end up with tiramisu in my hair?

"Oh, Amy, of course—I'm such a fan!" Jeanne said.

"And I, you. I mean, me too. Shit, I mean darn. I mean . . . I'm also a fan of yours."

She gave me a hug. Jeanne and I aren't likely to go dancing anytime soon, but this magnanimous little pirouette with her gave me a jolt of joy.

The world is full of far-off realities, which Jeanne Phillips, or I, or any advice-giver, should approach with as much tenderness as we can muster. When people write to me, they're sending me a snapshot of their lives. It's a generous gesture, because they are willingly sharing their weaknesses and secrets, and this sharing helps other people who will read their question and identify with what they are going through.

My own children rarely come to me for advice, and I try very hard not to offer it, unsolicited. But I don't think it is always easy to be my child, because of assumptions people make about what it's like to be the child of a professional know-it-all. When Emily was in high school in Chicago, more than once, a parent at a school event would see us together and recognize for the first time that she was my daughter (we have different last names). "It must be awful to be her daughter, always telling you what to do!" they would say, gesturing toward me. I think this type of comment is a failed half-joke, but

Emily was stung. "She's my mom. I like being her daughter," she would say softly.

Peter Sagal, host of *Wait Wait, Don't Tell Me!*, always tells me that I'm too nice. It's sort of a running gag between us. As far as I can tell, my supposed niceness in answering requests for advice is his biggest problem with my work. Peter knows me pretty well, but he and I might have different goals for my column. I assume he wants my work to be popular and entertaining. I labor—and have, for almost fifteen years—under the sincere desire to coach and encourage people toward some understanding of their problems, mistakes, or foibles. Peter sometimes compares my work unfavorably to advice-giver Dan Savage's column, which is very popular, edgy, and frequently snarky, mean-spirited, and very entertaining. But I don't want to be like that. I want to be myself.

In almost fifteen years of writing the "Ask Amy" column, two of my answers have gone viral. Both times I was answering letters that were so patently ridiculous and unkind that answering them was exceedingly easy. I just pushed back. I said what everybody else was thinking. One viral question was from a father worried about his gay son. I e-mailed back and forth with the letter writer several times before running the question in my column, asking additional questions in order to try to determine whether the letter was illegitimate or inflated. I determined that it was, sadly, sincere:

DEAR AMY: I recently discovered that my son, who is 17, is a homosexual. We are part of a church group and I fear that if people in that group find out they will make fun of me for having a gay child.

He won't listen to reason, and he will not stop being gay. I feel as if he is doing this just to get back at me for forgetting his birthday for the past three years—I have a busy work schedule.

Please help him make the right choice in life by not being gay. He won't listen to me, so maybe he will listen to you.

—Feeling Betrayed

DEAR BETRAYED: You could teach your son an important lesson by changing your own sexuality to show him how easy it is. Try it for the next year or so: Stop being a heterosexual to demonstrate to your son that a person's sexuality is a matter of choice—to be dictated by one's parents, the parents' church, and social pressure.

I assume that my suggestion will evoke a reaction that your sexuality is at the core of who you are. The same is true for your son. He has a right to be accepted by his parents for being exactly who he is.

When you "forget" a child's birthday, you are basically negating him as a person. It is as if you are saying that you have forgotten his presence in the world. How very sad for him.

Pressuring your son to change his sexuality is wrong. If you cannot learn to accept him as he is, it might be safest for him to live elsewhere. A group that could help you and your family figure out how to navigate this is PFLAG. This organization is founded for parents, families, friends, and allies of LGBT people and has helped countless families through this challenge. Please research and connect with a local chapter.

This was not the first question I had ever run in my column from a parent wishing a child would stop being gay, but this was the first time I got angry enough to frame the obvious response in a way that revealed my own disgust quite so nakedly. This column hit on a Friday, and I was in an airport when it started going viral.

The experience of seeing something I had written fly around the world to be shared and commented on literally thousands of times was surreal—and wonderful. I felt like Kathy Griffin on Oscar night. The column seemed to have a life of its own, and as I sat in the molded plastic chairs at the airport gate, I could watch as the column hit people's newsfeeds as they checked their phones. One woman sitting across from me recognized me from the column and excitedly grabbed a selfie. She had her own story of being rejected and thrown out of the house as a teenager. She said she wanted to call her mom and share my answer with her. While I was encouraging her to dial the phone, the woman seated beside me held up *her* phone: "Look—I got it, too!" she said. George Takei, the openly gay actor and GLBT advocate, shared my column with his huge Facebook following of over 5 million people. Ashton Kutcher pushed the Q and A out to his 17 million Twitter followers. And Peter Sagal also tweeted it out, telling his large following, "I always tell Amy to be meaner."

For several weeks after the original column ran, I continued to hear from hundreds of people from around the world who were celebrating my smackdown and sharing it with their circles. They e-mailed me with their own stories of rejection and heartache, and they all said, "It's about time."

I can lay down a line of snark when it's called for, but that is not who I want to be.

When I first started writing my advice column, I knew that I wanted to convey empathy to my readers. I wanted to write with the tone offered by my favorite advice-giver, the great Marguerite Kelly, whose column "Family Almanac" in the *Washington Post* was informative, compassionate, and helpful—and always kind and understanding. I wanted to be like my friend Gay, the seasoned nursery school teacher, whose knowledge and wisdom about parenting had been so influential, and my friend Nancy, who always makes the kindest assumptions about people, regardless of the shenanigans they pull. And of course my mother, Jane, who, when I was a newly single mother and Emily was a difficult toddler, pulled me aside and said to me quietly, "Remember, you are all she has."

In my earliest days of answering questions in my column, I wanted to act empathetic. And then, through time, helped along by my readers who trusted me so much and influenced by the course of my own life, I actually *became* empathetic.

Here is what it is like to be me: I am lucky enough to throw on my ding-dong dress and sit at a dinner near the president and to thoroughly enjoy that moment—knowing that it is only a moment (and not even a defining one). But I will always find some of my most meaningful moments of connection closer to home. The times I feel the best about my own life are when I've listened instead of talked and when I think I've acted well, instead of acting out. The circumstances of my own life, and especially surviving my losses, have shown me that there is no one way to get this thing nailed down. I do not have all the answers, but I'm learning as I go.

Chapter Twenty-Seven

Mother's Day

Stepmothers don't like Mother's Day. Some non-stepmothers also don't like Mother's Day, but *all* stepmothers face the day with dread and loathing. Mother's Day is the annual day of reckoning, when children in blended families get anxiety rashes from trying to figure out how to celebrate *all* of their mothers, and stepmothers try to prepare for the moment when they will be reminded of their legendary status as fairy-tale villains and the not quite "real" mothers to the children they love.

Mother's Day is the day *this* mother and stepmother wants to spend at the movies. Alone. *Fine,* I think. *Get me a card. Send me a text. Let's just get through this day of awkward until we have to face it again next year.*

This past Mother's Day, I slipped out of the house early to sing in the choir at church. Emily had written me a note from Chicago, and as she was the one girl of our five with whom I shared DNA, I was both tickled and also relieved to be done with the Mother's Day portion of Mother's Day. Even though it was shaping up to be an unseasonably warm and beautiful day in May—perfect for gardening or reading on the porch—I was mapping out my movie schedule for the afternoon.

Michaela sent me a text: *Meet up at the Slope at Cornell for a picnic at noon.* Okay. Very good. I freaking love picnics, especially if I don't have to make the food or pack it, or in fact do anything; if I can just show up and sit on the ground somewhere and eat pie directly out of the pan with a plastic fork. I drove to Cornell's campus—lush and greening and gorgeously blossom-struck on this hot spring day—and found the spot on a steep slope overlooking the spectacular blue-gray slash of Cayuga Lake and the vineyards and dairy farms on its opposite shore. I sat at the base of a large oak tree directly under Cornell's iconic 175-foot-tall clock tower, where students played its famous carillon several times a day.

Bruno was already there. Angela and my granddaughters Sparkle and Sprout, now six and three years old, clambered up the hillside to join us. Avila and Michaela showed up with a blanket and a bag of food from my favorite sandwich shop. Avila—now a senior in high school with a pocketful of college acceptances to choose from—pulled out a quart-sized container of coleslaw (my favorite food group) and a fork. She assured me that I wouldn't have to share it.

Day made.

My little granddaughters flung themselves onto my lap. Then they leapt up and threw acorns, and then started to roll down the hill, hopping up halfway down, giggling and dizzy, crazy with the day. These two little girls had become my favorite sidekicks. We shared overnights and trips to the library. We erected tents in the living room and played flashlight tag in our old farmhouse. Over the years, we had all tried various nicknames for the little girls to call this once-reluctant grandmother, but none of them seemed to stick. They simply called me "Amy" and I loved it.

Angela and Junior were both hardworking parents. I was proud of the lives they were making for themselves and their children. I had recently acknowledged my cranky and unkind reaction toward Angela when she was a teenager, going through such a tough time at home.

Angela told me that my response to her second pregnancy was actually worse than for the first.

"Oh no," I replied ruefully.

"Oh yes," she said.

Like the good mother I was still trying to become, I had asked this daughter to please forgive me. And like the good daughter she already was, Angela did me the great honor of granting forgiveness for my behavior during our early years together. Surely this was more than I deserved, and on this day of celebrating motherhood, I was impressed by her maturity and humbled by her forgiveness.

There were sweet and sentimental cards and gifts from everyone. It was such a perfect coming together in one moment that I was simply awash with happiness and gratitude. I even forgot to worry about what might be coming next—what black dog might be limping around the corner, ready to fling itself onto our family's path.

The massive clock at the top of the tower clanged one o'clock: *BONNNNNGGGG*. And then the carillon started to play. Mmmm, nice. It was Gershwin, "Someone to Watch over Me." The bells rang across the campus, and the sound swept down the slope and across the lake. I imagined the music entering the falling-down dairy barns and the farmhouses, running up wooden staircases, brushing over quilted beds and spilling out open windows before disappearing into the fields and forests beyond. I put my face in my hands because I didn't want the girls to see me cry. The concert continued: "Embraceable You," "Honeysuckle Rose," "Close to You," the theme from *Star Wars*. Quite simply, a musical sampling of everything I love.

Michaela had set this up in advance with her friend Renee, who played the carillon through her four years at Cornell and who, postgraduation, still had keys to the clock tower. Renee was up in the tower playing her heart out, and the bells were tolling for me.

We gathered up our things and our group entered the building and climbed the 161 steps to the top of the tower. We sat in folding chairs circling the large and complicated instrument, with its many wooden pedals and levers, pulleys and ding-donging bells suspended overhead. I felt the thrill of finally being inside a song.

I thought of my mother—she who taught me to love music and who had bequeathed me the soundtrack of show tunes and pop songs to accompany my life story. I also thought of Emily, a natural-born harmonizer, who knew the same songs that I knew. How they would have loved this.

The secret to a happy marriage is to marry someone who loves you and who believes in bringing the "better" through the "worse" of marriage. I have somehow managed to find that sweet and happy spot. My husband has taken me—broken, skeptical, complicated, and deeply flawed—and has never implied that I should be different. I know, without a shadow of a doubt, that my Mr. Darcy loves me, just as I am.

And these daughters of ours—all the girls who'd once danced in the kitchen? In my arrogance, I thought that all of the attention had been flowing one way, from parent to daughters. But they had been giving lavishly all along, by taking me in and by trusting me to become the parent they deserved to have. They had given me all they had, which was seven years of their lives. In the meantime, they had totally figured me out.

There are a lot of ways to be in a family. But here is how to BE a family: You have to spend time together. You have to try to be honest so that people trust you. You have to forgive others their failings and disappointments and ask for forgiveness for your own. You have to let things happen, to surrender to events, and accept that no matter what you do, life unspools anyway—whether you are alone and crying in your car, or holding hands with your beloved. You have to embrace those fleeting moments when everyone is healthy and happy. And sometimes, you have to make a spectacular celebration, just because you can.

Acknowledgments

Thank you to Mauro DiPreta and the team at Hachette Books. I am ever grateful to Mauro's editorial guidance and infallible judgment.

Thank you to Steve Mandell, my Ambassador of Quan. I am grateful for years of great advice and representation.

Thank you to the readers of my advice column, "Ask Amy." They have been generous with their own stories. They have trusted me, and have taught me so much.

Thank you to my loving husband, Bruno, and to our five wonderful daughters. First, they let me live with them, and then they let me write about it. I am forever grateful.